WHEN DUBLIN WASN'T DOUBLIN'

BY

TIM SELLS

ABOUT THE AUTHOR

The author is the Great-Great-Great Grandson of the founder of Dublin, John Sells. He is also the Great-Great-Great Grandson of Revolutionary War heroes, John Davis and Ann Simpson Davis, who, along with several of their children, moved to the Dublin area in 1816.

The author was born and raised in Dublin, Ohio, on the banks of the Scioto River. After graduating from Dublin High School in 1967, he briefly attended Louisiana State University but was forced to return to Dublin because of depression. He resumed his studies at Ohio State University where, in 1971, he was graduated *summa cum laude, Phi Beta Kappa, Sigma Epsilon Chapter.* He was named by the Ohio Staters, Inc., the Outstanding Student in the College of Humanities. He received a Fellowship to the Department of Romance Languages, but opted for a teaching assistantship at Ohio State. Shortly thereafter, he entered the United States Army. Upon his Honorable Discharge from the Army, he was stricken with his first bout of manic depression. More were to follow.

After the Army, the author worked as a juvenile probation officer with the Franklin County Court of Domestic Relations and Juvenile Delinquency and as an income maintenance worker with the Franklin County Welfare Department. Subsequently he secured a job with the State of Ohio where he devoted his next thirty years as a disabled veterans outreach worker.

The author retired in 2009. He has enjoyed volunteering the past few years teaching English as a Secondary Language at the Community Center, Vineyard Columbus Church, where he and his wife, Debbie, are members. He has maintained his hobbies and his love for baseball, fishing, swimming, reading, eating, sleeping, and all things Latin America. He is often heard to say: "I love to wake up in the morning with nothing to do, and go to bed at night and only have half of it done."

ACKNOWLEDGEMENTS

This book is dedicated to Dr. Kay Redfield Jamison...Professor of Psychiatry at the Johns Hopkins School of Medicine and co-author of the standard medical text. Dr. Kay Redfield Jamison is one of the foremost authorities on manic-depressive illness. She has also experienced it firsthand. For even while she was pursuing her career in academic medicine, Jamison found herself succumbing to the same exhilarating highs and catastrophic depressions that afflicted many of her patients, as her disorder launched her into ruinous spending sprees, episodes of violence, and an attempted suicide.

In *An Unquiet Mind* Jamison examines manic-depression from the dual perspectives of the healer and the healed, revealing its terrors and the cruel allure that at times prompted her to resist taking medication. She has emerged with a memoir of enormous candor, vividness, and wisdom, one of those rare books that has the power to transform lives—and even save them.

Back Jacket
An Unquiet Mind

Also, I would like to thank my beautiful and supportive wife Debora, my son Ryan, and my daughter Elizabeth for their understanding and patience. Special thanks to my friends in Dublin: Joe, Margaret, Mike, Casey, Johnny, and Laura Ryan; David and Christina Wolfe; Jim and Betty Weaver; David Geese; John Andrews; Mike Holmes and Bill Easterday. Special gratitude to Pastor Richard Nathan of the Vineyard Church of Columbus and my small men's group: Steve Lander, Bob Crawford, Jim Beightler, Tom Wyman, and Joe Decker.

I want to thank the Dublin Historical Society; Hal Sherman, Artist: Rick Franz and Brandon Brown, City of Dublin, Information Technology; The staff of the Ohio Historical Society, The Staff at the Columbus Metropolitan Library, Downtown and Dublin Branches; The staff at the Franklin County Recorder's Office; Fred Hahn, City of Dublin, Director of Parks and Open Space; and Fritz Harding; Richard Termeer; Walter Myers; Chi

Weber; Jim Richards; Danny Sells; Leona Jones; and Jim Thompson, for their help in providing materials used in the book.

I also want to thank Herbert Jones, President of the Dublin Historical Society; Chi Weber; Jim Richards; Clayton Rose; Jim Thompson; Lee and Barbara Headlee; Sandy Sells Corica; and Danny Sells, for taking the time to read my manuscript and for their helpful criticisms.

Also, a special thanks to Mrs. Angela Abel, Department of Veterans Affair Vocational Rehabilitation and Employment Counselor; The Volunteers of America, Homeless Veterans Reintegration Program; Doctors Jinous Eslami and Matthew Stevenson.

This book could not have been possible without the assistance and encouragement of my friend from Dublin, Don Rose. His efforts were tireless and inspirational.

Moreover, immense gratitude is due to Ms. Mimi Mullin for her expertise in proofing this book and correcting punctuation and grammar.

A LIST OF SOURCES
OF INFORMATION
CONTAINED IN THIS BOOK

History of Franklin County, Ohio - Historical Publishing Company - 1930 - Opha Moore

Dublin's Journey – The Printing Network, Pressworks – 2004 – City of Dublin, Peter Franklin & Elaine Kehoe

Last of the Wyandots – Linworth Methodist Church – Jim Thompson

A Brief History of your Neighborhood – Jim Thompson

Circus Town - The Short North Gazette - 2009 - Nancy Patzer

Various Articles – Shanachie, I, II - 1985, III - 1988, & IV – 1989 – Students of Dublin High School – Advisors, Joyce Hotchkiss and Scott Weber

Almost the Capital - The Columbus Dispatch Magazine – June 12, 1960

History of the John Davis and Ann Simpson Davis Family – 1954 – Newton Davis

Ann Simpson Davis American Heroine – Author Unknown

John Davis American Hero – Author Unknown

History of the Davis Homestead – Author Unknown

Step Back Into History, Dublin, Ohio – Dublin Historical Society Website

Pioneer Days Website

History of Dublin, Our Churches & Schools – As contained in the Dublin Sesquicentennial Program – 1960 – Newton Dominy

Records of Faye Eberly - As contained in the Dublin Sesquicentennial Program – 1960 – Faye Eberly

City of Dublin Web Sites

The Suburban News – As it Were – Ed Lantz

WOSU-TV – Columbus Neighborhoods – Franklinton

(614) Magazine – Columbus 200: Born on Valentine's Day – Robert Paschen

The 1854 Oregon Trail Diary of Winfield Scott Ebey -- Oregon-California Trails Association

CONTENTS

WHEN DUBLIN WASN'T DOUBLIN'

PREFACE

I was sitting in the lobby of the psychiatric ward of Mt. Carmel Hospital in Columbus, Ohio, waiting. I think I was waiting for dinner since it was around 3:30 PM. As psychiatric wards go, Mt. Carmel wasn't too bad. We had a television set, our own kitchen with a refrigerator stocked full of juices and snacks, and real clean tables and chairs. We even had lounge chairs. There were about four or five of us there then, and we were just waiting. I have heard it said that everyone is waiting for something, and I believe that to be true. Some people are waiting for the big ball game, while some people are waiting just to hear their name; but everybody is waitin' for somethin'.

Anyway, the lobby of Mt. Carmel's psychiatric ward was nice, much nicer of course than the old State Hospital up on the Hilltop in Columbus. That place looked like some kind of gothic back-drop for a horror movie, and it wasn't much better inside. I got disciplined in there a few times. There was a sign up on the wall that said, "No Patients beyond This Line." Well, I didn't have any patience; I was manic, that's why I was in there in the first place. I just walked under that line, and took a little stroll down the hallway and peaked into all of those caged windowed rooms. The inmates ran up and squished their faces right against mine like they were half crazy, which, I suppose, they were. Well, before too long the gentlemen in the white coats came and took me under their arms and put me into one of those locked rooms with the caged, windows. I couldn't figure that out. I didn't have any "patience"; why did they put me into one of those caged, windowed rooms?

On the other hand, I really liked the open wards at the VA Hospital in Chillicothe, Ohio. I really liked being with all of the other Vietnam Era

Veterans. Trouble was, I spent so much time in their locked wards I really didn't get to enjoy their company too much at first. I was real sick. When you are in an open ward in the VA Hospital in Chillicothe it's much different. They have a real nice golf course in Chillicothe and an Olympic swimming pool and a wonderful occupational therapy program and a real nice cafeteria—get about anything you want to eat and plenty of it. Funny thing, my psychiatrist at Mt. Carmel threatened to send me down there to Chillicothe once if I didn't behave. I wish he had; would have saved us both a lot of trouble. He also threatened to give me electro shock treatments on my brain if I didn't behave. I listened to him then, because I wanted to maintain some semblance of my so-called mind, and at Mt. Carmel, the group leaders would take you outside for walks if you were "nice."

Anyway, I was just sitting there in the midst of my bi-polar depression, and I don't think that there's anything much worse than to be depressed and feel all alone and that nobody understands you or even wants to. You just feel like a big glob of glue after it has set too long in the tube and gets all hard inside. Well, as I was thinking whether it was really worth living anymore or not, seriously, in that state of deep dark depression that I was experiencing, in through the doors of the ward walks this Catholic Sister in her full blown habit of black and white, carrying a deck of Bicycle playing cards. Funny thing, that room just exploded with sunshine when she strolled in and walked over to the table where we were sitting. She sat down, but never told us her name—didn't have a name tag, if I remember correctly. Now, I couldn't even tell you how old she was in that black and white habit of hers; she could have been anywhere between eighteen and eighty, but I do remember she had a lot of color in her cheeks. Must have been the "good life," I supposed.

"Well, who would like to play bridge?" she asked very pertly.

No one said a word. A couple of people kind of nodded off, like they were on drugs or something—which we all were.

"Certainly we have some bridge players here," she stated, as if it were the most common and easiest of games to play.

Again, there were just a couple of grunts, moans, nods of the head, and murmurs—"depression speak," I thought.

"Well, can anyone play hearts, spades, canasta, or even euchre?" she asked.

Nothing. No reply. By now I am wondering whether this nun hasn't been transferred to Columbus from some order out in Las Vegas. Maybe there was a special order of 'Casino Queens' out there or something. Also, even though I am pretty deeply depressed myself, I am starting to feel a little bit sorry for this sister because no one will even talk to her.

"I've played some hearts, Sister," I mumbled, under my breath.

"Oh, may God bless you, my child!" she exclaimed as if I had said something quite miraculous. "Now I can teach all of you how to play bridge," she said.

"Ain't bridge hard?" someone moaned.

"Yeah, I know it's hard," someone else grunted, "I've seen pictures of it diagrammed in the newspapers."

"Puff, puff," she exclaimed, "It's only hard if you think it's hard. It's actually quite easy and loads of fun. Everything is easy once you know how; it's just like in life itself; and I will teach you all how to play. And we will start our lessons with our hearts player here, and the rest of you will catch on quickly. I know you will. You just have to have faith, and then you can do it. That's all there is to it. Watch and see."

Well, by now, this Sister is reminding me of that Clint Eastwood movie where Shirley MacLaine dresses up as a nun in *Three Mules for Sister Sara*, and she leads Clint Eastwood all around the place looking for gold. She's not really a Sister or anything like it. She just fools Clint Eastwood into thinking so in order for him to do what she wants. Same thing with this sister. I mean, she walks into the room like Shirley Temple *On the Good Ship Lollipop* one minute, and the next moment she's riffling these cards like a riverboat gambler going from Natchez to New Orleans.

Finally, she looks at me and says, "and what is your name, my son?"

"My name is Tim, Sister," I reply.

"And where are you from?" she asks as she deals out the cards, licking her thumb.

"Aw Sister, you've never heard of the town I'm from," I respond. "It's just a little place outside of Columbus."

"Small?" she asks, "How big?" she asks again.

"Little," I say.

"Little?" she asks.

"It's not very big, Sister!" I maintain.

"Well, is it big enough to have a name?" she asks.

"Yeah, Sister. It's got a name all right. We call it Dublin." I respond.

"Dublin you say?" she asks, licking her thumbs again, flipping out the cards.

"Yeah, Sister, we call it Dublin."

"Well, laddie, if it's Dublin where you're from, then you are entirely mistaken about its size."

"No I'm not, Sister. I've lived there all my life. My family even founded the place."

"Well, laddie, you must have been a playin' with too many leprechauns when you were a wee child because everyone knows that Dublin is the fastest growin' city in the world."

"Sister, you're crazy!" I exclaimed, "You belong in here with us. You don't know anything about Dublin."

"But I most certainly do, laddie" she said, "Everyone knows that Dublin is doublin' every day!"

Well, in the midst of my bi-polar, depressed state, what she uttered flew right over my head, but that Sister threw her head back and hee-hawed so hard that tears came to her eyes and she could barely catch her breath. She just went on cackling like a barnyard rooster (or hen, in her case) for what seemed like five or ten minutes. Finally, she caught her breath.

"Pretty good one, eh, laddie?" she managed to catch her breath.

"Pretty good one, Sister." I finally caught on. Then the rest of the group started laughing, "Doublin' every day!" they chortled, "Dublin's doublin' every day!"

Well, I suppose the joke was on me, but I never forgot the good Sister's words, prophetic as they proved to be. It seems to me as though Dublin has been "doublin'" every day since then.

What I would like to do in this little book of stories is to share with you, my readers, what it was like When Dublin Wasn't Doublin' every day, as it seems to be doing now: that is, when Dublin was a village, not a city. I am not a "deep" man, but I do believe that life is a series of stories: some good and some bad. I think human beings were made to enter into the stories of one another: some from chapter upon chapter, and some for just a few lines. And, I do believe that everyone has a story to tell, and that they are all important. Everyone is waiting for something, and everyone has a story to tell. So much for those who say there are no absolutes in life.

One thing I want to warn you about, though, is that when I think back on my days growing up in Dublin, I occasionally slip into thinking in the vernacular of Dublin that I grew up with and that tends to spill over into my writing. I hope you won't be bothered by it.

As I told the Sister, my family founded Dublin. I will tell you the story of how Dublin began and how my family was involved in the early years of the town in CHAPTER 10 - THE BEGINNING OF DUBLIN. It's an interesting story, if I must say.

INTRODUCTION

S o, to whet my reader's appetite so he or she will continue reading, let me tell you one of my favorite stories about my grandfather, or the old man, as my relatives used to call him. His real name was Amaziah Hutchinson Sells (born April 22, 1867, died August 10, 1951). The Dublin folks called him 'Ams' for short. He was a pretty "eccentric" individual as you will see, and he was married to my Grandma Florence Mary (Polly) Davis on February 4, 1891. She was given the nickname of Polly and everybody knew her by that name; in fact it is on her tombstone.

My beloved Grandma Polly was born on July 11, 1873, and she died on June 6, 1932. She was the daughter of Joseph W. Davis and Mary Jane Butt Davis. If you do the numbers, you'll see Grandma Polly was just fifty-nine when she died. The old man lived for eighty-four years. My Grandma Polly had fifteen children, near as I can figure; it's no wonder she died so young—took a lot out of her. The old man was tough. After Grandma Polly died, the Old Man up and married his housekeeper, Eddie. I don't know why, but everybody called her Aunt Eddie. So, I thought my step-grandmother was my aunt for what must have been twenty years. I grew up confused. Some people say that Grandma Polly had as many as twenty children. That's kind of high, I think, even for her and the old man. Some say sixteen, and some say fourteen. Maybe she had some still births in there? I don't rightly know. My papers say fifteen, so let's go by that. It's enough for three basketball teams. She had a brood. It's all a mystery to me. As you will no doubt see, there were a lot of strange and mysterious things that happened on the Sells' Farm. I will read to you from an obituary that I have of my Grandma Polly:

"Florence Mary Davis, daughter of Joseph Watts Davis and Mary B. Davis, was born on the ancestral Davis farm two miles southeast of Dublin on the east bank of the Scioto River, July 11, 1873. Here she spent all of her girlhood and married and passed away June 6, 1932, at the age of 59 years, 11 months and 26 days. She attended high school at Dublin, and was a student at Otterbein College at Westerville. On February 4, 1891, occurred her marriage to A. H. Sells. Mrs. Sells was the mother of sixteen children, all but one of whom with her husband survives her. She is also survived by two sisters and three brothers...Internment will be in the Davis cemetery on Riverside Drive."

"Your grandmother was six feet tall and weighed three hundred pounds when she died": those were about the first words I ever heard about my grandmother. I once asked my dad what Grandma Polly was like, and he said, "Heck, how should I know? I was the youngest of all the kids. I hardly knew her. I was raised by a nanny and your oldest aunt, your Aunt Ruth. I do know my mother never turned away a hobo. She always would feed a hobo and give him a place to sleep out in the barn in the hayloft, and the old man would put him to work the next day if he was still there in the morning. Hobos could live and work on the Farm as long as they wanted to."

This description of my Grandma Polly from my dad sounds a lot like what I read In the *History of the Davis and Simpson Families* compiled by Newton Davis in 1954. Newton was Grandma Polly's brother. We will refer to his work later, but for now let's look at the excerpt about Grandma Polly on page 37:

"Born July 11, 1873, A strong and robust child and grew to be a large woman. Went to Perry 3 School and then to Otterbein at Westerville. She was a good worker and full of fun and good cheer, always helpful to others. She enjoyed music and played some on the organ and piano. When father and mother were sick so long she helped care for them, along with the other work. She married Ams Sells about 1891, and always lived at the Davis home, never had another place. She raised a family of fifteen children during twenty-six years, always taking good care of them and her housework, with all the problems involved with the farm work. She was a devoted Mother and gave to all the children the best of her life. She was interested in the Church and Schools and tried to lift up the general tone and spirit of the community to a high level. Polly was honest and upright in all her doings and had a very keen sense of honor and uprightness. She made a trip to

Florida and had a good visit except that she had some blood poisoning that bothered her for a long time. Ams Sells ran the farm and took care of the business. They bought Uncle Charles' Farm East and that added much to the work of the farm. Polly took sick in 1931, suffering from a heart condition. She died suddenly in 1932 and was buried in the Davis Cemetery and a beautiful marker was put up by the children..."

Anyway, Grandma Polly married the old man, and, to this day, I don't know why. In the pictures I've seen, he was just a gnarly, wiry, bald headed thing 'bout the same height of my dad (5'11"). Heard he was eccentric and cantankerous, yet he had a soft side to him. Obviously, he was very virile. I am just about certain that this "young" man, who became the old man, had a strain of mania in him as the remainder of this story will bear out.

Now, as most of you readers know, the big difference between eccentricity and mental imbalance is money, or in his case, land. He had a lot of land, though not much money. When the old man got to be around sixty, he figured out he had enough kids and farmhands to work the Farm, and he decided to quit working. "Early retirement" they call it now. Not only did he quit working, but he decided to quit

AMAZIAH SELLS THE OLD MAN

wearing clothes. Sounds a little bizarre, I know, but he just woke up one morning and threw all of his clothes away, except for a pair of his old leather shoes. Before you become too aghast, what he did beforehand was order seven robes from Sears and Roebuck, a different colored robe for each day of the week. He would wear a yellow robe on Monday, a blue robe on Tuesday, an orange robe on Wednesday, and so on and so forth, so the story goes. He kept his days straight that way, I imagine. What I find most interesting, though, is how he would try to color-coordinate himself. You see, he only had that one pair of shoes, and on occasion, when business dictated, he would have to leave his reclusive estate, the Sells Farm, and go downtown to Columbus. So, if he had to go downtown to do business, and if it were a Monday, for example, he would have one of the boys or girls paint his shoes yellow in order to match his yellow robe. Thus, he was always dressed for the occasion, and he became, in his mind at least, a veritable, agrarian, social pacesetter—the Howard Hughes of his day, if you will. This behavior, eccentric, amusing, or "ill," as it may seem, would be carried over into the next generation of Sellses, and the next. That's the bloodline I sprang from.

But every town or village seemed to have its "characters" like the old man back in the days when Dublin Wasn't Doublin'. It was different then. People had more time to develop themselves and their peculiar ways. Psychologists and sociologists and psychiatrists didn't stamp labels on people then like they do now. Then, towns had terms like "rare" or "odd" or "weird" for people like the old man who did not, or would not, conform to the larger "normal" society. But, on the other hand, we now have psychotropic medicines which can deal with a lot of "aberrant" behaviors, and mental illnesses, and I thank God for that.

This book of stories is not just about the people of Dublin, and some of its characters, but it is for everyone who once lived in a town or village that may have later become a city. Look up on the street signs to see the names of some of these "different" people, Look at the names on the street signs that you pass by; pay attention to the names of the schools in your area; heck, try to even figure out why certain malls have the names they do. Let your imaginations run wild. How did that school get its name? What was the person like behind the name on that old road? How's come that strange sounding street is named the way it is?

So, let me try to take you back through time to when people never locked their doors, back to the times when, if you got up early enough, you could talk the bread man into dropping off a dozen extra glazed donuts, or you could talk the milkman into giving you a quart of chocolate milk. Ask around about some of the "real characters" in your city when it was once a village or small town. Ask your mom or dad about some of those "strange kin" of theirs, in their own family, which they may be a little bit reluctant to talk about. Then lean back and listen to them share with you about "Weird Uncle Willie" or "Jumpin' Aunt Julie." Now that's real family time, and it's a whole lot more fun than watchin' TV or playin' video games, believe me. So, my reader friends, let your minds meander as you learn about Dublin,

When It Wasn't Doublin'…and just imagine your own home town before it became a city.

Now, any book about Dublin, of course, would not be complete without paying homage to the great muses, the 'little creatures', who inspire all of the tales, trials, and tribulations of this sleepy, little Irish hamlet:

ODE TO THE LEPRECHAUNS

The stories that I will tell you
Do you think that they are true?
Or am I really a Leprechaun
Sent to play tricks on you?

And the words that're in this book,
How do you know they were said?
Most of the people who spoke them,
Why, they're already dead.

Imagination, of course, is in here;
And exaggeration is in here, too.
But isn't that the Leprechaun's way,
To entertain and play a trick on you?

So put on your reading glasses,
And peer down your doubting nose.
Check my lines for syntax,
And correct my faulty prose.

You may think the tale unbelievable,
Like rolls of 7's that go tumblin'.
But these stories could only be written,
On the emerald felt of Dublin.

Yet if you're so sure there's a false one,
That you'd swear on the Blarney Stone.
Remember the Leprechauns of Dublin
When you're out at night alone.

So please don't dismiss me quickly,
And rapidly write off my diction.
In Dublin the saying holds true:
Truth can be stranger than fiction....

CHAPTER 1

THE SCIOTO RIVER

I was born in 1949 and grew up in Dublin (except for a brief period when we lived in Worthington). From the time I was born until I was five we lived at 38 South High Street, in Dublin. Then we moved to Worthington, where we lived for one year and then moved to 74 Marion Street, back in Dublin. We lived at 74 Marion Street until I was about 11, at which time my dad rented a house at 6052 Dublin Road, located back a long lane and near the Scioto River. I don't know who owned the house, but I always think of it as the Blankenship house, since they lived there before us. When I was a freshman in high school we moved to 5175 River Forest Road and that is where we lived when I graduated from Dublin High School in 1967. After I graduated from school my dad and mom moved to the Snouffer's at 7700 Dublin Road (now Donegal Cliffs) and I lived there on and off.

Growing up, I think that my best days were when we lived on the banks of the Scioto River in the old Blankenship home. Growing up, I don't ever remember my dad telling me he loved me: he just built me a raft, by hand. Now, this was in the days well before all those factory-built pontoon boats you see puttering around Hoover or Alum Creek Reservoirs, this was a real raft and, we called her the "African Queen."

My dad could do about anything mechanical, and he sure knew how to weld. "The African Queen" which was named after the movie of the same name, starring Humphrey Bogart and Katherine Hepburn, was built with six fifty-five gallon drums, three on a side, all welded expertly together. The front drums were cut and welded, on each side, at a forty-five degree angle so that the Queen could glide effortlessly through the Scioto. The iron frame was welded tightly so that the flooring could be made of a series of planks that would slide in horizontally and fit snugly. This proved to be very important because when it rained, and that's when the fish bite, water would run right through the Queen. Thus, you never had to bail her out. And even if it did rain, so what? My dad had somehow welded a frame or some contraption above to hold a very sturdy roof. And, you had to have a roof, because my dad had a couch sitting right underneath it. My dad welded a hand pump on the side of the raft, very similar to the hand pump we used to have in the middle of Dublin above Dr. Karrer's house, in case we needed water to wash our hands or perhaps clean fish. He welded an iron bar horizontally across the front, in front of the couch, for extra stability and so we could lean our fishing poles against it to see when we got a strike from a fish.

But, I think the most ingenious thing he did was to devise a system of anchoring the Queen, anywhere, and under any conditions. If you know anything about fishing, you know how hard it is to anchor your boat in the right spot so that you can fish where the fish are. Well, my dad, being the plumber that he was, and knowing all about pipes, welded two big pipes vertically, on the front of the Queen, one on each side. Then, quite brilliantly, I thought, he had inserted inside the two big pipes of greater circumference, two very long pipes of smaller circumference that rose high in the air. These long, high, skinny pipes were perforated at certain intervals by a series of holes that had been drilled in them, and marked to show the depth of water you were in when you dropped them down. The inner poles were secured, when traveling by pins run through their holes and the holes in the larger, holding pipes. Thus, the inner pipes slid down easily inside the outer pipes when you pulled the pins and easily anchored down into the bottom of the Scioto. The beauty of it all was that when you arrived at your destination you could swing the Queen in an arc against the current, straighten her up to the east and west, pull the pins, down went the inner poles, and you were anchored— for good. And, you knew how deep the water was also. I believe you could have done jumping jacks and summersaults on the Queen, and she wouldn't have budged. She withstood some bad storms, but was always faithful. "A thing of beauty and a joy forever" that's what she was. She was equipped with a thirty-five horsepower Evinrude, but the Queen was never in a hurry.

She stalked her prey methodically, much like the "Pequod" did for the great white whale in *Moby Dick*. And of course, when she was out at "sea," she always let her true colors be known: she flew the Red, White, and Blue.

The Queen's destination was usually the "Riffles," a special place where the water ran fast and where my dad and I went, because that was where the fish were. It is located just downstream from Joe Dixon's.

We kept the African Queen docked in a little inlet on the east side of our yard. It was a very big yard, on the west side of the Scioto. So, when I think of the Scioto River, I think a lot about the African Queen. Whether my dad built that raft for me, or for himself, I guess I'll never know. What difference does it make? All I know is that we were together when we were on it, and I could use it whenever I wanted; but, of course, I liked fishing with my dad the most.

There were a ton of small mouth bass up in the Riffles, and we used to fish for them off the Queen with soft craws. The Riffles was a very special, almost a sacred place, for my dad and me, and the fish that lived up there were majestic. There were giant smallmouth bass that would jump from the water three or four times trying to spit the hook. There swam the denizens of the deep—huge carp (or bugle-mouth bass as we called them), and of course down in the channel, with their tails weaving back and forth, were channel, blue, and shovel head catfish—and they got to be behemoths. My dad and I fished for smallmouth, but I think what he really liked to tie into were giant carp. And, like father like son, I inherited that trait.

Every now and then, I would see him reach down in the craw box and pick out the biggest, softest soft craw he could find. Now a carp craw is not the same as a bass craw. A bass craw is smaller, generally, and a little tougher. You can catch bass on peelers–harder craws. But a big, fat, soft craw—well, they don't move too fast, and it's hard for a big carp to resist them. Anyway, he would toss that big old soft craw out there just off the quick running water of the Riffles, into an eddy. You had to be careful, when those craws were real soft, that you didn't throw them off your hook.—it would cost you a fortune nowadays. Then, my dad would open the bail up on his reel (he mostly used big Zebco 88s) and wait, and wait, and wait. You kept your bail open when you fished in the Riffles; that is, if you valued your rod and reel. A big cat, or carp, or even a big small mouth could hit a craw so hard and so quickly that he could take your rod and reel with him. Bye-bye. That's all she wrote.

Well, after a while, if you were lucky, you heard about the most beautiful sound there is in the natural world, the unmistakable sound of line being stripped off your reel at close to supersonic speed. It was a sound mostly like a whir, but with a little bit of a stitch in it—hard to describe. The very tip of your pole would be bouncing quickly, throbbing, almost pulsating. You knew it was a big fish, and a big fish needs a lot of line. My dad would stand up and pick up his pole. I would set the hook a lot quicker than him; he had the nerves of a cat burglar. He had fought through France and Germany; he knew how to wait. Just when I thought the fish would drop the craw, dad would snap that pole back like a bullwhip, and it would immediately double down and over—looked like a parabola. He would laugh, and I think he would have played those fish for an hour if he could have.

You never knew what you might hook in the Riffles, a big channel cat, or blue cat or shovelhead cat, a big bass, a carp, a snapping turtle, or even, God forbid, a giant dogfish. I was always hoping that my dad would have a big cat on, but about every time they turned out to be carp. Carp and cats stay down a long time when you fight them, whereas a small mouth is apt to come up quickly to swim upstream to try to spit the hook. Well, my dad never was disappointed to catch a carp; he would laugh, and sometimes even talk to them, and chortle a little while he fought them.

When you catch a big fish, as you might know, you don't use a net—you use a gaff, which is kind of like a hay hook. We

LEFT TO RIGHT – BILL EASTERDAY, 25 POUND CARP, SMALLER CARP, ME

would gaff those carp up on the queen, and they would flop all over the place. The Queen never moved, during all of it. She remained steadfast, like the elegant lady she was.

Well, you're probably wondering how big these carp were that we caught up in the Riffles. I imagine the ones we caught there were around twenty pounds, the biggest ones, maybe twenty-five to thirty pounds. I caught one at twenty-five pounds during high water further up the river, behind the quarry at Mrs. Snouffer's, which is now Donegal Cliffs. I saw my friend, Bill Easterday, catch a twenty-five pounder at the same place. We got our picture in the *Columbus Dispatch* for that one because we kind of tag-teamed that old bugger. He caught himself up in some brush—carp are smart and wily critters—and I waded out and freed him up so Bill could reel him in. Red Trabue, the "Hunting and Fishing" writer for the *Columbus Dispatch* and host of the *Outdoor Show* on WBNS-TV, God bless him, took our picture over at Carl Finkes' Bait Store on Riverside Drive. "You can look it up," as Casey Stengel, the manager of the New York Yankees, used to say.

I know a beautiful Dublin family who live along the river on Riverside Drive, about half a mile north, and across the river from the old Snouffer quarry, Joe, Margaret and Laura Ryan. That's where I keep my boat now, and where I presently do most of my fishing. Believe me when I tell you that I have caught some whoppers up there, too: carp, smallmouth, shovelhead, saugeye, and channel cats. It's a beautiful stretch of river, right out of *Field and Stream* and teaming with wild life. I will be forever indebted to them for letting me keep my little boat there.

Well, the African Queen and catching carp, heck, that is just a little bit about what the mighty Scioto River was, when I was growing up, and When Dublin Wasn't Doublin'. I would like to share with you, a few more stories about the river—the river that was pretty important in the founding of Dublin. For the sake of brevity—and I could talk about the river forever—I would like to just talk about some things south of the Dublin Bridge because that is the part of the river I know best, and hope you will appreciate these anecdotes.

However, before I get started with these stories, I want to address the current "carp crisis" that threatens the Great Lakes fishing industries. I am going to josh you a little now, but I was thinking that if the United States Army, the Corps of Engineers, that is, would let me and three of my boyhood carp fishing buddies—Jim Terrell, Mike Holmes, and Bill Easterday—re-enlist we could at least put a dent in that carp population up there. My weapon of choice would be a Mitchell 300 with 12 pound test line, a six and one-half foot boron rod, and an unlimited supply of soft craws. They say these Asian carp are only eating plankton and grass, but I don't care where they're from, I never saw any carp turn down a big, fat, juicy soft craw.

When I see pictures of these carp jumping out of the water and smacking people upside the head, well, it reminds me of that Walt Disney movie, *Dumbo, The Flying Elephant.* If you remember, Dumbo (all the other elephants made fun of him because he had such big ears—"bullying" even then) goes flying by, flapping his ears, and there are these three crows sitting up on a telephone line that see him. One crow turns to the other and says, "I've seen a horse fly." The other one looks back at the first one and says, "I've seen a house fly." And finally, the last one turns his head around, and says, "But I ain't never seen an elephant fly!" And until this day, I have never seen a carp fly in person, but there are pictures of them flying on the television set, so it must be true. Seriously though, folks, this is a serious problem, and the powers that be need all of our support to keep the Asian carps out of our Great Lakes.

LEFT TO RIGHT – THE LORD MAYOR OF DUBLIN, IRELAND, LOIS, AND JOE DIXON AT THE 1975 ST. PATRICK'S DAY FESTIVITIES IN DUBLIN, IRELAND

Now I want to tell you a story that took place on the Scioto, and that involves a truly great figure in the annals of Dublin history, Joe Dixon, one of the great mayors of Dublin. Joe was a true Southern Gentleman. He hailed from Georgia. I loved to listen to that smooth, Southern drawl of his. And you can't mention Joe without mentioning his beautiful wife, Lois, who recently passed away. Those two were the epitome of Southern hospitality.

Anyway, one evening, I believe it was after a baseball tournament game Dublin High School had played (Dublin was always playing in baseball tournaments back then), Dave Wolfe, my best friend and right fielder on the team, came down to my house on the river. He had his fishin' pole with him, as always, and even though it was a little bit late, we decided to take the Queen up to the Riffles. On this particular night, my big brother Mike went with us. I don't know why, but that night he brought along a Mossberg .22 Carbine Rifle and a seven-shot clip. Anyway, we had some pretty good craws, so up the Scioto we went. I swung the old Queen around in the Riffles, anchored her, and we tossed out our lines.

We waited and talked. I forget what we talked about, mostly baseball, I imagine. I don't think we ever talked about girls too much then, although David was going with this pretty little girl named Donna Sebastian who lived down on Thornhill Lane, south of Dublin, where the Roses, the Prouts, and the Essigs used to live. Donna would always give Dave a little peck on the cheek beside the school bus when Dublin had an away game. I guess it was for good luck, but I never wanted any girl doing something like that to me, especially in public. Of course, David was three years older than me, and much more a "man of the world," so to speak. Back then, girls were kind of like alien beings, and nobody really knew too much about them anyway, or wanted to. I'd just as soon throw a rock at one of them down at the bus stop as actually talk to one.

We might have talked about cars; everybody liked cars, fast cars. Dave's brother, Dubby, had a Corvette; now that was something to talk about. Jim Abbot had a 409 Chevrolet Bel Air, like the kind the Beach Boys used to sing about. I don't know if Jim ever lost a race in that car. Now, Sawmill Road was the place all the races were held. If you look at it now, you'll figure out why: from Henderson Road due north it runs very, very straight and true until it gets to Route 161 and there wasn't hardly any traffic on it back then, especially late at night and in the early morning. But I do not recommend street car racing; it's too dangerous.

Anyway, we were probably talkin' about the Dodgers, Dave's team, or the Yankees, my team, when Dave got this tremendous strike that almost jerked his pole clean into the water—with the bail open. He jumped up off the couch, and held his pole still. You could hear that line peeling off the spool from the far end of the Queen. He must have let ninety to one hundred yards of line shoot out before he snapped that pole back for as much as he was worth. I never saw him swing a baseball bat that hard! Immediately, his pole bent over double and the drag on his reel just whined and whined. I thought that the ball bearings in that reel were going to melt. But, he wasn't getting that fish turned around. Z,Z,Z, went that drag! I had seen fish in the Riffles that you just couldn't turn, and I was hoping this wasn't one of them. I was also hoping that Dave had a lot of line on that spool. And I didn't know what pound test he was using; I was hoping it was, at the very least, ten pound test. With ten pound test, a real good rod, a double Palomar knot, and a good reel with a precise drag, you can catch a pretty big fish in the river, but there's a lot of luck involved: and you really have to play that fish perfectly. Finally, after what seemed like one hundred and fifty yards or so, the fish slowed and circled in deep water. Remember, in the Riffles, you are fighting against a current, too. Anyway, now it became like a tug of war, like the way you fight big fish in the Great Lakes or in the Ocean. You pull your pole up ever so slowly, drop it down and reel in the slack as quickly as you can as you drop the pole down, keeping the fish's head up, always up. Pull slowly, drop and reel. Pull slowly, drop and reel. Then, invariably, big fish will dive on you, and your drag will start to buzz all over again. Then, when the fish stops, you start the whole process all over again: pull up slowly, drop and crank in the line ever so quickly. But, try as he might, Dave couldn't get that fish to surface, and I thought that we would never even get to see it, let alone get him on board. Finally, after all the pulling, and drag burning, and reeling, and sweating, I thought I saw him surface. "Over there," I shouted, "to the left and close to the bank." Kind of reminded me of Ahab when he saw Moby Dick breaching through his telescope way out in the ocean: "He beckons, men, he beckons!" We all looked, and thought we saw something slightly breaking water.

But then, a horrible thought hit us all, and I think, all at the same time: we didn't have a net, and we didn't have a gaff! What were we to do with this Monster of the Scioto even if we did bring him close enough to the Queen to land him? Just then, he dove again, deep into the murky depths. "Bring him up, Dave; bring him up. I know what to do!" shouted my big brother.

"Bring him up?" I thought to myself, as if he were talking about a nine inch bluegill. This fish was a leviathan and strong as an ox. But, after much effort, Dave did bring him up again. He circled about thirty yards south of the Queen. We flashed our little flashlight in his direction, barely seeing him, but it was enough for my brother. Without hesitating, he let loose a clip of .22 longs. It was to no avail, and only served to irritate the leviathan and cause him to dive once again.

We just didn't know what to do. But, suddenly, I thought of something, and maybe I shouldn't have. "Let's go get Joe Dixon; he'll know what to do," I shouted. "Yeah, yeah," everyone agreed, "Joe Dixon will know what to do." Now, I still believe that it was a good idea, but there were a couple of problems with it: First, it was probably about 1:00 or 2:00 in the morning; and second, although it was May, the water was still cold and it was swift. Then there was the matter of just who was going to go get Joe? Still, we had an awful big fish hooked that we had fought for a long, long time. To make a long story short, I drew the short straw, so, in I went. I managed to stand the cold and fight my way through the current and climb up to Joe's house, about two or three hundred yards north of the Riffles. Even though I hated to, I rang Joe's doorbell.

Now, right here, I'd like to stray a bit to share a few words about this man who was one of the finest mayors of Dublin. Joe was from Georgia, as I have said, and had that beautiful soft, Southern accent. He and his lovely wife, Lois, were friends of my family. They didn't know any strangers. My father and Joe were very close. They both had grown up on farms and had a lot of other things in common. My father took a backhoe and dug Joe's back patio, a patio of solid limestone, when just about everyone around said it couldn't be done. There was another member in the Dixon family besides Joe and Lois—Bill, their Irish setter. Bill was, hands down, the smartest dog I ever saw, smarter than some of the people in Dublin I knew at that time. "Bill," Joe would say, "Go tend bar." And he would do it. Bill would go and bring you a beer. That dog would do anything Joe asked him to do. I always liked to visit the Dixons because they always made you feel right at home, just like Joe Ryan and his family do for me and my son now.

Bill came to the door first and then went upstairs and woke up Joe. It was really late, or early, depending on how you looked at it. Out of breath,

I told Joe what our problem was. He didn't grumble, he didn't hesitate, he just said, "Let me go get my canoe out and I'll take along a big net. We'll see if we can't get him up together." He went and got into some clothes. Then we slid the canoe into the water and headed down the river. Joe used his flashlight to spot Dave's line and we drifted and paddled over to where the line entered the murky water. Joe managed to bring the fish up enough to make out what he was, and then Dave's line just snapped. "It was a big carp, boys" Joe said, "a real, real big one." There's nothing worse than hearing your line snap. Sometimes it will crack real loud like a rifle shot, and sometimes you will barely hear it; but the results are the same—dead silence, impotence. We just headed home after that. What was there to fish for? We'd already hooked the biggest fish we had ever known, but I can remember that I never really felt too bad about losing that fish. After all, we had all worked together as a team and we had done everything we knew how to do, and Joe Dixon had even pitched in and helped. And most important of all, and thanks to Joe, we knew that it was a carp, and not a catfish.

Well, by now, you're probably thinking that this little collection of stories about Dublin When it Wasn't Doublin' came right out of *Field and Stream*. But, the truth is, it seemed like back in those days, everything revolved around the beautiful Scioto River. For example, I was sitting in Mrs. Dulin's fifth grade class one day; I was just sitting there, I wasn't doing anything bad, when in walked these two rather formal looking gentlemen—along with the principal. I can't tell you who the principal was, but it was either Mr. McGarvey or Mr. Grizzell. I do remember that when we lived right in the middle of Dublin, between Leor Cole's and John Herron's stores, the superintendent, Mr. Love, lived nearby us. Anyway, immediately, when I saw these three, this trio of terror, I tried to backtrack in my mind real quickly for something egregious I had done, or failed to do, some grave sin of commission or omission. Because, you see, in the fifth grade, I was in a contest to see who could get the most whacks from the paddle of Mrs. Dulin. When Dublin Wasn't Doublin', and you kept acting up in class, you got whacks with the paddle. Usually Mr. Rosnagle, the shop teacher, would hand-make the paddles—those instruments of terror. Now, it might sound cruel to you now, but in those days, that was just the way it was. I never minded getting whacks from Mrs. Dulin; she couldn't hit you hard enough to warm your rear end, and I always really believed that it hurt her more than it hurt me (you know, that's what they always say—beforehand). My two main "whacks" competitors were Greg Hewlitt and Jim Peffers, Anyway, we were in a race and got the whacks for the fun of it.

But, back to the terrible trio who had entered the classroom: I just knew they were looking for me. And, sure enough, they were. When you're a criminal, you get a certain "sixth sense," but still, I couldn't think of anything that I had done that wrong, recently. "Timmy," the principal said, "We need to see you out in the hall." Well, I am sure you've all had that feeling, like the bottom of your stomach has just fallen out. Seeing the principal was one thing, but accompanied by these two other guys in suits was enough to make a young kid cry. This is the way John Dillinger must have felt, I thought to myself, when he got caught. I got up and walked through the door into the hallway.

"We are all going on a little trip under the Dublin Bridge," the principal said, or words to that effect. "Well," I thought, "that's perfect; that's about the most desolate place in Dublin."

"We're going to take your picture," one of the "suits" said. Man, I thought, a mug shot at such an early age.

"And a Miss Becky Eberly is going to be with you," the other guy said.

Hold on, I thought, this couldn't be all bad. Becky Eberly, who lived over on Grandview Drive, never got into trouble. She was such a pretty little girl—a little "young" for me.

"You're going to be on the cover of the *Columbus Dispatch Sunday Magazine*. Miss Becky is a seventh generation Eberly, and you are a seventh generation Sells. Dublin was founded in 1810, and since it's 1960, you are going to have a Sesquicentennial. Your town, is now 150 years old," they told us. So, it was down to the Scioto River, the source of it all, and under the Bridge where the spring is, where we used to pick watercress for watercress sandwiches. In the picture which, sure enough, appeared on the cover of the *Columbus Dispatch Sunday Magazine*, you can see me bent down on one knee handing up to Becky a cup of water in a tin cup. The photo was in color, and Becky had a little red dress on; I had one of my favorite shirts on that had turtles on it. The caption of the picture, I believe, read something like this: "Their Forefathers Drank Here." I still have the picture.

THE COLUMBUS DISPATCH
Sunday
MAGAZINE
JUNE 17, 1960

HERE THEIR FOREFATHERS DRANK

Well, my dad framed that magazine picture, and, for the Sesquicentennial Parade, he made a float for Becky and me based on it. I remember that
the float was complete with running water. And I also remember that Carol
Finkes, daughter of Carl Finkes' of Dublin Bait Store fame, was selected to
be queen of the 1960 Dublin Sesquicentennial.

I share this little snippet with you because, it seemed when Dublin
Wasn't Doublin', just about everything centered on the Scioto River. And, I
loved the Dublin Bridge. You could go down there and shoot pigeons, and

pick soft craws, and catch hard craws and boil them in an old coffee can and eat them, and go swimming south of the Dublin Bridge off the old rock in the channel above the Riffles.

We used to fish for carp with dough balls under the bridge. Don Delewese used to make the dough balls with anise in them. We were told it was against the law to put anise in dough balls, but it didn't seem to bother Don any. Bobby Beiriger was always with us, and he had a Zebco reel that sounded like an alarm clock when he cast it. We would just fish and fish all day long for those "bugle mouthed bass," and Don and Bobby would catch one every now and then. Funny thing, I don't think I ever caught a carp under the bridge on a dough ball. What I did do though, might seem a little

DUBLIN BRIDGE

"gross" to you. We would fish all day long; we didn't have anything else to do, and about two or three in the afternoon I would get really hungry—really hungry. So, being the indiscriminate and voracious eater that I have always been, that all Sellses have always been, I ate my dough balls. They really weren't too bad, and the anise gave them a bit of a tang. They filled me up. I always made sure, when we divided them up before we split up to go to our favorite spots that I got a little extra. I figured if a carp could eat them, so could I. After all, carp ate crawdads and people did too—at least the tails. If any of my friends noticed that I didn't have any dough ball left at the end of the afternoon, and I hadn't caught any carp either, they never said anything. Heck, they probably ate dough balls too.

When I couldn't pick any soft craws and I wanted to do some serious carp fishing, then I had to go to a bait store. Growing up, I spent a lot of my time in bait stores, and I still do. Of course, the owners of the bait stores that were near-by, the ones that I went to, were my friends': Carl Finkes, Barb Finkes, Carol Finkes, and Emerson Armstrong. Carl's bait store was up on Riverside Drive north of Dublin, on the northeast corner of where Hard Road now intersects with Riverside Drive. He and my dad were friends. Carl let me go to the back of the store where they kept the soft craws in big galvanized tanks under a stream of constant running water. They had to be kept under running water in order to make sure the craws stayed soft and the peelers remained a little tough. Many times hard craws would kick their shells while in the tubs. I liked Carl a lot, but he had our old dog King up there, who I will tell you about later, and I was always on the lookout for him.

After Carl left, his wife Barb took over the bait store. She always brought the craws out for me to pick in little wood and screen cages. There was a gnarly old guy who she let sleep up there. His name was Tex. You could about always see him around the Wyandotte Inn, the White Cottage[1] or, of course, the Zoo Bar (at various times known as The Hut, The Dam Site, and The Bogey Inn, but known to me as the Zoo Bar). Barb was kind; she would take in about anything or anyone. 'Course she didn't have to worry much with King being up there. Funny thing Barb did, though: she paid fisherman 50 cents a pound for carp and 40 cents a pound for catfish. Never could figure that out; catfish taste a whole lot better than carp. She must have had her reasons. Anyway, one summer I almost bankrupted her. I brought seventeen carp, all over five pounds, into her bait store. I didn't take any money though; just swapped her for soft craws. After Barb Finkes left, Carl and Barb's daughter, Carol, took over.

My other bait store was owned by Emerson Armstrong. It was located at the mouth of the driveway on the Sells Farm. Back then (and today), I had a craw box which was made of hard, pressed cardboard and filled with damp, sphagnum moss to keep the craws lively on a warm afternoon. I would drive my boat across the river, dock her (there wasn't any sense in locking her—people didn't steal things back When Dublin Wasn't Doublin'), climb up the river bank beside the quarry, and get to Emerson's store. Back then, it seemed like every bait store had a little bell on the screen door that rang when someone came in. The conversation usually went about like this:

"Hello, Son," Emmie would say. In those days, old folks usually called little boys "son," and I was no exception. Seemed like we were all one big family, and, of course, I never figured out who was related to who. "It Takes a Village...."

"Hi, Emmie," I would say, "'I'll be needing some soft craws."

"What I figured, Son. You know where I keep 'em," Emmie always let me pick my own craws.

"Fisherman's dozen, Emmie?" I would ask.

---

1   The White Cottage was located at 9215 Dublin Road in Shawnee Hills. The building is now occupied by Jimmy V's Grill and Pub.

"Fisherman's dozen," he would reply.

One day I went to the back of the store and picked out seven juicy, big old lobster craws for carp and catfish, and six feisty peelers for smallmouth. Cost me a dollar. I should have picked 'em the night before but I had a ballgame and the Yankees were playing the Angels on the radio. Fell asleep with the radio on.

"See you later, Emmie. Thanks."

"See you, Son. Don't get your line snapped."

"I won't; got a good drag."

Next time I walked into Emerson's to get some craws, he didn't seem so happy. "Last time you come in here pickin' craws out of the tanks, you had oil and gas on your hands, didn't you?" he asked.

I thought real hard. Emmie was right. Before I had come over, I had filled my gas tank with oil and gas and must not have wiped my hands.

"Yes Sir," was all I could say.

"Son, I lost a lot of craws because of that oil and gas mixture bein' in the tanks. Always make sure that your hands are clean before you put them in the tanks. Lots of soap and water and rinse 'em good. Pretend you're a doctor."

"The bottom of my stomach fell out when Emmie reprimanded me. I had betrayed the trust of a bait store owner. I felt so bad I wished I could get a paddling.

"I am so sorry, Emmie," I sniffled.

"Oh, don't fret, Son. We all make mistakes. Go on back there and get your craws. And get a fisherman's dozen while you're back there."

Heck, Emmie was just like Mose Myers, who we will encounter later.

Well, enough about carp; you can probably tell by now that they were one of my favorite fish. What I would like to do now, to give you a snapshot of what it was like to grow up on the Scioto when Dublin Wasn't Dublin', is to paint you a picture of a pretty typical day in my life on the banks of the great Scioto River when I was about 12 years old and living at the Blankenship house at 6052 Dublin Road.

I used to wake up around 9:00 AM, unless the Yankees had a game the night before on the Coast, and I was up late listening to it on the radio. I would go down and have breakfast of coffee and toast, and walk down to the river. Now, I forgot to tell you this, but I had two boats. Besides the Queen, I had about an eleven foot aluminum boat with a twenty-five horsepower Mercury engine on it. If I had any craws, I would use them; if not, I would use night crawlers. Back in those days, you could always pick night crawlers at night after a rain, but it was harder to pick craws. You picked craws at night, too. The soft ones would come in to shore on the banks of the river to kick their shells. Of course, sometimes you would pick a hard craw, and, man, they could really pinch your fingers! The trick was to slide your fingers up their tails and grab them just below their pinchers. Anyway, I would putter up to the Riffles in my aluminum boat or in the Queen, and I might troll a little along the way along the west bank where it was deepest. Well, now I would just keep fishing until I got hungry for lunch. I could almost always catch some channel catfish, bullheads, rock bass, or bluegills. To catch smallmouth you had to get up there real early, when they were feedin', but I was lazy, even back then, and I liked to sleep late—still do.

When I got hungry enough, I came home, and ate lunch. I liked to eat bologna sandwiches, or tomato, cheese, and mayonnaise sandwiches. I liked to eat a lot. I would lie down for a while; heck, I was about worn out by then, and I would read—mostly baseball books or baseball magazines. If a friend came down, we would play. If not, I would just lie around the house and read about baseball while my mom was watching soap operas. Many times, I would be in this blissful state, just lying around, not doing anything in particular, when the phone would ring. "Dave Wolfe wants to talk to you," my mama would shout. Well, that only meant one thing. "You need to go out and cut the grass," Dave would tell me, "We're going to play 'bloop ball' tonight." "Bloop ball," as opposed to "wiffle ball," is played with a solid plastic ball and a plastic bat. A bloop ball has a lot more action on it as it comes to the plate, and is much more difficult to hit. Dave worked downtown at Yeager's during the summers, and he really liked to play bloop ball—almost as much as I did. "OK," I would say, "what time are we playin'?" "After dinner," he would say. Well, as much as I hated to interrupt my "activities," I would get up and go mow the bloop ball diamond. It was just part of our yard, but I thought it was a really beautiful diamond, and I will elaborate upon it later. Suffice it to say for now; we played a lot of bloop ball.

Later in the afternoon, if the spirit moved me, I would go down to the river and hit rocks or buckeyes across the river. I had a wooden bat which was split down the middle, down the grain. I got it from the Dublin High School Baseball Team. I could swing it pretty fast. Anyway, it was a lot of fun, and I am sure that it really taught me a lot of eye-hand coordination. I would toss a small rock or buckeye up in the air, and swing as hard as I could. It got to the point where I almost never missed, even the smallest pebble, much smaller than a pea. What was really cool, though, was I could always tell when I really got a hold of one—you didn't hear it plunk into the river; you heard it go cascading down the opposite shoreline of rocks and trees. That was a "shot"; a home run. I could hit buckeyes and rocks for hours and hours.

If I wasn't hitting rocks or buckeyes, you might find me walking along the shoreline looking for clams or salamanders or such. Sometimes, if a friend came down, we would walk down the shore a way to Dr. Dix's land and fish for bullheads. Dr. Dix was a brain surgeon. You could about always catch bullheads, even in the late afternoon. We would fish until my friend had to leave. Then I would just mess around until dinner. I liked to throw things—rocks, buckeyes, whatever. I would pick out targets and throw. I would get a rubber ball and throw it against the barn imagining that I was playing in games between the Yankees and Dodgers or Yankees and Reds or Yankees and Tigers—I knew all their lineups, it was a lot easier back then, not so many teams, no free agency.

Dinner came, I ate, and then I ran out and played bloop ball. Well, we played until we couldn't see the ball. We just played and played and played. And we always played to win. You really learned how to run the bases when you played bloop ball. Jim Weaver, when he was

LEFT TO RIGHT: ME, DAVID WOLFE, DON DELAWESE

not under the spell of his blonde haired enchantress, Marta Cook, was the best base runner I have ever seen. Man, Weaver could fly down to first base! Later, after we had all graduated from high school, we played softball together in adult leagues. Weaver was so fast that all he would try to do was just hit a ground ball to the left side of the opposing team's infield. There was not a shortstop or third baseman in those adult leagues who could throw him out. Not only was he fast, but since he hit left handed, he was falling three to four steps toward first base by the time that the ball took its first bounce in the infield. He ran the bases the way Jackie Robinson did: with speed, precision, and aggression. He knew how to cut the corners of the bases when he ran, and his hook slide was just like Ty Cobb's. Anyway, we played bloop ball until you couldn't see at night, and then my friends went home.

Sometimes, like I said earlier, we would go night fishing off the Queen, but usually my friends went home. Me, well, I would get something more to eat, and go up to my room to see if I couldn't dial in the Yankees. I could get them easy when they played Detroit, Cleveland, and Chicago, but it was a stretch to bring them in from New York City itself. But, on those occasions, I was in heaven when I heard the voices of Mel Allen and Red Barber and, later, Phil Rizzuto. I loved baseball. I still do. When I woke up on a morning of a day when there was a little league game, or pony league game, I would just about cry if it was raining. I loved to play that game, and I loved to listen to my Yankees play. Most of the time I would fall asleep listening to them play. What a lullaby. Remember, I had had a "hard" day, hadn't I? If I did fall asleep before the end of the game, what do you think I did the very first thing in the morning, while drinking my coffee? I got ahold of the sports section and read the box scores. I have often thought, during the course of my life, that, if I had read the financial pages as diligently as I read the sports section, I could have become a billionaire. But, of this I am sure: I would not have had nearly as much fun!

Well, so much for "a day in the life" while living on the Scioto; now I would like to share with you a certain night on the Scioto. Remember that silver boat I was talkin' to you about, the little silver boat I had along with the African Queen? Strange, I never did know how that boat got to my house; one morning it was just there (must have been the little creatures). It didn't have a license on it and I don't know if it even had any letters or numbers on the side. Anyway, I loved that boat, too. Like I said, it had a 25 horse-power Mercury on the back, and she was only about eleven feet long. She was really light, and she could fly. When I sat way in the back and goosed the throttle, she must have looked like a silver banana going down the Scioto

River. Then, after 'bout a hundred yards, she would trim off, and then she would really cut through the water—like one of those cigarette boats they have down in Miami Beach. She was a beauty, but you know, I never named her. Boats got to have a name. Of course, the "African Queen," she just kept on rollin', like "Proud Mary," but I never named my little silver, aluminum boat. Maybe if I would have named her, she wouldn't have gotten away from me when the high waters came. At the very least, I could have called her "The Boat With No Name." I guess I was ungrateful at that age, and the Leprechauns that dropped that boat off, well, maybe they just wanted to teach me a lesson. Whatever, let's get back to that night on the Scioto, and what I learned to use that little silver boat for.

There was a time, believe it or not, When Dublin Wasn't Doublin' that there were no fast food restaurants around: no McDonalds, no Burger Kings, no Kentucky Fried Chickens—nothin'. We just had the Dublin Nite Club, the Wyandot Inn, and the White Cottage at which to eat. Then, miracle of all miracles, up sprang, at the east end of Fishinger Bridge, the Burger Boy Food-O-Rama, or BBF, as it was affectionately called. They had great hamburgers, and French fries and milkshakes and whatever, and they served the food fast! I loved to eat there whenever I had someone to take me. I was young at the time, and couldn't drive. I developed a craving for that food; I just couldn't eat enough of it. All the Sellses, as I may have mentioned earlier, are rather renowned for their prodigious appetites. When I was really hungry, things were fine if someone had a car and we could go to the BBF. Just wonderful! However, many times I would get a BBF craving at night when there were no friends around, there were no cars, and there was no way to get to the BBF. It was just excruciating the way my stomach would rumble and twist—thought the fish could pick up the vibration through the boat if I was fishing. Anyway, one summer night, when I was fishing out in my little silver boat and pretty near doubled over with hunger pains, when I would not have known that I had a bite, even if my pole stood straight up on its end and made a pirouette, I had—the word they use for it down there at the university is—an "epiphany!" I had plenty of gas in the engine, had a few dollars on me, and though I didn't have a light, I didn't need one because the moon was out, so I hoisted anchor, and just let that little silver boat "set sail" for the BBF, which was about five miles south of where I was. Well, it was a ride! Seemed like it took about twenty-five minutes, and

I kept my eyes open for the River Patrol all the way. I didn't have lights and my boat wasn't licensed. I lay down in the back of the boat, since the breeze off the river was chilly (especially when I repeated this run in September and early October). After a long, cold, moonlit journey, I beached her at the foot of Fishinger Bridge, and made my way up the hill, a pretty steep hill, if I remember correctly. But at the end, there she was—the beautiful BBF. Well, after a journey so perilous and full of fright (the River Patrol), I made it worthwhile. Up to the counter I went—a real swashbuckler. "Four hamburgers, two fries, and two milkshakes," I bellowed, hearty-ho! I got my booty, trotted down the hill, fired up my little skiff, and headed back up the Scioto. When I docked her beside the Queen, I ran up to the house, and it was only then that I devoured my prize. I tried to eat slowly, but I never could, and it was no matter that my catch was somewhat cooled by the ride. This was real grub, so hearty-hey!!

Can you think of a better place to grow up than on the Scioto River? I don't even remember using a bicycle that much; I had a boat and a raft. My friends would come down, and we would fish off the Queen. I used to swim off her and dive right into the Scioto. I can remember lying down on the African Queen couch, late at night or early in the morning, with my fishing line wrapped around my finger, just about asleep, when a big cat would come cruising by and practically jerk my arm out of its socket. Biggest problem I had was keeping my dogs off the Queen when I went fishing—had to keep them locked up in the basement. If not, they would follow me up and down the riverbank and swim out to the Queen when I anchored her. They would swim—they were Labradors—around the Queen until you pulled them aboard. And when you landed a fish, well, they were all over the place, doing a "war" dance, dancin' and barkin' and so on.

The Blankenship Home was eventually bought and remodeled by one of the truly great statesmen in Ohio history, Secretary of State Ted W. Brown, and I really liked him. He would come down to where we docked the boats after a hard day of work, remodeling a barn on the property, and then the house that we lived in which he bought, and he would have a beer or two. I liked Mr. Brown because he had a great sense of humor, and what was best of all; he never took himself too seriously. I'm pretty sure that he was good friends with our governor then, Governor James A. Rhodes, because they both hailed from Jackson County. I never saw the governor, though, only at the State Fair, riding around in his golf cart. Anyway, on some occasions after a few beers, Mr. Brown would tell me that he was going to make me the Honorary Lieutenant Governor of Kentucky, or some such imaginary title. I thought that was pretty nice of him even though I didn't know exactly what he was referring to. He would always ask me how I was doing when we were down there together by the Queen, he sitting under the shelter house, and he seemed to take a real interest in how I was doing in school and sports. But you know, as much as I liked Mr. Brown, I never needed any honorary title or nothing like that when I was growing up down at the Blankenship's House on the banks of the Scioto River. Heck, I was Huck Finn and I never even knew it!

CHAPTER 2

THE DAVIS FARM

Well, back to story time. I suppose that I was not the first Sells to enjoy the richness of the Scioto River, nor will I be the last. I have taught my son how to fish the Scioto, and, of course, taught him how to play baseball. I taught him how to cross the street, too. We were walking down the sidewalk one day, and I was holding his hand. We had just stepped off the curb to cross the street when I looked down to see a squirrel, or what used to be a squirrel, all gnarled up like he had been run over by one of those FedEx trucks—a couple of times. Anyway, Ryan, my son, looked down at that squirrel and then he looked up at me. "You see that squirrel, Ryan?" I asked him. He said, "Yes, Daddy." I said, "Ryan, that squirrel tried to cross the road, but he only looked one way. You have to look both ways when you cross the road." He said, "Yes, Daddy." I never had any trouble with him crossing the street after that.

Anyway, before I digressed, I was getting ready to tell you about a place that is sacred to me. Just south of Friendship Village, on the east side of Riverside Drive, surrounded by stark limestone borders, sits the Davis Family Cemetery. To me, it's a sacred place, and if you will bear with me and read a little more history, I think that you will understand why. I have extracted the following information concerning the history of the John Davis and Mary Ann Simpson Davis family from a lengthy document compiled in 1954 by Newton Davis, my Grandma Polly's brother, except where I indicate a different source. Newton and Grandma Polly were great grandchildren of John Davis and Mary Ann Simpson Davis (my great-great-great grandparents):

"Mary Ann Simpson—Davis was born in December 20, 1764, and died June 6, 1851, at age 86 years, 6 months. She was a lovely young woman, had some schooling, was a good writer as is indicated by her handwritten poems and letters…. She loved music and poetry and enjoyed the life of a farm woman along with the other members of the family. Her pictures show her to be a very good-looking woman with features of strength and good character. Her family was patriotic who espoused the colonial cause and she had a warm heart for the cause of Liberty and Freedom.

**ANN SIMPSON
DAVIS**

"When the British soldiers came into Bucks County [Pennsylvania] to get food and pillage the people, Mary Ann decided that she would like a part in winning the war. At the age of 15 she went to Valley Forge on horseback and volunteered to General Washington who accepted her as a horse messenger to carry messages into the lines of the British and to the other Generals on the field. She became acquainted with General Lafayette at Valley Forge and also the other leaders who were there. She often in later life told of her work and the people that she knew….

"She rode into Philadelphia delivering messages that were in vegetables or in bullets that she held in her mouth. She often had to swallow them when searched by British soldiers. She sold vegetables and other products. She often looked like an old woman, dressed in old clothes that made her look old. She was never afraid of anyone nor any condition. She rode night and day to deliver messages to the generals wherever they were in the field. She stayed some place around Valley Forge and knew General and Mrs. Washington very well and was in the headquarters where she met Alexander Hamilton and others who were with General Washington.

"She can well be called the Original Revolutionary WAC. [Women's Army Corps]. There were a few women who did service like this but very few who were so close to the leaders of the Revolutionary War.

"She rode her horse as well as any man and performed her duty like a good patriot. She was highly respected by the men in the Army, and… a faithful Messenger, trying to help to win the Liberty and Freedom for which the men were fighting.

"She returned home after the War service and was at her father's home when John Davis came to claim her for his bride. The wooing was successful as no doubt these two young people had met at Valley Forge and other places and were ready to consummate their plans with the wedding that took place at the home of her father and mother in Solesbury Township (Pennsylvania) where they lived. They were married on June 26, 1783, by the Reverend James Boyd, minister of the Presbyterian Church at Newton, who rode to their home for the nuptials."

Ann was a redhead. That probably doesn't surprise you. All the red heads I have ever known are strong-minded.

Concerning John Davis, The Newton Davis document says:

"He was born September 6, 1760 and died January 27, 1832, at age 71 years, 4 months. He was the sixth son of eight children. He lived at home and had some schooling in the local school. He worked on his father's farm. He was a sturdy and strong youth who knew that his heart was on the side of the colonial cause and was ready to help with the cause of the Revolution as soon as opportunity came.

"He enlisted for service on June 4, 1776 and reenlisted in December, 1776.

"He carried the flag in the boat with General Washington across the Delaware River on the "Do or Die Campaign" to attack the Hessians at Trenton.

"He spent that winter at Valley Forge. He was then 16 years old. He was close to General Washington.

"He served for the entire war. He was at the Battle of Brandy-wine and helped to carry General Lafayette from the field when he was wounded. He fought at Princeton, Monmouth, and the entire campaign in New Jersey.

"At the battle of Bergan Point he was wounded in his foot. He never fully recovered from this wound. However, he continued to serve in the war until its conclusion.

"He was at the home of William Neely when Colonel James Monroe, who later became president, was brought there after being wounded and he helped to care for him.

"He fought at Yorktown where he served under General Lafayette.

"He was a brave and loyal soldier and did his bit for Liberty and Freedom."

I hope that you are not tired of reading history. You have to admit, though, these are pretty good stories in and of themselves.

After their marriage in 1783, John and Ann Simpson Davis lived in Pennsylvania until 1796 when they moved to Maryland. They had nine children, born in the years indicated: Sarah, 1784; William, 1785; John, 1788; Ann, 1790; Samuel, 1792; Joshua, 1796; Samuel, 1798; Joseph, 1802; and Elizabeth, 1805. All of the children were born while they lived in Pennsylvania and Maryland.

Sarah married Phillip Warfield in 1801; where they settled is unknown. Ann married Basil Brown in 1807, in Maryland; they settled in the Dublin area on Post Road. William married Mary (Polly) Sullivan in 1809 in Delaware, Ohio. They moved to the Dublin area, on the east side of the Scioto in 1817. John married Amy Hart in 1818 and settled in Pennsylvania. He became a U. S. Senator. The first child by the name of Samuel died in his infancy.

In 1816 John and Ann Davis moved from Maryland to Ohio. At the time of their move to Ohio, John was 56 years old and Ann was 52. Their oldest child was 32 and their youngest was 11. The four youngest children moved to Ohio with them; Joshua, age 20; Samuel, 18; Joseph, 13 and Elizabeth 11.

When John, Ann and the four youngest children moved to Ohio, they first lived at Berkshire, in Delaware County, on a farm owned by Joseph Eaton, a schoolmate of John. In 1817, while the family was living in Berkshire, Joshua married Joseph Eaton's cousin, Edith DeFord. Joshua and Edith stayed in Delaware County.

After two years living in Delaware County, John and Ann acquired land granted to them for their service in the Revolutionary War and they and the three remaining children moved to the newly acquired land.

> "This land was… one mile south of Dublin, in Franklin County, twelve miles from Columbus. Here the land was well wooded and the ground rich. The farm fronted on the Scioto River for almost a mile then back east, covering the hills in a beautiful scenic display. The trees were maple, sugar, oak and walnut with many other kinds. The farm covered several hundred acres and brought forth a job of woodcutting that continued for fifty years. A log house was built near the river road on the west side and not far from the river where there was very good fishing, plenty of deer, and all wild animals upon which they lived for many years. They had all kinds of fruit and vegetables. Several acres of fruit trees were planted after Johnny Appleseed came through and left quantities of seeds of all kinds."

The following is taken from another document entitled *John Davis Hero* (author unknown).

> "The next ten years were strenuous years for the Davis family. Land was cleared, a two story log cabin was built [along with] barns for animals. Fields were fenced and cultivated. Flax was planted and cloth made for their clothing, sheep raised, sheared and the wool made into yarn and cloth for warm clothing…."

Joshua died in 1823 at the age of 27, leaving Edith a widow with four small children. "John laid out a family burial plat south of the home on a shale bank. His son, Joshua was the first to be buried there." And thus began the Davis Cemetery.

Elizabeth married James Coleman in 1823 and moved to Springfield, Illinois. Samuel married a daughter of John Sells, Sr., Matilda Sells, in 1825, bought some land from his parents on the north side of the farm, built a house on it, and lived there.

That left only Joseph living with John and Ann. However, in 1827, Joseph married his brother Joshua's widow, Edith, and brought her and the four children[2] to live with Ann and John.

**ANN SIMPSON DAVIS HOUSE
(IT WAS TORN DOWN WHEN
FRIENDSHIP VILLAGE WAS BUILT.)**

"John and Ann dreamed of a permanent house, one like Ann's home in Newton, Pennsylvania. But John died in 1832 so did not live to realize their dream. Ann, Ede (Edith) and Josey (Joseph) fulfilled this dream. The brick house was started in 1837 and finished in1842. Ann knew every brick that went into the house....A special room off the kitchen was built for her. There was a fireplace where she could toast her toes and smoke her pipe at night sitting in her favorite chair. Her maple cord bed and the dower chest with the secret drawer was there and the walnut cupboard John had made for her when they moved into the log house, in which she stored her cherished things. She spent the last nine years in her dream house. Only John was missing. When John died Ann wrote in her bible "John and I lived together 48 years and 7 months, June 26, 1783 to January 27, 1832. She was content visiting her children, piecing quilts, writing letters to grandchildren and nieces. I have many of the letters she received. Among those in the secret drawer was one from G. Washington which she prized highly, commenting on her services to him and his generals."

2   The children of Joshua and Edith were, Mary Ann Davis, born in1818, and married to Siles Hutchinson in 1847; John Washington Davis, born 1n 1820, and married to Orpha Wright in 1846; William Davis, born in 1821, and died in 1841; and Joshua Davis, Jr., born in 1823, and married to Eleanor Hall in 1849.

Edith had three more children after her marriage to Joseph, including Joseph Watts Davis, the father of my Grandma Polly[3]. Joseph and Edith Davis raised their family on the Farm. Edith Davis died in 1874 at age 77 and Joseph Davis died in July, 1892 at age 90.

Joseph Watts Davis was born in 1838 and was raised on the Farm. He married Mary Jane Butt in 1861. He served in the Civil War as a Captain and was stationed at Camp Chase in Columbus.

JOSEPH DAVIS

Standing L to R: Florence (Polly), Will, Pat & Shell Davis
Seated L to R: Annie, Joseph, Marry Jane Butts Davis, & Newton E. (Ted) Davis

THE JOSEPH WATTS DAVIS FAMILY

He and Mary Jane lived on the Farm throughout their married life and raised their eight children there.

The children of Joseph Watts Davis and Mary Jane Butt Davis were:

William Wilshire Davis (nicknamed Will), born in 1863. He married Ethel Arts, but was later divorced. He then married Helen Kraft and moved to Florida. Later, he went west, did some gold mining, and then had a horse ranch with his brother Pat. He died in 1937.

3   The children of Edith and Joseph Davis, besides Joseph Watts Davis, were: Martha Jane Davis, born in 1828, married to Geroge Marquis in 1848 and died in 1892; Frank Davis, born in 1831, moved to Iowa 1n 1855, married Julia Clark in 1857;

Edith Gertrude Davis (nicknamed Gertie), born in 1865. She moved to Florida. She married Charles Tydings in 1889. She died in 1946.

Percy Shellenbarger Davis (nicknamed Shell), born in 1868. He traveled with the Ringling Brothers Circus for 20 years as a member of their band. He also died in 1937.

Wilson Riley Davis (nicknamed Pat), born in 1870. He went west to Idaho and Montana, became a cowboy, had a horse ranch with his brother Will, and then returned to Dublin and married Annie Bower. He and Annie had one child, Joseph, who died at age 7. He also died in 1937 (as did his brothers Will & Shell). His death was ruled to have been by an accidental gunshot. I will tell you more about him and his death later in the book.

Florence Mary Davis Sells (nicknamed Polly), my Grandma Polly, born 1873.

Newton Eads Davis, born in 1876. He married Florence Hiffner in 1900, and authored the *History of the Davis and Simpson Families*.

Frederick Ralph Davis, born in 1879. He died at age 8, in 1887.

Annie Davis, born in 1883. She was raised in Florida by her sister Gertie, after their mother died.

THE DUBLIN CORNET BAND

In 1879, according to the document compiled by his son, Newton Davis, "Joseph Watts Davis organized the Dublin Cornet Band and made their wagon, or had it made, and bought the uniforms and instruments for the band." Mary Davis died in 1891. Joseph Watts Davis died in January, 1892, six months before his father died.

So John Davis (September 6, 1760 – January 27, 1832) and Ann Simpson Davis (December 20, 1764 – June 6, 1851) were my great-great-great grandparents; Joseph Davis (January 27, 1802 – June 29, 1892) and Edith Davis (August 9, 1797 – August 14, 1874) were my great-great grandparents; and Joseph Watts Davis (June 19, 1838 – January 25, 1892) and his wife, Mary Butt Davis (July 10, 1842 – October 14, 1891), were my great grandparents. They are all buried in the Davis Cemetery. My grandmother Polly is buried there also.

Grandma Polly was 19 years old when her grandfather Joseph died, her father having died 6 months earlier. She was already married to Amaziah Sells and they were living at the Farm. They acquired the farm after the death of Joseph and continued to live there. They both lived there until they died.

So the Davis Farm became the Sells Farm and the brick farmhouse built by Ann Simpson Davis and Joseph and Edith Davis, after John's death, is the house that my dad was raised in. The farm was much bigger when John and Ann Simpson Davis were living than it was when it was the Sells Farm because, over the years, portions of the original farm had been parceled out to family members or sold off. One document I have, entitled *Ann Simpson Davis – A Revolutionary Heroine* (author unknown) says that the original farm was 1,100 acres, but that may be an exaggeration.

I am very proud of my great-great-great grandmother and grandfather Davis. There is now a Dublin middle school named after Ann Simpson Davis. She is listed as a patriot of the American Revolution, and there is a local chapter of the National Society of the Daughters of the American Revolution named for her. There is also a chapter of the National Society of the Children of the American Revolution named after John Davis. It would be a great privilege for me to be buried some day with them in the Davis Cemetery, but you never can tell. There are a lot of unknowns in the world.

Now, weren't those stories worth the reading? It's nice to know I have Davis blood in me. Another thing I wanted to tell you about the Davis His-torical Cemetery is that when I recently visited it, I almost got run over on Riverside Drive. I parked my car on the west side of the road on the berm, got out and walked north to the cemetery, but when I went to cross over Riverside Drive, it was like the Indianapo-

THE DAVIS CEMETERY

lis Speedway. I was sure there had to be an easier way of getting in there and I am happy to report that since my visit an asphalt parking area has been added off Riverside Drive that makes access to the cemetery much easier, and safer too. It needs to be entered as you are driving north on Riverside drive.

Anyway, in regards to the graveyard, I am told there aren't just Davises and Sellses buried in there. I have heard that there were runaway slaves buried there too, as the old brick farmhouse on the Farm was part of the Underground Railroad. There are many unmarked headstones in the cemetery. Are they the headstones of runaway slaves? I would be happy if they were. I am sure that the escaped slaves would have been treated well on the Farm. In Sellsville, where my family wintered the Sells Brothers Circus, which I will tell you about in the next chapter, many African-American Americans were placed in positions of supervision. Also, I know that across the Scioto River on Riverview Street, Dr. Pinney, an abolitionist, harbored runaway slaves. Kind of makes me feel good knowing that there's all kinds buried in that cemetery, not just Sellses or Davises. It is nice to know that the Sellses and Davises were culturally diverse even way back when. I wouldn't be surprised if there are a few hobos in there too. Grandma Polly took everyone in. My cousin Dick Sells used to come up from Lancaster to mow the cemetery. Perry Township takes care of it now. The "Ann Simpson Davis DAR Chapter" plants flowers there annually.

Before I quit talking to you about graveyards, I would like to say a little more about the Dublin Cemetery which is right smack in the middle of Dublin, next to the Dublin Community Church, right off Route 161.

All the great names of Dublin are represented in that Cemetery: the Headlees, the Orrs, the Lepperts, the Geeses, the Pinneys, the Tullers, the Tuttles, and I could go on and on. I understand burying space is at a premium nowadays—people just dying to get in there.

I know that cemetery pretty well since the first job I ever had was running Bobby Joe Bailey and Willie Millers' coon dogs around and around and around in that graveyard. The dogs plumb wore me out; I wasn't more than six or seven then. They would bellow and howl and bark, but I just kept running around behind holding on to their leashes. The first tombstone you see when you come into the Dublin Cemetery is that of the real old man, Ludwick Sells, and I saw his name so many times while I was running those dogs around in circles that it got seared in my mind. Funny thing, those dogs always seemed to want to stop and to pee on his tombstone after a while. But, Willie and Bobby Joe paid me pretty good, so I didn't mind.

Now, there are also a whole slew of Sellses buried in there, including my Great-Great-Great-Great-Grandparents, Ludwick Sells and Catherine Deardorff Sells; my Great-Great-Great-Grandparents, John Sells and Elizabeth Stroup Sells; my Great-Great-Grandparents, John Sells, Jr. and Marinda Hutchinson Sells; my Great-Grandparents, Richard Hannibal Sells and Amanda Rachel Bower Sells; and my Grandfather, Amaziah Sells. Grandma Polly and Grandpa Amaziah are not buried together. Apparently she wanted to be with the Davises and he wanted to be with the Sellses.

My Great-Great-Great Grandfather, John Sells, founded Dublin. In CHAPTER 10 - THE BEGINNING OF DUBLIN, you will read about John Sells, and some of the other members of the Sells family and about the early years of Dublin. You will also learn that the Wyandot Indian Chief, Leatherlips, who was the chief of the Indians living in the Dublin area, was executed by Indian warriors, solely because he wanted to be at peace with the settlers of Dublin. You will also hear about how Dublin almost became the capital of Ohio, and find out why it lost out to Columbus.

My dad, Robert Sells (1918-1998), and my mom, Darline Sells (1922-1987), and my big brother, Pat Sells (1948-1949), are also buried in the Dublin Cemetery. My big brother Pat died in his crib when he was around 21 months old. My mom left his crib for just a second, near as I can tell, and he reached up and pulled some window drapes down on himself and smothered to death. I had just been born when it happened. I don't think my mother ever recovered from that tragedy, and I believe that it may have added greatly to her later problems. Anyway, our footstones in the Dublin Cemetery are all pink granite, and there is one extra plot there, I think, maybe for me if I so choose. When we buried my dad, I remember Gary Headlee and Jimmy Headlee were there. Those Headlees are everywhere and I never could keep them straight. Gary asked me if there was anything I wanted to have buried in with my dad's ashes. I seemed to always have baseballs in my car because of my son Ryan, so I threw Gary a baseball, and Gary tossed it in the hole. My dad loved baseball, as you will see later. My dad's footstone is simple, yet very meaningful: "Robert L. Sells, 1918-1998, US Army." The War was the defining moment in his life: his college, his Master's Degree, and his Ph.D.

CHAPTER 3

THE SELLS BROTHERS CIRCUS

Now, before I continue with my recollections of Dublin When It Wasn't Doublin', I would like to touch upon a subject of great interest to just about anyone who has ever heard the name of Sells, especially in Central Ohio—The Sells Brothers Circus, at one time the second largest circus in the country. The circus was founded by the same Sells family that founded Dublin. I would like to thank the fine people of Dublin who helped me begin this recounting with a book the City put out: *Dublin's Journey*, Peter D. Franklin and Elaine Kehoe, co-authors. Another source for what follows concerning the circus is a series of articles which were in the *Short North Gazette* entitled *Circus Town*, written by Nancy Panzer. I would like to share with you some stories about the circus that I extracted from these sources, and of course, relate some stories that I heard growing up.

Ludwick Sells was my grandfather of six generations ago, and John Sells was his son (and my fifth generation grandfather). It is John Sells who is formally credited with the founding of Dublin in 1810. John had four brothers who also helped settle Dublin —Peter, Benjamin, Samuel and William. Benjamin had a son named Peter. This Peter's sons, Lewis, Ephraim, William Allen and Peter were the founders, owners and operators of the circus, making them my '2nd cousins, thrice removed'. Following are excerpts from the "Circus World" articles.

"...One of Ludwick grandsons, Peter, moved from Dublin to Columbus in 1834 and found employment as a truck gardener and Methodist lay preacher. He raised eleven children and was quite prosperous. Peter had five sons, and all of them served in the American Civil War. One died in Andersonville Prison, but the other four survived and were residents of Columbus in the late 1800s. Three of them, Ephraim, William Allen, and Lewis, were in the auction business and followed circus troupes around the country in order to take advantage of the audiences they attracted. After one failed attempt at running their own circus show, they enlisted the help of their brother Peter, the youngest of the family...

"The brothers became fascinated by a man named 'Cannonball George Richards', a performer who billed himself as a "percussive aerialist." In other words, he shot himself out of cannon on a daily basis....In 1871 the brothers purchased the act and some equipment and animals and started the circus....The first show was in Columbus at the intersection of State St and High St....

"Before long the Brothers felt that they needed an elephant to make the show complete, and in 1873 purchased their first of many pachyderms to come. Elephants became somewhat of a passion for the Sells Brothers and less than a decade later they had eight. The show grew and by 1878 they were being transported by rail rather than by wagons over the road....In 1887 the title of the show was changed to:

"Sells Brothers World Conquering And All Overshadowing Three Ring Circus, Real Roman Hippodrome, Indian Village and Pawnee Bill's Famous Original Wild West Show"....

"By 1890 the Sells Brothers Circus was the second largest circus in America.

"At its height, the show had a 328 foot big top, six other large tents, 322 workers, 64 performers, 50 cages of wild animals, 13 elephants and 7 camels.... Sideshow features included giants, tattooed people, a magician, midgets, a snake charmer, a knife throwing husband and wife team, Hindoo giants, a "wild man" and another man who had rocks broken on his head.

"The Circus enjoyed great success and was particularly popular in the Midwest, West, and even made a tour to Australia.

THE SELLS BROTHERS – PETER, LEWIS, EPHRAIM, AND WILLIAM ALLEN

"The Sells Circus was different from many other circuses in the respect that it did not winter in Sarasota, Florida as many others did at the time. [Winter quarters for the circus were located in the Columbus area at "Sellsville," an unincorporated area, bounded by the Olentangy River on the east, 5th Avenue on the south, and King Avenue on the north, and containing approximately 1,000 acres.]…"

"On Sundays, local residents were allowed to visit the Ring Barn, where animal trainers rehearsed. Winter quarters were lively, full of animals, colorful residents and visitors.

"The people [of Sellsville] occasionally bore witness to some humorous and frightening (unrehearsed) animal acts. During the height of the show's popularity, the menagerie [at Sellsville] included 18 elephants, pumas, black panthers, hyenas, antelope, lions, tigers, leopards, zebras, bears, rhinoceroses, sea lions, monkeys, hippopotamuses and around 250 horses…Sometimes animals did escape….One resident reportedly ran into five escaped polar bears on his way home from work, and another family had their front porch torn off by a stray elephant

"In 1900, in Sellsville, a giant bull elephant, Sid, grabbed his trainer, Patsy Forepaugh, raised him up with his trunk and threw him against a wall, breaking the wall and killing Patsy. A year later, Sid killed another man at the Pan-American Exposition in Buffalo, N.Y. Sid's offenses were not deemed punishable by death, and he continued to perform.

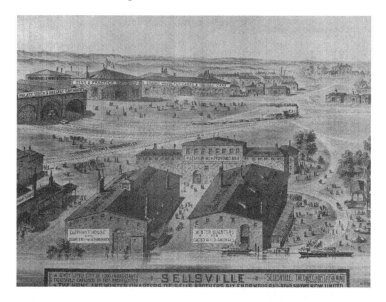

**SELLSVILLE: THE WINTER HOME FOR
THE SELLS BROTHERS'S CIRCUS
BETWEEN 5TH AVE. AND KING AVE.,
WEST OF THE OLENTAGY RIVER**

"The Sells Brothers Circus evolved and took on elements of the Wild West Show....Occasionally, the Wild West Shows got a little bit too wild. One day in Clinton, Iowa, a pistol used by the performers was mistakenly loaded with real bullets (as a matter of protocol, blanks were normally used). The discharge [seriously injured] three people, including the wife of the County Attorney. The show was hurriedly torn down and hustled across state lines. For several years afterward, the Sells brothers didn't include Iowa in their itinerary.

"In the very late 19th Century, the Sells Brothers Circus began to decline. A disastrous trip to Australia proved to be ominous when an outbreak of glanders, a contagious disease, killed most of the animals. Ephraim Sells died in 1898. Barnum and Bailey bought into the Show shortly thereafter. When Peter, aged 59, and Allen both passed in 1904, Lewis Sells sold the remaining shares to James Bailey for $150,000.00 in cash. Bailey then sold a half interest to the Ringling Brothers. Bailey died in 1906 and the Ringling Brothers bought the other half interest and the Sells Brothers Circus became part of the "Ringling Brothers, Barnum and Bailey's Greatest Show on Earth," from *Circus Town*.

To this day, whenever the Ringling Brothers Circus comes to Columbus they give a "tip of the hat" to the Sells Brothers Circus by parading their elephants through Sellsville. This year they unloaded them from their train at Goodale Blvd. and Grandview Ave. and paraded up Grandview Ave. to 3rd Ave., then east on 3rd

THE AUTHOR AND THE RINGLING BROS. ELEPHANTS

Ave. to Eastview Ave. and from there, north to Lane Ave. and then to Shottenstein Arena. I was there and saw them.

In 1895, Peter Sells built a mansion at 755 Dennison Avenue in Columbus. The magnificent edifice was built for his wife, Mary, and their daughter, Florence. He and Mary had wed in 1878 at Canton, Missouri.

After a relatively short time, Mary tired of the circus life, and apparently tired of her husband, Peter, or of his being gone all the time tending to circus business (and maybe she got tired of having so many Sellses as relatives.). What ensued was a scandal fit for *Entertainment Tonight*. Mary Sells was reported to have taken not one, but two lovers during Peter's forays into the circus and business world. It was, as they say, a nasty, nasty divorce, and Peter got just about everything, and Mary received practically nothing. The divorce was granted in 1900 and Peter received the mansion at 755 Dennison Ave. He lived there with his daughter, Florence until 1902, when he sold it. He had a stroke in 1904 and died.

So, the Sells Brothers Circus and Peter were gone, but, pray tell, what became of the Circus House? The answer is that it continued as a private residence until 1925; then for the next 28 years, it was used as a meeting facility for the United Commercial Travelers; from 1953 through 1959, the

**THE CIRCUS HOUSE
755 DENNISON AVE.
(CORNER OF BUTTLES
AND DENNISON)**

Fraternal Order of Police occupied the building; during 1960 and 1961 it was used by the House of Hope as a shelter house for alcoholics; in 1962 it was vacant; then, for the next 33 years, from 1963 through 1996, it served as a nursery school with a private residence on the second floor. In 1997 the owners of the property began a project to restore it to its original grandeur as a private residence. It has been used as a home from then, until the present.

Now, before I quit talkin' to you about the circus, there's something else I would like to say. I was readin' in *Dublin's Journey* (p.47) that, before establishing Sellsville, the Sells Brothers used to winter their circus along Route 161 west of Linworth, on the grounds of what is now the Brookside Country Club. I never knew that, and to me, it makes the Sells Circus more of a Dublin thing than a Columbus thing, what with Ludwick Sells being the great-grandfather of Lewis, Ephraim, William Allen, and Peter.

And Bill Moose is another Dublin connection. Bill Moose, a full blooded Wyandot Indian traveled with the circus for 9 years as "Indian Bill." I learned about Bill Moose from a book entitled *Last of The Wyandots*, published by The Linworth United Methodist Church Historical Society. The following information was extracted from that book:

> Bill Moose's parents were part of Leatherlips' tribe that lived in Dublin. According to Bill, his father was born in about 1771 and died in 1871 and his mother was born in about 1766 and died in 1872. They were part of Leatherlips' tribe at the time he was executed. They moved from the Dublin area to Upper Sandusky sometime between 1810 and 1837. They lived out the remainder of their lives in Upper Sandusky, refusing to leave when the government relocated the rest of the tribe to Kansas in 1843. Bill was born in Upper Sandusky in 1837. Occasionally, Bill's parents and

Bill traveled to Dublin to visit Leatherlips' grave, during which visits they camped in the vicinity of Bright Road and Riverside Drive where their tribe had last lived. They also visited other sites in the Dublin area which were special to the Wyandots. After his parents died, Bill decided to relocate back to Central Ohio, his ancestral home. He lived along the Olentangy River, in a place called the "High Banks," but spent a lot of time in the Dublin area camping and visiting with folks whose ancestors had been friends of his parents and the other members of the Dublin area Wyandot Indians. He lived out the rest of his life in Central Ohio, except for the 9 years he

BILL MOOSE
"INDIAN BILL"

traveled with the Sells Brothers Circus as 'Indian Bill'. He is said to have been the 'Last of the Wyandots" because after the Wyandots were relocated to Kansas and later to Oklahoma they were mixed with other tribes and because of intermarriage with other tribes there were no other full blooded Wyandots by the time Bill died, in 1937, just shy of his 100th birthday. By the time of his death he was well known and highly regarded in the Central Ohio community. It was estimated that more than 10,000 people came to the funeral home to pay their respects to him.

I forgot to tell you what I heard and what I saw down at the Columbus Theater of Arts this past summer. Ms. Annie Oakley got her start as a sharpshooter in the Sells Brothers Circus. I saw a coin that she had shot which they had on display. Oakley quit the circus in 1895 (*Dublin Journey*, p.48). Now, I don't think that Annie Oakley could shoot as well as my great Uncle Pat Davis could, but that's another story you'll be hearing shortly. Well, there's a lot more that could be said about the Sells Circus, and if you are interested, you can go "on-line," as they say now days, and even buy yourself some posters of the Sells Circus, if you are so inclined —most of 'em have elephants in them. In the Sells Circus, instead of racin' horses, I guess they used to race elephants—now, ain't that somethin'?

I remember as a child that when we had family reunions and other family get-togethers—when we weren't fighting one another—I would hear stories about the circus. The fact that I came from such a big family, and the fact that we once had a circus, well, that made me feel we were a little "different" from other families. My dad always loved elephants, too, and I imagine he pestered the old man about getting one for the Farm, but the old man never did. Guess he already had enough critters and kids to take care of.

Anyway, my family did have a big circus with lots of elephants and big cats and like I said, I heard that instead of having horse races they would have elephant races. I heard that at the circus winter home near what is now called Victorian Village during the winter, the Sells Brothers would keep the big cats in the carriage houses. And I heard that the people of Sellsville occasionally had to put up with some unrehearsed animal acts.

I guess what I am most proud of about the Sells Circus is that Sellsville was an integrated community. "The school, located on Virginia Avenue near Chambers Road, was called the Polkadot School because the enrollment was of an equal number of black children and white children. Some of the older black residents had been slaves who came to Central Ohio by way of the Underground Railroad. The community had a 21-piece black band called the Clippers, and a black baseball team called the Sellsville Sluggers, *Circus Town*, p.5.

Anytime that you walk into the Columbus Metropolitan Library downtown on Grant Avenue, you will see, cascading down the staircase, a portrait of Lewis, Ephraim, William Allen, and Peter, my kin of long ago.

I read an article recently in the *Columbus Dispatch*, published in connection with the celebration of the 200th birthday of Columbus, about "the great flood of the Olentangy River in February, 1883" and how it affected Sellsville. Of course Sellsville was on the west bank of the Olentangy River. According to the article, the flood caused quite a panic there. I suppose it was pretty hard movin' the big elephants up to the high ground and I reckon it was just as difficult corralin' the lions, tigers, and bears. And then there were the camels, orangutans, monkeys, and chimpanzees. I wonder what they did with them. At least there weren't any unicorns.

Lots of people ask me about the circus. I guess it was the "magical mystery tour" of its day. I often wonder what kind of inspiration caused the brothers to set out to form a circus. It must have taken a lot of energy. I can't help but believe that to have that much energy Lewis, Ephraim, William Allen, and Peter had to have had something extra running through their veins like Ludwick and his sons, but we'll never know. Maybe they were just "Circus People"; or maybe they were just Sellses.

CHAPTER 4

THE SELLS FARM

S ince we have been talking about the miraculous and the magical, perhaps it is time we speak of some truly wondrous events that happened
on the Sells Farm that added to the folklore of Dublin, unique at least
throughout Central Ohio, if not the whole of the state, if not the whole of
the United States of America. Now, I am speaking of things that happened
on the Sells Farm during the latter part of the 1800's and early 1900's.

The Farm was south of Martin
Road on the east side of Riverside
Drive where "Friendship Village" is
now. It was known as the "Sells
Farm" when I was growing up, but
as you have just read, it was the
Davis Farm before it was the Sells
Farm. Of course, The Sells Farm
was run by the old man, Amaziah,
who we have discussed earlier. The
old man had the great fortune of
marrying my grandmother, Florence Mary Davis, the daughter of

**THE SELLS FARM
(THE OLD DAVIS FARM)**

Joseph Watts and Mary B. Davis. Grandma Polly, as she was affectionately
known, spent all of her life on the Farm in Dublin, and she passed away in
1932. Like I said earlier, she was said to have been six feet tall and weighed

three hundred pounds when she went to see the Lord. I guess you would have been that big, too, if you had birthed that many children. She attended Dublin School and Otterbein College in Westerville, Ohio.

They had their own little menagerie on the Sells Farm, and I suppose the old man was the ringleader of his own three-ring circus, not to be confused with the Sells Brothers Circus. The first thing I remember about the Farm is hunting. You see, back then, when I was a kid, there were many farms around Dublin: the Tullers, the Tuttles, the Lepperts, The Frantzes, the McCoys, the McKitricks, the Geeses, and on and on and on. Now days, there aren't any farms like those, but back then we had farms, and we always had lots of places to hunt. Now, I'm going to tell you right off that I wasn't a hunter, but I did like to get out and walk around—no telling what you might see. On a big farm, you always had plenty of creeks, fence rows, wheat, corn, and beans, and there is no better place for birds than that— pheasants and quail and doves and even woodcocks now and then. On those farms, it seemed there were big cock pheasants about everywhere you stepped, and coveys of quail around just about every creek bed or thatch of high grass. Rabbits? Everywhere there was a rabbit. They lived all over those farms, especially in those briar or wood patches where you could kick them out. It would get cold out hunting, but it was worth it. And all those pheasants were corn fed. But, I must confess, I didn't follow in the Sells' tradition of being a crack shot, and I don't remember ever shooting anything when I went hunting. For me, it was the thrill of the thing. I would be walking around, keeping' my shotgun pointed down, and all of a sudden there would be a big whoosh and terrible whir in the air at the same time and it would be a big old cock pheasant taking off. It would darn near make me wet my pants, and then there would be three or four or five rounds shot off by the other hunters, and then I would fire my shotgun—just for the heck of it. And quail? They were worse! Quietly creeping through the woods, sometimes you had a dog and sometimes you didn't, but if you did, and if he came to point, then you knew there was a covey very close. I swear, I would get ready, I would raise my shotgun, I would hold my breath, then, well, all of a sudden all heck broke loose! There would be five, six, seven quail take off all at the same time. It about scared me to death, just the sound of it, and I would try to pick out one to hit, like they told me to do, aim to hit just one, but I always ended up shooting right in the middle of the whole covey. So, there you have it, never shot a pheasant and never shot a quail. Shot at them, but never hit one. I sure did like to eat them though; there are few things better than a pheasant or three or four quail. My dad and my brother were great hunters. Of course, my dad used a shotgun called the "Yankey Tank." It was a sawed-off 12 gauge shotgun, an automatic. He never missed much with that. But, my dad didn't hunt much after he came home from the War.

Now, I will tell you a story my dad shared with me, it's what he told me, anyways. It seems as though, at the end of the working day, when the boys didn't have anything to do, and with fifteen children, my dad being the youngest, there wasn't a whole lot to do to keep the boys occupied. So, I guess what they liked to do, being in the so called "prime" of their lives, was wrestle with one another and sometimes have bare-fisted fights to see who was the toughest on the Farm. Now, the old man would supervise them, and if things got "out of hand," well, he would just crack his bullwhip. It sounds like something the old man would do. He would sit in his rocking chair with his bullwhip in hand. I guess this is not too unusual given the fact that my great grandfather was a teamster on a mule train and familiar with the use of bullwhips. Now, this may sound a little harsh, and maybe even abusive, but bear in mind that there were no social service agencies back in those days. Anyway, when things did get out of hand, as I was told, it was not uncommon for one of the boys to feel a sting on his legs from the old man's bullwhip. My dad told me that one evening when the boys were out wrestling and he was out there just standing on the periphery and watching, he felt a sharp sting on his leg, and it really hurt.

"What did you do?" I asked

"Well, I didn't do anything at first," he said. "I just turned around and made a loop behind the brick farmhouse. I picked up a brick because there were always bricks lying around there. I snuck up behind the old man in his rocking chair, and I hit him as hard as I could with that brick upside his head so that he flew right out of his chair. I figured that I had killed him, I hit him hard; so I ran away. I eventually made my way up to Delaware where I joined the National Guard. When we declared war in 1941, I was already in the Army."

My aunts and my uncles, well, it was a clan and they were wild. I surely wish I would have had the chance to know my Grandma Polly Davis. "What was Grandma Polly like?" I used to ask my dad. "How the heck should

I know? Like I told you before, I was the last born, and I was raised by a nanny and your Aunt Ruth." "And your dad, what was he like?" I asked my dad. "Well, after, and even during the War, we got along pretty well. Funny thing about the old man, when your Grandma died, there was a lot of turmoil about this and that in the family: who was going to get this and that, how was the land going to be split up, was there going to be a new will? You know what the old man did? He just up and married his housekeeper, Eddie. You always called her Aunt Eddie, but she wasn't your aunt. She used to be the old man's housekeeper. He just did what he wanted to do. He made me an overseer of the Farm before he died. He used to come to our house when we lived right in the middle of Dublin between Cole's and Herron's, and he would watch TV with us since we had one of the first TVs in Dublin. I believe that Harold Shriver had the first."

On the farm was this big, big brick house that had been built by my Davis ancestors, and it sat in the northeast corner of the Farm. "Do you know how many bedrooms that farmhouse had in it?" My dad once asked me. "No," I responded. "Well," he said, "it had twenty bedrooms in it, and they were all heated by coal fireplaces. Do you know who got to carry twenty buckets of coal up every night to heat those rooms, and who had to clean out those same fireplaces every morning?" he asked. "No." I said. "Well," he said, "I did because I was the youngest. Now, I am going to ask you another question: did you ever wonder why we never used a fireplace in any house we ever lived in?" "No," I said. "Well, think about it," he said. I did, and I finally figured it out. The farmhouse was huge. It had two large adjoining kitchens, fully equipped. My dad told me that when it came time to thresh wheat, grandma, my aunts, and lots of neighbors' wives and daughters from nearby farms would be in the kitchens fixing food to feed up to seventy men, all at the same time.

Speaking of which, there were plenty of things that I would like to have seen on the Farm. I would like to have seen a couple of the boys returning from the Linworth, Ohio, train junction with a couple kegs of oysters in the back of their wagon for the old man (as if he needed any) for Thanksgiving and Christmas. Yes, and I would have liked to have seen the same boys coming back from Linworth with stalks and stalks of bananas for everyone on the farm to eat—wonder how many bananas they would have had to load in the backs of those wagons. I would like to have seen the old man driving his machine around the Farm. Friend of mine, Pete Hall, who taught me how to catch crappies and big catfish, was going north on Riverside Drive one evening, he told me, when the old man pulled out in front of Pete and wrecked Pete's car. "Get it fixed and send me the bill," was all the old man said. Well, Pete said that he got his car fixed and sent the old man the bill, but the old man never paid him. Maybe the old man forgot, or maybe the old man thought Pete would just take it out in trade by the food he ate on the Farm. Anyway, Pete never held it against me. The old man was just strange. People are strange, especially when you are a stranger to them.

But, getting back to threshing wheat, I think that is what I would most like to have seen on the farm—everybody working together, community spirit, something special to Dublin and other small villages. It's something we don't seem to have much of these days. Anyway, I went "on-line" for some research. I thought I would refresh your memories and mine of what hard work and friendship and community are all about, things we used to have a lot of "When Dublin Wasn't Doublin'." What follows was extracted from this website:

(http://www.livinghistoryfarm.org/farmingin the20's/machines_06.htm)

Harvesting Wheat

> "Winter wheat is planted in the fall, grows through the spring and is ready for harvest in the middle of summer. So, harvesting wheat is hot, dusty labor. In the 1920's the harvest took several steps, lots of neighbors and all their wives and daughters to feed and support the threshers. The process began with a horse drawn (and later tractor-drawn) binder that would cut the wheat stalks and gather them into bundles. The bundles would be stacked into windrows to dry. Then later all the neighbors would gather with a huge thresh-ing machine that would separate the wheat kernels from the straw stalks. The women and girls would cook huge meals for the crew. Today, the work can be done by one person on a combine, another to drive the truck to the elevator and another to cook. When the wheat was ripe you would cut it and run it through another part of the binder and put it into bundles and tie a string around it. And it would be kicked off into windrows. Then in the evenings, you would go out and put these bundles up in piles so they could dry out, maybe eight, ten, or a dozen bundles in what they call a shuck.

Later on, you would go out in the fields with your bundle rack and pick these up and then run them through a threshing machine and that separated the wheat from the straw.

"While the men and boys worked in field, farm women and girls faced long hours in a steamy hot kitchen, preparing meals for hungry field hands. With no microwave oven, refrigerator, or frozen foods to ease the work, the women cooked and baked for several days in a row, fixing huge meals for the threshing crews. As with field work, neighbor women shared the cooking and kitchen work. At threshing time, even children helped. Older boys loaded bundles of wheat into the threshing cylinder and piled up straw that was used later for livestock bedding and to stuff mattresses. Older girls worked in the kitchen, helping cook platters of fried chicken, potatoes and gravy, beans, squash, homemade bread and butter, pies and cakes and much more to feed the hungry workers. Little girls ran back and forth to the field, carrying sandwiches and snacks to workers, and little boys hauled jugs of cool water to workers in the hot, dusty fields." (Darrell Ronne).

"A big, huge, threshing machine—it was a huge old steam engine that run it. The man that run that, if you happened to be threshing at your place, he'd come before breakfast, and he would fire up that steam engine so he'd get enough steam so he could run that day. And then you had to, the ladies had to feed him and the man that run the separator, breakfast. And then of course, they had to feed all them hungry men at noon, and there would be, well there'd be twelve running the racks and there would be some that were hauling the grain away and the one doing the separator. And the poor ladies, they sure had to work hard to feed all those people." (Harvey Pickrel).

I most certainly would have liked to have seen that, surely would! Everybody working together, side by side! Can't say though that I'd liked to have actually taken part in the threshing, or even working in the kitchen—I've always been the kind to shy away from hard work. Smartest thing an old timer ever told me was this: "Son, there's three things you should stay away from in this world— a shovel, a sledge hammer, and a spud bar." I took his advice. But, on the other hand, for threshing wheat, I guess I could have been the water boy. I think I could have handled that—providing that the water bucket wasn't too awful heavy.

There was always plenty of work and all kinds of action on the Farm, all sorts of people and kin coming and going, kind of like a bus station I suppose. I am told that during the First World War an army regiment camped out on the Farm. I don't doubt it. I am told that my Uncle Ted liked to go down to the regiment and wrestle with the soldiers to see who was the toughest and I am told that when the army regiment left, they let us have a lot of their surplus goods for the Farm. I'm sure they were put to good use.

There were also some pretty unusual things that took place on the Farm. I was told by Jim McCoy, about as reliable a source that you could find in Dublin at the time, and who had a farm just south of the Sells' Farm on Case Road, that the old man had a bull that was downright mean and ugly—a real killer. If the boys (or girls) ever tried to cut through one of "his" fields he'd try to pin them against a fence and gore them. One day, I guess the boys decided they had had enough of being chased around by this bull and being scared out of their wits whenever they were cutting through his fields and that they ought to do something about it. Well, somehow, they managed to get him cornered in the barn late one afternoon, and forced him into one of the holding stalls. I guess that old bull bellowed and bellowed, but he hadn't seen anything yet. The boys managed to jump on top of him, wrestle him down, and pound a ring through his nose. I guess they thought that would take a little spunk out of that big critter. Just the opposite happened. He got really mad then: kicking, snorting, and frothing at the mouth. Well, this made the boys tickled to death; I expect they were lying on the barn floor doubled up with laughter. I guess the more that bull bellowed, the harder they laughed. Then one of them came up with the bright idea of hog-tying him with a rope like you would a calf at the rodeo. After they had hog-tied the bull, they just looked at one another. "What are we going to do with him now?" they probably asked one another. "Well, let's just string that bugger up!" they all shouted. They all joined in, whooping and hollering. "Yeah, let's string that big bugger up and teach him a lesson or two that he'll never forget." So, as Jim McCoy told me, they took the thickest rope they could find, tied it to the bull's back legs, threw the rope over the main beam of the barn, and grabbed hold of it, held on for dear life, backed up, little by little, pulled with all their might, and finally got the bull off the ground. By now, that big bull was up in the air, swinging back and forth. Every time he would swing back and forth, he would bellow like he was caught in a fence. Of course, the boys would give him a little shove now and then to make sure he enjoyed his ride. Every time that bull brayed and grunted and snorted, I imagine the boys would just fall down on the barn floor laughing. Imagine that sight! I guess the circus was alive and well after all those years: "Step right up, step right up, ladies and gentleman, and see the Eighth Wonder of the World, the one ton, Dublin, Tumblin' Bull. He will snort and bellow. He's not a nice fellow. See him fly with ease WITHOUT a trapeze!" Well, the boys laughed so long and so hard that they couldn't laugh anymore. I imagine their ribs started aching and their knees got weak' from laughing so much. They finally cut the bull down, and let him run out through barn doors. I bet you, though, that after he got "strung up," that bull was never as mean and cantankerous as he had been. I doubt he ever chased the boys again when they cut through one of "his" fields—even if they had on red shirts. That was the kind of fun they used to have on the Farm, When Dublin Wasn't Doublin'.

"What was it like during the Depression?" I once asked my dad.

"Didn't know we had one," he said, "See, on the Farm we had dairy cattle, which I milked, beef cattle, wheat, corn, beans, orchards, and all kinds of canned vegetables from the gardens which your grandma and the girls took care of. We had heat. Your Aunt Blanche ran a coal business, so we had plenty of coal. Your uncles worked hard, of course, and a lot of them had fingers or thumbs missin' from working with farm machinery. They played hard too. Nobody could play the piano like your Uncle Dolly, and it seemed like your Uncle Dan always had a "hot" car, which he would wreck.

"And, like I told you, your Grandma Polly never turned away anyone who was hungry. There were lots of hobos back then. Everyone helped out everyone else, especially during threshing time and corn harvesting time."

I am sure that there was always dynamite on the Farm, as there were plenty of stumps and such around to be cleared, and I have always been amazed that there weren't any deaths on the Farm—that I know of. I do know that, across Riverside Drive, there is a quarry, and my dad fell down that quarry and lived. The quarry is almost fifty feet deep. I suppose the trees and shrubs helped break his fall. He did suffer a dent in his head. I know, because I used to cut his hair. Also, I came to believe, especially later in his life, that the fall might have had something to do with his rather, shall we say, "peculiar" behaviors.

Later, we had an outdoor picture show next to the Farm. It was just north of the Davis Cemetery and was called the Riverside Drive-In, but we just referred to it as the "Side." Fill up the trunk with your buddies, pay your dollar, inch your car up the little viewing slope, attach that tinny old speaker, and watch the movie. It seemed like *The Hustler* played there forever. The "Side" was just across the Scioto from the Blankenships', our house, so I could take my boat across the river, walk up the cliff, and walk into the theater. That's what I think my brother and his friends did, too.

Well, let's just re-cap what we had on the Farm before we leave it, though it will continue to "crop" up throughout the course of these stories. On the Farm itself, we had beautiful trees, streams, pasture, and rows and rows of corn. We had the old man walking up and down the porch in one of his robes, maybe with his bullwhip in hand; we had Grandma Polly gently working away in one of the two kitchens; we had the boys wrestling around on the ground with one another after chore time; we had all the girls engaged in some sort of industrious activity (remember Aunt Blanche and her coal route). There were probably blasts of dynamite going on as stumps were being cleared out (probably sounded like the original "cannon ball man" in the Sells Brothers Circus; we had the youngest, my dad, carrying buckets of coal up to the twenty rooms; we had farm machinery of all kinds and a finger or two being lost from one of my uncles; we had many out buildings with black snakes slithering around inside or just sleeping; "we had cats and rats but no elephants and sure as you're born, not even one unicorn." I am sure that my father fantasized about having his own elephant on the farm as a boy; he loved elephants, but it was not meant to be. We had the fish of the seas across Riverside Drive in the Scioto River, and we had the fowl of the air with all the pheasants and quail. We had hobos sleeping in the haylofts, singing their songs. There was a bull with a ring in his nose swinging from the beam in the barn. There were hogs, and dairy cattle, and beef cattle, and chickens, and geese, and ducks, and fox—all kinds of critters. There was hard work, but there was play, and thanks to Grandma Polly, plenty of love to go around. If God blesses the beasts and the children, why, He certainly blessed the Sells Farm.

And on the Farm, we had one more thing; we had a special horse. His name was Ole Porter. I once asked my dad how many miles he had to walk to the schoolhouse in Dublin.

"Never walked to school," he told me, "had a horse, Ole Porter."

"What kind of a horse was he?" I asked.

"He was a special horse," my dad said. "The old man gave him to me."

"I mean, what kind of a horse was he: a big black stallion, a quarter horse, a Tennessee Walker?" I asked.

"No, Porter was just a farm horse we kept around the Farm, but the old man liked him."

"Well, what was it that was so special about that horse?"

"The old man would feed him apples and carrots and sometimes give him a little sugar."

"Why would he do that?"

"The old man always made sure that horse had plenty of oats."

"Why did he treat him so different then? "

"He liked him."

"Why did he like him so much?"

"Because Porter was smart."

"Smarter than the rest of the horses on the Farm?"

"Sure was."

"Well how did he get so smart?"

"Same way everybody gets smart."

"How's that."

"How's that? You ought to know that."

"I don't know. How did Porter get so smart?"

"Porter went to school, just like you do."

"What do you mean he went to school?"

"Well, every day, when it got time for me to go to school, I would strap my books over my back, and go jump on Ole Porter, and whisper in his ear, 'Porter, it's time to go to school now,' and off we would go. He would kind of half trot and half walk to the school. He knew the way. It must have been because he had taken some of my brothers and sisters there. He was a real gentle horse, Porter was. Then, I'd look out the window around 2:30 or 3:00 in the afternoon, and there would be Porter outside in the schoolyard, just munching on some grass, waiting to take me home. Ole Porter was a special horse, and the old man liked him. I never walked to school."

CHAPTER 5

MY AUNTS AND UNCLES

Now on the Farm, as I have told you, there were fifteen boys and girls. The boys were, as near as I can tell, Jab, Joe, Lewis, Ted, Jim, Dick, Dan, Don, and my Dad Bob, the last born. The girls were Ruth, Mary, John D., Nan, Ann, and Blanch. They turned out to be my uncles and aunts. Like I said, some people say that there were only fourteen boys and girls. An obituary from the *Columbus Dispatch* said that there were sixteen. Also, I have heard tell that there were as many as twenty of them. Maybe there were some still-births along the way. I don't know for sure. I get confused as to how many there actually were. Confusion seems to be a natural state of mind for me.

Well, I believe that it was when I first attended a family reunion that I grasped, for the first time, what it meant to be "confused," and I have suffered from that malady ever since. I would meet uncles who I never knew were my uncles, unknown uncles married to my aunts, first cousins I had never seen before, second cousins likewise, and even far distant third cousins. I even had a fifth cousin, a Count Bower. Never knew there were counts in the family, but it did not surprise me any. We had everything else. I don't know if I ever had first cousins who married one another. I don't think so, or first cousins who married second cousins, but I wouldn't be surprised. I had cousins who I had always thought were my uncles, and uncles who I thought were my cousins. Everyone would be talking real loud, and swearing and yelling and laughing and crying; well, it was just too much. Invariably, someone would accuse the other of cheating in cards, or never returning a tool or piece of equipment that they had "borrowed," or they would start talking about how the Farm should be run, and a hellacious fistfight would break out. I remember that there was a vast, vast

SELLS FAMILY REUNION - 1950

quantity of food at these reunions since the Sells men were renowned for their prodigious appetites: chickens, hams, geese, ducks, fish, turkeys, breads, cakes, pies, vegetables, casseroles, salads, fruits, and many, many more offerings. It was like some sort of medieval feast. However, the men would always find things to complain about: "chicken's too dry," "ham's too fat," "steak's too boney," "not enough lard in this pie crust," "bread's too hard," "cake's too flat," "nobody could cook like my mother," and so on and so on. And, when they started talking about splitting up the Farm and selling it, well, I am going to leave it to your fertile imaginations what those "reunions" degenerated into. Half of the older brothers and sisters wanted to sell the Farm and get their money before they died, and the other more prosperous ones wanted to keep the Farm as an investment since it was prime real estate on Riverside Drive just south of Route 161 and would bring a good price in the future. I know that my dad, my Aunt Blanch, and my Aunt Nan never wanted to sell the Farm, and they would fight their brothers tooth and nail over that issue. Suffice it to say, to this day I find it very difficult to distinguish kin, of anyone's family, and I find family reunions a little difficult to handle.

I never knew the old man, and I never knew Grandma Polly, but I did know most of my aunts and uncles, and I knew some of them pretty well. I'll tell you about the aunts I knew best and then I will talk about the uncles I knew.

My Aunt Ruth was the oldest, and was always quite formal, prim and proper, and she lived to be well into her nineties. For some reason, she and my dad did not get along. As I have said, my Aunt Ruth more or less raised my dad since grandma was old when she had him. Maybe my dad rebelled against my Aunt Ruth; I don't know. I do know that Aunt Ruth always sent me birthday cards with coins in them, dimes, and she baked me cookies. And, she was a Christian woman. She shared a lot of the early stories about Dublin with a historian, a Mr. Hartman, I believe, but my dad had his doubts about the accuracy of those stories. She was pretty old when she told them.

I had an Aunt Dutch (Ann) who lived out in Monterrey, California, with my Uncle Eddy. My Aunt Dutch would blow into our house for a "week," and it seemed like she stayed there for months on end. When they named her "Dutch," they named her right. She was a German dynamo. She never stopped—work, work, work—with steam coming out of her ears. She was always rearranging things in our house, which I do not think pleased my mom, but my mom lacked the fortitude to confront Dutch. Anyway, my Aunt Dutch loved and idolized her "Baby Brother Bob," so, what were we to do? I remember one day she backed our family's car right into my big brother Mike's car and put a dent into it. My brother had a temper, and really didn't care for Aunt Dutch. Aunt Dutch stormed into the house, "Oh, you big block-headed *#*#*#! Why did you park your car in the driveway where I could hit it?" My brother looked at her and said, "Listen, *#*#*#, when I see your name on our mailbox, I'll start listening to what you have to say. Until then, leave me alone." She always referred to me with endearing terms like "little sneak" and "little block-headed *#*#*#." Anyway, I think it was hard on my mom for Aunt Dutch to be there. Let us just invert a popular refrain and say that her "brief" visits turned out to be "long and gruesome." But, Aunt Dutch did have one redeeming quality: she was a great cook, and I think she mellowed as she got older. Aunt Dutch had a beautiful daughter, I guess she was my cousin, and her name was Jeanette. Jeanette was real "artsy', and for a time lived down on campus at Ohio State. It was rumored that she was married to a Russian spy (remember that this was during the Cold War), but those rumors were never substantiated. She was eventually divorced from him. My cousin Jeanette had a pretty neat son called Billy. I guess he was my second cousin, right? I get confused about aunts, uncles, and first, second, and third cousins.

What can I say about my Aunt Blanche—she ran a coal route, and married an eligible bachelor of Dublin during those times, Jim Geideman, who was the high school basketball coach for Chi Weber, Chuck Hill, and other young men of Dublin. Chi told me that Jim Geideman was, at one time, one of Dublin's most eligible bachelors and that once my Aunt Blanche set eyes on him, he didn't stand a chance. Aunt Blanche was a beautiful blond-haired, young lady in her own right, and when she saw what she wanted, she was not to be denied.

I had an Aunt Nan, too, and boy, she was something! She was beautiful, as all of the Sells girls were, but she was different; she was more refined. Aunt Nan married my Uncle Ken Hovey, and Uncle Ken, a graduate of Brown University in Rhode Island, took the patent out on "Muzak," the canned music you hear in the elevators and such. Uncle Ken died at a very early age, which left my Aunt Nan a very wealthy young good looking widow, and she was no wall flower. To make a long story short, Aunt Nan was remarried seven times; all with pre-nuptial agreements, I am told. I always liked Aunt Nan, and she wanted one of us to go on to Brown, but, of course, I just wasn't smart enough. One time Aunt Nan caught a five hundred pound marlin off the coast of Australia, and that made her pretty neat in my eyes. She was, so to speak, very much of a gadabout. She had houses all over the United States, at one time or another: Vermont, Ft. Myers Beach, Indianapolis, and Ocala, and she would also go to Switzerland a lot.

I also had an Aunt Florence—better known as Aunt "John D." From what I heard, the old man was so enamored with John D. Rockefeller that he decided to give her that nickname, since she was born on his birthday." Everybody called her "John D." I had an "Aunt" Eddie, too, but she wasn't really my aunt. Aunt Eddie was the housekeeper and the old man married her after Grandma Polly died. One of my aunts told me that when the old man finally died, Aunt Eddie called up Aunt John D. and said, "John D., your dad is gone." Aunt John D. started yelling, "Where'd he go; where'd he go?"

Aunt Nan and Aunt Blanche are buried in the Davis Cemetery.

I had my favorite uncles, and rank them according to the degree of the eccentricities they manifested; their peculiarities that I came to love:

Uncle Joe, Uncle Dan, Uncle Ted, and my Great Uncle Pat. But before I tell you about them, let me tell you a little bit about some of my other uncles.

I had an Uncle Dick who lived out in San Francisco after he retired from the Navy. Uncle Dick was the only one of my uncles who had much hair on his head, so he stuck out. (Uncle Jim, a farmer in Mt. Sterling, Ohio, had a little hair on his head, though he was missing most of it. He was missing some fingers too, which he lost as a boy on the Farm). Anyway, my Uncle Dick retired as a Chief Petty Officer from the Navy. During his service, he had worked with Admiral Halsey. Uncle Dick had been all over the world. He developed a taste for the beetle nut and it stained his teeth, but I guess it didn't bother his wife, Nora. Their house out in San Francisco looked more like a curio shop than a dwelling as Uncle Dick would bring back souvenirs for Aunt Nora from where ever he happened to have been. Before I shipped out for Korea, (which beat shipping out to Vietnam by a long shot), Uncle Dick and Aunt Nora just dropped everything for a week and showed me all around San Francisco, and they knew San Francisco. It was a wonderful week, and one that I will never forget. It made me forget all about what might have been going on back in Dublin. So, San Francisco remains one of my favorite cities to this day, although I am still a little partial to Austin, Texas, where my mom and dad met.

I also had an Uncle Lester, "Jab" who was the oldest of the boys. He lived down in Washington Court House. I loved going down there because he married my Aunt Lucy, and she was probably one of the greatest cooks of the Sells "outlaw" women.

Sorry for the interruption; I told you that I had a lot of uncles, and they just keep popping up. Anyway, now I will tell you about my more eccentric uncles. I loved my Uncle Joe. He spent most of his time down around New Orleans. He married my Aunt Inez from New Orleans who had a Master's Degree in secretarial sciences. The cool thing about Uncle Joe was that when he came up from New Orleans to Dublin to visit us, he always came up in a caravan. By that, I mean he came up in two cars, rather than one. I don't remember exactly, but my Aunt Inez must have been driving the other car. He would drive one car and work on it while he was here in Dublin, and he used the other car to go get parts for the car he was working on.

Pretty cool, and he was always in a good mood—maybe too good. Every time he would walk behind me, he would pull my hair and just cackle like a rooster. But it hurt! It was OK by him, though, he didn't have a hair on his head—like most Sellses. (If the reader will look on-line and see the posters of the Sells Brothers Circus, he or she will see that we came by our baldness honestly.) Uncle Joe always wore an old straw, short-brimmed, hat. Maybe that was the style at the time in Louisiana; I don't know.

Uncle Joe took me to see Billy Graham when Billy Graham was at Jet Stadium here in Columbus. I remember Billy preaching, especially that he pointed his finger and said, "God loves you, and you, and you!" I will never forget that. Now, I do not know what kind of dynamic went on between my Aunt Inez and my Uncle Joe, but I do remember that they were married and divorced three times. I remember one afternoon that we went to the Burger Boy Food-O-Rama, the BBF, the same one that I use to take my silver boat to on the banks of the Scioto. Uncle Joe wanted some hamburgers, so he took my brother Kelly, Aunt Inez, and me there to get some. Well, it was winter, maybe January or February, and there was ice on the sidewalk where you went into the restaurant. We went in single file, like penguins: Uncle Joe first, my brother Kelly, me, and Aunt Inez trailing behind. Well, when I made it through the door, I turned around, there wasn't any Aunt Inez! She was sprawled out on the icy sidewalk some paces back, squirming around on her back like a lizard—a Louisiana lizard. I ran back to see if she was OK, and she was fine, just shook up. But, old Uncle Joe, he merely turned around and gave out that cackle laugh of his: "She never has learned how to walk in the snow," was all he said. He didn't miss a beat, and kept right on walking in to get his hamburgers. I guess he was pretty hungry.

One more story I remember about Uncle Joe and Aunt Inez, which I will tell you in order to chronicle their on again and off again marriage(s). I guess down South they have a lot of Piggly Wiggly" stores, although I haven't seen any of them up here. Maybe Uncle Joe wasn't too fond of them; I don't know. Anyway, they were staying somewhere near the quarry; it had to be near there for this to have taken place. I guess Aunt Inez had just stuffed old Uncle Joe with about all he could possibly eat for dinner, and a Sells can eat a lot. After Uncle Joe got done with his meal, and pushed himself away from the table, Aunt Inez looked up at him and said, in that sweet Louisiana drawl of hers, "Well, how did you like all of that, my little Piggly Wiggly?" Well, for some strange reason, Uncle Joe did not take kindly to those words, as a matter of fact; I guess he took them as an insult from a Southerner to a Yankee. He jumped out of his chair (no small feat for a man of his bulk), and grabbed Aunt Inez, as the story has been told to me, and said, "I ain't no doggone Piggly Wiggly," and ran her out of the house in a headlock and shoved her down the quarry. Of course, she wasn't the first to take a dive down the quarry; if you will remember; my dad had done it previously, but by accident. But, the Leprechauns of Dublin, not being against southerners, saved this beautiful Louisiana lady from an abysmal demise. I don't know if this incident precipitated one of their divorces, but it certainly was "grounds" for one.

While my Uncle Joe was callous, my Uncle Dan was the exact opposite. He gave new meaning to the phrase "laid back." He liked to come over to wherever we lived—Marion Street, the Blankenship house down by the River, River Forest, and at the Snouffer's—to talk to my mom and dad. He really liked talking to my mom, and he was a great listener. I can remember that Uncle Dan was always nice to my mama, and the two of them would just talk and talk over iced tea or coffee. He treated her like one of her brothers down in Texas would have treated her—the baby of the family. He taught her how to fry fish, and how to make other dishes the Sellses liked. My dad tended to get all fired up about things—rant, swear, and rave. In contrast, Uncle Dan never got fired up about anything; he was always cool, calm and collected. He reminded me of a Franciscan Friar. Maybe that's why my dad liked my Uncle Dan so much, and because my Uncle Dan always stuck by him. The two played off one another. When they would talk about what to do with the Farm, when the proverbial *merde* would hit the fan, they stood fast together. Uncle Dan was a great listener, but I enjoyed the way he spoke. He had a distinctive nasal twang to his voice that I found unique, and an affirmative way of ending all of his sentences:

"Got some tomatoes to bring you, Darline, I do," he would say, or "Danny Lee and I are going to bring the boat down tonight to catch some bullheads, we are." Or, "Sandy went to Cedar Point, she did."

If the definition of being a good husband in the 1950's and 1960's was synonymous with being a good provider, there was no better husband than Uncle Dan. He worked at The Columbus Bolt Works for forty years. My dad would arrive home late at night or in the wee hours of the morning, often drunk and belligerent. On the other hand, Uncle Dan was always under control and easy going. Many times I wished that I could have lived with my Uncle Dan, who was so much like me, and my Aunt Gerry, who was so outgoing and so active in the church and community. I often thought that Danny Lee, whom my dad loved above all of his other nephews, would have made a better son for him than I did.

I can't talk about my Uncle Dan without talking about my Aunt Gerry—two peas in a pod. I love my Aunt Gerry. I can see her now in that big kitchen of hers fixing me something to eat. Her fruit cakes and fresh coffee were my favorites though she would fix me anything I wanted. I loved to hear her laugh. Just like her son Danny Lee, when she laughed, it made me laugh. As she would be chatting and moving around in that big kitchen with no wasted motion, Aunt Helen, her sister would be rocking back and forth in her chair. My Aunt Gerry took special care of her sister Helen. Sometimes, I would come over to see Aunt Gerry when I was depressed and feeling bad, and we would sit out on the front steps and, well, just sit. Sometimes, it's good to have someone close that you don't feel you have to talk to. I always felt good being around my Aunt Gerry. We'd be silent for a while, and then I'd start telling her stories about what was happening in the Army down at Fort Knox. Little by little, she'd laugh and ask questions, and I'd try to explain to her about Army things, and then we'd really start laughing together.

My Aunt Gerry was one of the great, all-time euchre players in Dublin. If euchre had "life masters" like bridge does, my Aunt Gerry would be one. I remember a time, after I had just gotten back from the VA Hospital in Chillicothe, when Aunt Gerry and I and a few others drove up to Centerburg to play euchre. Imagine driving all that way just to play euchre. I asked my Aunt Gerry recently if she ever cheated when she played euchre; she firmly denied it. I have never heard anyone admit that they cheated at euchre, but you can't tell me that some of them don't cheat when they play. However, I will give my Aunt Gerry the benefit of the doubt because I love her.

It'd hard to talk about my laid-back Uncle Dan and his euchre playin' wife without mentioning the princess of their family—Sandy Sue. I can hear my Aunt Gerry now, yelling out the screen door, "Sandy Sue, Sandy Sue?" She sure enough was something to catch your eye, and still is to this day. Blonde, flaxen, waxen hair to go along with the biggest, blue Sells eyes you ever did see! She has a smile that'd light up Old Man's Cave. She was a million dollar baby! The reason I didn't mention her when I was telling about going over to see my Aunt Gerry is because she was never home: cheerleading, Cedar Point, dates with innumerable boyfriends, etc. She got a job with Delta Air Lines as a flight attendant after she graduated from Kent State University. Didn't surprise me any. They were lucky to get her. She used to work the Germany/United States flights. There was not a man who could catch her until she was ready to be caught, and she ended up having two of the cutest little toe-headed kids I ever did see. They are all grown up now. Sandy is married and living well. A thing of beauty is a joy forever. My, how time does fly.

Uncle Dan, Aunt Gerry and Cousin Sandy are three of the four kin I was closest to when I grew up in Dublin, but I think I may have saved the best for last—Uncle Dan and Aunt Gerry's other child, my favorite cousin, and my dad's favorite "other son," Danny Lee. I am going to tell you a story that will show what Danny Lee meant to me when I was young.

It happened one lazy afternoon at the Shawnee Hills Swimming Pool. When Dublin Wasn't Dublin, all summer activities centered around the Shawnee Hills Swimming Pool. It was a hot July afternoon, and I was lying beside my girlfriend on the grass at the east end of the pool, where the diving boards were. We were listening to music from our transistor radio—The Beatles, The Rolling Stones, Herman's Hermits and doing a little hugging and kissing (every now and then), a nice way for a young man and his girlfriend to spend an afternoon. I learned though that sooner or later, my girlfriend wanted to talk to me and the stuff she wanted to talk about was boring: so and so is going on a camping trip to the Grand Canyon; I want to get this and that new clothes for the coming school year; I'm still trying to decide what to study when I go to college, and I haven't even decided what college I want to go to – not exciting stuff! And, she wanted me to look at her while she talked to me! Why couldn't she just close her mouth, and let me kiss her? To tell you the truth, I don't think things have really changed that much between men and women since those days up in Shawnee Hills. Anyway, I was listening to my girlfriend go on and on when, from up over the hill on Dublin Rd south of the pool I heard what I thought was a low flying jet airplane. The sound was deafening, and everyone ran to the fence at the east end of the pool. The roar increased to a full crescendo pitch. Then we saw, literally shooting down the hill, its source – it was Danny Lee Sells lying down on that huge motorcycle of his, at full speed, steering it with his feet! Everyone's jaw dropped. No one could believe what they had just seen! But it wasn't over yet. The roar faded gradually into the distance, almost stopped, and then slowly rose up again to jet engine

THE SHAWNEE HILLS SWIMMING POOL

level. Down the hill from the north came Danny Lee. This time he was standing up on the back seat of the motor cycle, and bent over with his hands grasping the handlebar. This time all his fans clapped and cheered for more. But the roar faded into the distance, never to be heard again. Did those at the pool actually see what they thought they saw or, was it a figment of their imagination? The legend of the Dublin Dare Devil lives on....

After many years of marriage, my Uncle Dan and Aunt Gerry divorced. This grieved me greatly. My Uncle Dan married a widow woman, by the name of Ruth. She took good care of him, and she also made great pies, which endeared her to me. They had a little land with a pond on it up in Delaware County. I spent a lot of time up there. Sometimes I spent the weekends and slept on the porch. I remember that Uncle Dan liked ham and we ate a lot of ham. Uncle Dan and I watched a lot of TV together. He usually wore long underwear, regardless of the season. I always lay on the carpet looking up at my Uncle Dan in his contour chair in front of the TV. He was the closest thing to a grandfather that I had.

One day I was lying around, I wasn't doing anything, maybe I was eating something, when Uncle Dan looked at me and asked," You, what are you doin'?"

"Me?"

"Yeah, you," he said.

"Nothing," I said.

"You never do anything," he said.

"I know," I said.

"Well," he said, "you go out to that lake, and you catch six bass all this long (he held out his hands). We're going to eat fish tonight."

Well, I don't know if he thought I was a magician, or endowed with some inalienable outdoor rights. Maybe he was just tired of me lying around not doing anything. Anyway, out I went. I always kept some night crawlers around, along with artificial bait, and since Uncle Dan never let anyone else fish that pond, the fish were pretty ravenous. I slid his boat into the pond, and worked the shorelines and weed beds with a night crawler on a harness. I caught six bass pretty quickly. Heck, I think I could have caught a hundred and six if I stayed out long enough. I liked that boat because it was fiberglass and it was pretty quiet. An aluminum boat is real noisy. Anyway, I brought the fish back in, cleaned them, and gave them to Uncle Dan to fry. Nobody could fry fish like my Uncle Dan. Bass sure are good to eat, especially when caught in the early spring. Well, this procedure went on for as long as Uncle Dan lived. "You, go catch four fish this long." "You, go catch three big fish, this long," and so on and so on. So, we ate a lot of fish, and we ate a lot of ham, and we ate a lot of pies. Life couldn't get much better. And, at least while fishing, I couldn't be accused of not "doing anything." I made my contribution to the cause, so to speak.

One thing we always watched on television, and I never could figure out why, was bowling. On Saturday afternoons there was always a bowling tournament on the TV, and Uncle Dan wouldn't miss it. He would lie there in his contour chair, in his long underwear, kind of like his version of the old man—winter, spring, summer, and fall—and watch bowling. That bowling ball would go up and down, up and down, over and over, over and over. Of course, I would have preferred to watch baseball, but, after all, it was his house I was in and it was his food I was eating, so bowling was OK with me. One day I was just lying around, I wasn't doing anything, when he said, "You."

"Yeah," I said.

"What are you doing?" he asked.

"You know me, Uncle Dan, I'm not doing anything," I responded. I figured he wanted me to go out and catch some fish, but he fooled me this time.

"The grass is high, it is," he said.

"Yes it is," I said.

"You know how to mow grass?" he asked.

"A little," I replied.

"You go outside and mow the grass, do it," he said.

"OK," I said. I was not accustomed at all to doing any kind of manual labor when I went to Uncle Dan's, least of all mowing grass, which I have never cared to do.

I got the lawn mower started, no small feat, and preceded to mow the grass down. The grass was high, very high, so high that you could barely see in front of you. I don't think that I had gone more than five feet or so when I hit some immovable object. It just wouldn't budge. I made my way through the grass—I could have used a machete or at least a corn cutter—when low and behold I gazed upon the immovable object. It was nothing other than a bowling ball, black with three holes in it. I tossed it out of the way, re-started the mower, and proceeded about another six or seven feet when I ran against another impediment—another bowling ball. I stopped the lawnmower and did a reconnaissance of the yard. There were bowling balls all over the place. Now, even for a Sells, this struck me as odd. I went inside and asked my Aunt Ruth about my uncle's seeming fascination for bowling and bowling balls. "He just likes bowling balls," if I remember correctly, was all she said. "But he doesn't bowl, Aunt Ruth," I replied. She just shrugged her shoulders. It was another mystery.

Uncle Dan is buried in the Davis Cemetery.

So, there was Uncle Joe in his caravan; there was Uncle Dan the bowling fan; and then there was Uncle Ted with his beer in a can. Uncle Ted always drank Pabst Blue Ribbon Beer. He drank more beer than anyone I had ever seen, including my dad. My dad didn't have a favorite beer. If you would have asked my dad what his favorite beer was, he would probably have told you, "the next one." Uncle Ted just drank Pabst—lots of it—and it showed. He stood a mere 5 foot 3 inches, but weighed in the proximity of two hundred fifty pounds. He had a short, squat body, with a rather long protruding neck, which gave him, to me at least, the appearance of a snapping turtle. He was a walking parabola, but he dressed sharply: black polished shoes, a crease in his trousers (a belt the length of a small clothes line), clean white shirt, and a sporty grey fedora to cover his bald head. He had no teeth, but was able to gum down about anything set before him. He had worked at the Yeager Machine Shop for forty years as a machinist. He drove a faded 1951 Chevrolet coupe with a rusted out floorboard. He was sharp of wit with an edge of sarcasm in his voice at times, but he loved his baby brother, Bob, and my mom, my brothers, and me. I think that's why, during his later years, he spent so much of his time at our home in River Forest. He also loved baseball. He talked a lot about the Saint Louis Cardinals, especially the Gas House Gang. In his younger days he played for Dublin's Dirty Dozen Baseball Team along with my uncle Dan. Also, when he was younger my Uncle Ted was no stranger to fisticuffs. In fact, my dad said that of all the Selles Ted was the toughest. He got started in the fight game at an early age, as witnessed by the adjoining newspaper article.

He loved to go fishing; so, how could I not love him? Of all of my aunts and uncles, it was only Uncle Ted who came to my big, ten-year-old birthday party, with all of my friends, when I lived down on the river at the Blankenships'. He would watch me play baseball and even bloop ball up at River Forest. He gave me silver dollars for Christmas and for my birthday—wish I would have kept them. He was something.

My Uncle Ted came up every weekend to play cribbage or gin rummy with my dad. Mostly they played cribbage—

Fight With School Teacher

A fist fight between Emory Corbin, 21, a Dublin school teacher and Ted Sells, 16, one of his pupils, which resulted in the teacher being "beat-up" was told about in juvenile court Friday.

Sells, who is the son of A. H. Sells, a farmer south of Dublin, was in juvenile court as the result of an affidavit filed by Corbin, charging him with incongruity.

The altercation, for which various explanations are given, took place Wednesday morning during recess at the Dublin School and finished up on the street when bystanders came to the rescue of Corbin.

Judge Black continued the case until Tuesday.

—*Ohio State Journal*
Friday, December 1, 1916

TED SELLS WINS BY KO

for money, of course. Now I learned to play cribbage one summer after I had broken my arm playing baseball, when we were living down at the Blank-enships', so often I sat and watched my uncle and my dad play. It is probably the best two-handed card game that there is, though it can be played with three or four people. Also, unlike other card games, there is a certain song in the air when cribbage is played: "Fifteen-two, the rest won't do; fifteen-four, shut the door; count the crib, your cut, your play, dud riffle, skunked, stink holed, pass, pass, pass…" Well, it is just a great game, and there's nothing worse than getting caught in the stink hole or getting skunked. My Uncle Ted and my dad could play forever, from early evening until morning of the next day, and maybe some more. My Uncle Ted was probably just as good a card player as my dad. Uncle Ted could play just about any card game there was, and he would usually win. I am sure that he frequented the back rooms of the Dublin Nite Club as my dad did. I guess, growing up on the Farm, you had to learn how to play cards, and that probably helped my dad a lot when he was in the Army. There were always enough kids around the Farm to start a game of cards; and that was probably the safest thing they could do. I imagine it was better than fighting one another, although I am sure that cards led to fighting on more than one occasion.

Uncle Ted used to come up on Sunday mornings in his "machine," as he put it. My mother would make either a big breakfast in the morning, or big dinner of fried chicken in the afternoon with chicken gravy, mashed potatoes, vegetables, and pie. My mama could make the best pecan pies that I have ever tasted. Anyway, for his contribution, Uncle Ted would always bring up a head of lettuce. He would bring a head of lettuce every time. "Looks like pretty good lettuce, Darline" he would say. Funny thing, I don't ever remember eating any salad. After dinner, Uncle Ted and my dad would start playing cribbage. I will never forget the one Sunday Uncle Ted didn't show up for Sunday dinner. No call. (No e-mail, no text message, Dublin Wasn't Doublin' then). He just did not come up. My dad was not one to pry, so he let it pass. Well, next Sunday came, and just like clockwork, here came Uncle Ted rolling into the driveway in his machine with his head of lettuce in hand.

"Ted, where in the heck were you last week?" my dad asked, with a little bellow in his voice.

"Bob, it was rainin' outside," Uncle Ted replied.

"Ted, it don't rain inside. What do you mean 'it was rainin' outside'," my dad asked?

"Well, I don't like to drive in da rain," Uncle Ted responded.

"Well why don't you like to drive in the rain?" my dad asked.

"I ain't got no windshield wipers on my machine, Bob," Uncle Ted stated, in an apologetic tone, his head cast down on his chest.

"Ted, it's not like you're destitute. You worked for forty years. Spend a dollar and go get a pair of windshield wipers," my dad said.

Uncle Ted's chin was still down against his chest, almost in penitence, and his elbows were resting upon my mother's best dish cloths, when he slowly looked up at his brother, "Bob, why should I? I don't like to drive in the rain..."

I have played and re-played that little bit of conversation over and over in my mind for many years, and it ranks up there with some of the great pieces of logic that I have ever heard. I always looked at Uncle Ted in a different light after I heard him defend his position.

I seemed to get along pretty well with my Uncle Ted, maybe it was because we both really liked fishing and baseball. Sometimes he would even let me play cribbage with him. That was like playing with a life master in bridge.

One afternoon Uncle Ted slipped in through the kitchen door, no small feat for a man of his girth, and as usual, put his calloused elbows on the kitchen counter, on my mom's dish-cloths, of course. He looked really sad, which was unusual for him.

"What's the matter, Uncle Ted?; you look pretty down," I asked.

"I just got back from seein' Doc Carpenter. He said I got to lose some weight," he said.

"Well, Uncle Ted, it probably wouldn't hurt you to drop a few pounds," I replied.

"Yeah, dat's what he said all right; he said I need to go on a diet."

"Sounds OK to me," I said.

"Yeah," he replied, in that soft bellow of his, like a bullfrog, "whats' dat you're makin' over dere, Timbo?" He asked.

I had the ice cream out and some bananas. "Oh, I'm goin' to make me a banana split."

"Yeah, looks pretty good," he said. "I always liked dem splits when I could eat 'em. They sure are good," Uncle Ted said, "Yeah, ain't dat Napoleon ice cream you're usin': vanilla, chocolate, and strawberry? Dat's my favorite."

"Sure is, Uncle Ted. You want me to fix you a little bowl?"

"Little bowl wouldn't hurt none would it, Timbo?" he asked.

"Aw, I don't think so, Uncle Ted."

"You know somethin', Timbo? Bananas are good for you 'cause dey got a lot of 'tassium in 'em," he said.

"You want a banana, Uncle Ted?"

"Oh, maybe half of one," he replied.

I opened the refrigerator door, and he was staring at me like a duck at a June bug.

"What's dat you gettin' out of dat fridgerator, Timbo?"

"Oh, I'm getting some Hershey's chocolate syrup," I said.

"Chocolate's good for you, too," he said. I read dat in a magazine."

"You want some chocolate on your ice cream and banana, Uncle Ted?" I asked.

"Oh, go on ahead if you want. Pour a little on it," he said.

"What's dat you're foolin' with now?" he asked.

"Crushed peanuts," I said.

"Peanuts got a lot of protein in 'em," he said.

"You want some on your ice cream and bananas and chocolate syrup?" I asked.

"Oh, ifin' you want to put 'em dere, go on ahead," he replied.

"Now what you got, Timbo?" he asked.

"I got some whipped cream."

"It looks real pretty like when you put it on your ice cream, don't it? Looks like a little sail boat up on the O'Shaughnessy Dam."

"You want some whipped cream on your ice cream and banana and chocolate and peanuts?" I asked.

"Oh, I suppose; it does look pretty," he responded.

"Now, what's dat you got, Timbo?" he inquired

"I got some maraschino cherries, Uncle Ted. I suppose you want some of them on your banana split too?"

"Oh, no, no, no!" he half shouted, "Dem cherries got too much sugar in 'em! I told you dat I was on a diet, but you just slide over here what you got made for me, and I'll see what she tastes like."

Once, my Mom and my dad went away on a long vacation around the United States in their recreational vehicle, and Uncle Ted, in all of his glory, was left in charge of his "Brother Bob's" house. I will not say that the patient was running the asylum, but it was close. I just don't know what it is about the Sellses, although I am starting to experience it myself now, but Uncle Ted saw fit to clad himself during that time only in his long underwear (remember now the old man in his robes, Uncle Dan in his long johns, and my dad, in his "jumpers," which we will come to later). No matter the time or temperature, Uncle Ted kept wearing that long underwear.

My little brother Kelly said, "Uncle Ted, if you take a bath I can wash your long underwear for you.

"Yeah, well, I'm fixin' to take a me a baff, Kellog," he said, "soon as I get 'round to it."

"When's that?" Kelly would ask.

"Well, I'm goin' to draw me some baff water pretty soon."

"Uncle Ted, the sooner you take a bath, the sooner I can wash your long underwear for you. You've been wearin' those things for quite a while now, and I'll get 'em nice and clean and soft for you."

"'Preciate the offer, Kellog, but I'll take me a baff soon as I can."

I never could figure out about Uncle Ted and his baths. Even though it seemed he didn't make it into the bathtub very often, he smelled clean enough and looked clean enough; at least to me he did. I figured that he must have been more like a fat cat than a snapping turtle. He still moved quickly like a cat when he wanted, and cats don't take baths.

I always seemed to get along quite well with Uncle Jolly as he came to be called. I thought he had some great, though peculiar qualities about him. For example, he would seldom shut the bathroom door when he disposed of his excess Pabst Blue Ribbon. Doubtless, my mother found this disconcerting. However, when I remembered his logic regarding the use and non-use of windshield wipers, I believed that I understood his reasoning: why shut a door when you've just got to open it up again? Moreover, here was a man who could consume vast, vast quantities of beer and not give the slightest indication of inebriation. His Pabst Blue Ribbon often accompanied him to our home with his head of lettuce. Also, he was never without his beloved transistor radio, held together by black tape. With it, he could stand out in the kitchen, lean his elbows on the kitchen counter, listen to the Saint Louis Cardinals, and drink his beer, while he waited for his Brother Bob to get home to play cribbage. There wasn't much about baseball that he didn't know. He knew the "inside" game, or "small" ball. He talked on and on about Cobb, Speaker, Ruth, and Gehrig; but his favorite group was the Cardinals' Gashouse Gang with Dizzy Dean. When he talked about them, well, that's about the only time I ever saw his eyes light up. So, Uncle Ted and I would talk sports, play a little cribbage (he considered me a lightweight), and maybe he would take a stroll outside to watch us play bloop ball. It didn't matter to me how eccentric Uncle Ted was, I loved him. He used to fish off the O'Shaughnessy Dam before this practice was outlawed, and he caught a lot of fish from the south side. One day he even took me out crappie fishing by the western stone wall of the zoo, but it seemed that all he did was keep asking me to do things for him in the boat: "Get me dat knife, get me a big minnow out of dat bucket, pick up dat anchor and swing it around, get me a split shot, get me dem pliers" After about an hour of this, I turned around to him and said: "Uncle Ted, I came out here to fish with you, not work for you." Well, I think he took it the right way. Anyway, we both started catching some crappies after that. Looking back, though, I shouldn't have been so harsh with him; he was a pretty big man, and he couldn't move around in the boat like he could when he was younger.

Finally, there is this little story which, I believe, captures the essence of Uncle Jolly and his stay with us when he was the guardian of his "Brother Bob's" house. Uncle Jolly was not a "Merry Old Soul" when he rode herd over his Brother Bob's house. He made sure that everyone dotted their "i's" and crossed their "t's," and that everyone, minus himself, of course, abided by the law. Uncle Jolly was a man of the law, and used to be a constable for the town, When Dublin Wasn't Doublin'. He gave out lots of speeding tickets and was part of the reason Dublin was known as a speed trap in those days. Well, I think his taking on the role of the policeman of our house may have set him on a collision course with my little brother, Kelly. Kelly was pretty much of a free spirit in those days, and I am happy to say, he has remained so to this day. Well, Kelly, or "Kellog" as he was affectionately dubbed by Uncle Ted, had the habit of sleeping in until just before his ride came for school. He would bolt out of the house like a streak, without even paying homage to the Great One, Uncle Jolly, whose elbows were always resting on our rounded kitchen counter. I noticed that Uncle Jolly had probably propped his elbows on so many bars in his lifetime that they were literally calloused. So, Uncle Jolly assumed a command post such that he could almost take in the whole house, with his reptilian neck swiveling around like a turret on a tank. He would turn that crusty old neck very slowly, not missing a thing, in almost a complete circle of surveillance with those calloused elbows of his planted firmly on the kitchen countertop. It would have been an interesting study in physics to figure out how many pounds per square inch of force he was putting on those countertops. My mother, needless to say, was not happy to see Uncle Ted use her dish-towels for elbow pads.

Anyway, Kelly would streak out the door, hit the automatic door opener, and off he would be for a day at school. As for Uncle Ted, who knows how he spent his days? He did like to read western novels, read the newspaper (the sports page), and talk to a few of his retired friends. But who knows what he actually did? What I do know is that he was the sentinel of his Brother Bob's home. And then, after the monotony of watching Kelly's morning dash to school day after day, I believe that an epiphany of sorts came to Uncle Ted, or as the French say, a *raison d' etre*. Uncle Ted observed, with that steady and unblinking turtle like gaze of his, that Kelly never shut the garage door after his departure. And with the door up, horror upon horror, what flew into the garage but flies. There were flies everywhere in the garage, especially on the window-sills, but worst of all, they seemed to congregate outside the door that led into our living room. So, any time when someone would open that door, flies would come in. Now, Uncle Ted had found his purpose in life! Now, Uncle Ted had found his reason for being! Now he would find permanent grace in the eyes of his precious Brother Bob. Uncle Ted set out to kill every fly that flew into his brother's house! Every one!

There was only one problem. After repeated warnings from the "Terminator," Kelly kept leaving the garage door open. More flies in the garage, more flies in the house, and many more swings for Uncle Ted and that ubiquitous flyswatter. I don't remember during those times that I ever saw Uncle Ted without a fly swatter in his hand. It was as though he had grown another appendage. Maybe, in his Dirty Dozen days, he could have gotten them all; maybe when he was in his prime at Yeager Machine, he could have gotten them all, maybe,...but those days were gone. He just didn't have the swing that he once did. And as they say: 'If it ain't in the swing, you ain't got a thing." And, what was worse, the flies that got into the house and managed to escape his relentless swats, well, those flies might lay eggs that would hatch into more flies. And Kellog remained impervious to his Uncle Jolly's pleas to close the garage door. Oh, every now and then he would close it, but it was not a regular thing for him.

As a result of the continuing saga of the flies and the danger of falling short of his Brother Bob's expectations, things came to a head. Finally, there was a summit of sorts between Kelly and Uncle Ted:

"Kellog, I need to talk to you 'bout somethin' very important."

"OK; so talk," Kelly said.

"When your Mom and your dad left on der vacation, dey put me in charge of dis place."

"I know."

"Well, dat's OK with me. I took charge," Uncle Ted said.

"Yeah, you did."

"I watch things."

"I know."

"And I been watchin' you, Kellog," Uncle Ted said.

"And I been watchin' you, too, Uncle Ted," Kelly said.

"Well, what I been watchin' is how every time you leave for school you leave dat garage door open."

"So?"

"When you leave dat garage door open, flies get in dat garage."

"Yeah."

"Dat garage can hold a lot of flies."

"I suppose it can," Kelly said.

"Well, did you know dat every time someone opens da door of dat living room attached to dat garage, flies gets into dis house?"

"I suppose that could happen too," Kelly responded.

"You suppose dat could happen! You suppose dat could happen!" Uncle Jolly raised his voice.

"Yeah, it could happen," Kelly said.

"Well, Mr. Smarty Pants, what do you think happens to dem flies when dey gets into dis house?"

"I don't know. They're flies; I guess they fly around."

"Dey don't fly around the house! No, dey don't!" shouted Uncle Ted.

"So where do they fly?" asked Kelly.

"Dem flies fly right under my flyswatter. You see it, right here?"

"Yeah," Kelly said, "I see your flyswatter." The flyswatter was thick and gnarly with fly blood and guts caked to the bottom.

"Kellog, da reason I tell you dis is dis: I killed thirteen flies today, and my brother Bob don't pay me to swat flies."

And that was Uncle Ted, or Uncle Jolly, when he was affectionately known as the Sultan of Fly Swatting. Like I said, Uncle Ted did not get the name of "Uncle Jolly" without cause. It sometimes seemed as though he had something sarcastic to say about anyone and anything, except, of course, his beloved Brother Bob. For example, one day, Dave Wolfe was at our house and Uncle Jolly came in and saw Dave with his head sticking inside our refrigerator. "Yeah, David, didn't I see you kissin' that skinny little ugly girl behind the oak tree the last time I was up here?" David blushed and just shook his head and grinned; he knew Uncle Jolly; he had given him his nickname. Or, sometimes after reading an article in the newspaper or hearing about some sort of event on the radio, Uncle Jolly would let fly with his favorite of all phrases, "ain't dat da ####." He would get skunked playing cribbage or get caught in the stink hole: "ain't dat da ####." His vocabulary, though limited, was extremely graphic.

Before they were divorced, Uncle Ted and my Aunt Midge had lived in Old Dublin, just north of the intersection of Bridge Street and High Street. My Aunt Midge was a beautiful lady, and must have had the patience of Job considering who she had married. She used to babysit for Mike, Kelly and me when we lived on Marion Street. Aunt Midge was a seamstress, and she could make about anything, and cook about anything.

They had two children, Pixie and Tippy. Pixie was a cheerleader for my Uncle Jim Geideman's basketball team, the one Chi Weber and Chuck Hill played on. Tippy married Pauline King who had spent most of her childhood in an orphanage, but later came to live with the Judge Rose, Sr. family in Dublin. Tippy was always up to something, a typical Sells. I heard that he was a great ice skater.

After my Uncle Ted left my Aunt Midge, he lived down on Maynard Avenue just north of the Ohio State campus. He liked to feed peanuts to all the squirrels that lived down there with him. I was in Florida when Uncle Ted died; he was 77 years old. For a man who smoked heavily and consumed vast quantities of beer, he lived a long time. Pixie had him cremated, and she kept his ashes around her house for a long time. I don't know where his ashes are now, or what happened to them. Funny thing, though, my dad said he actually went to see Uncle Ted "get the heat." I didn't know that you could do that. My dad said that Uncle Ted's belly just blew up in front of him when they gave him the gas. There must have been a lot of Pabst Blue Ribbon left in him. "Yeah, Uncle Ted," he was my favorite uncle.

MY UNCLES AND MY DAD WITH THE OLD MAN

Now of all my uncles, I guess the one that I have always been most fascinated by was an uncle who I never knew, but had heard a whole bunch of stories about—my Great Uncle Pat Davis. Pat Davis, the brother of my Grandma Polly Davis, was a cowboy. From what I understand, he went out West at an early age, and stayed there for many years. He became a cowboy—a 'rootin', 'tootin' cowboy. After he grew older, maybe a little homesick for his kin, he returned to the Farm where his sister, Grandma Polly, was and where he had grown up.

Uncle Pat, being a cowboy and all, well, he was just a crack shot, with a pistol or a rifle or any kind of firearm. His weapon of choice was a U.S. Army issued Colt .45 pistol. My Dad told me that Pat used to like to stand on the Dublin Bridge and shoot paint turtles when they would stick their heads up out of the water—just shoot their heads off. I don't think he was sadistic, he was just a man of few words who liked to shoot his pistol, and let it do his talking for him.

My dad told me the story of when, one year, my Grandma Polly, who dearly loved her Brother Pat, was fixing a Christmas Dinner and said: "Pat, these turkeys would really taste a whole lot better if we had some quail to stuff in them"

"That a fact?" he responded, after he cleared his throat. My dad said that Uncle Pat always had to clear his throat before he talked; maybe it had gotten a lot of dust in it from him being out west so long, herding cattle. "Well, it's pert near a blizzard a 'blowin' out there now, Polly, but we'll see what we can do for you," he said.

"Bobby (to my dad), go fetch a gun."

"The 12 gauge, Uncle Pat?"

"No, no."

"What then?"

"Just get that .22 single shot rifle."

"Uncle Pat, you can't shoot a whole covey of quail with a single shot rifle."

"Ain't gonna shoot 'em all at once; gonna shoot 'em one at a time. You drive the old man's car, and just let her coast along the creek bed with the wind to our face, away from them birds. When we see a covey walkin' up the creek bed, I'll just shoot the last one in line. With the wind blowin', the one ahead will never even turn around." Well, that's just what Uncle Pat did, so I heard, and that's how Grandma Polly got her quail to stuff the turkeys.

And Uncle Pat was just around the Farm. My dad never told me that he ever worked while living there. Of course, being the favorite of my Grandma Polly, maybe he didn't have to.

I don't know exactly when my Great Uncle Pat got married, but he did, and it was to my Great Aunt Annie Bower, and I heard she was Uncle Pat's match: she liked to chew tobacco and she liked to go crappie fishing below the quarry in the Scioto River. They got themselves a house in Dublin. Uncle Pat and Aunt Annie had, I guess you could say, a "tumultuous" marriage, probably not unlike the one between Uncle Joe and Aunt Inez. Anyway, one day Pat and Annie were home and Annie had this little yapper dog that was carrying on. For some reason, Uncle Pat never took kindly to Aunt Annie's yapper dog, and of course, he always had that pistol around. I guess that dog must have started barking one afternoon, or something, and Pat couldn't take it anymore. He got up, cleared his throat, and said, "Annie, I'm gonna have to shoot that dog." Annie jumped up with her arms flailing at the ceiling and cried, "Pat, you can't shoot that dog. That's my dog. You shoot that dog, Pat, and you're goin' have to shoot me too!" Uncle Pat cleared his throat again, stared at Annie, and then he stared at the dog: "Shoot you both." was all he said, and walked away. Well, I don't think Uncle Pat ever did shoot the dog, but given his reputation, or lack thereof, I wouldn't have put it past him.

Besides being a man well-acquainted with firearms of all sorts, Uncle Pat was quite a whiskey drinker, a gambler, and a womanizer. My dad's final story about Uncle Pat just chilled me to the bone. It all got started when Aunt Annie went to see Dr. Karrer, yes, the same Dr. Karrer who brought me into this world. Annie found out that she had the cancer. I don't know how long she kept it from Uncle Pat, or from anyone else for that matter, but finally I guess it got so bad that she had to tell him. I think they were in the front room of their home in Dublin when she told him the bad news. From what my dad told me, Uncle Pat was lying on the couch with his hands folded behind his head. After he heard what she had to say, Pat just cleared his throat and said, "Annie, ain't it funny. It's just down right funny that after all these years of you tellin' me—that because of my drinkin', and smokin', and gamblin', and chasin' after other women—I just wasn't goin' to live very long, now just lookie here; I'm goin' to outlive you, Annie!" Well, I don't believe, from what I was later told, that Aunt Annie took too kindly to Uncle Pat's remarks. She didn't say another word, she just went into the bedroom, took out Pat's Army Colt .45, came out into the living room, laid the barrel up against his temple and blew his head clean off. "I'll be darned if he was goin' to outlive me!" she was reported to have later said. Of course, the police came right away, and Dr. Karrer arrived shortly thereafter. I guess the police were going to handcuff Annie and haul her to jail. "No need for that," whispered Dr. Karrer, "she'll be dead in three months," and she was. Uncle Pat's death was reported as an accidental shooting. And, I suppose that's "The Ballad of Pat and Annie."

CHAPTER 6

MY DOGS

When I put the chapters down for this little book of recollections of Dublin When It Wasn't Doublin', my reader will notice that I listed "My Dogs" before "My Friends." Now, it wasn't in order of importance, let me assure you; I just had dogs before I had any real friends. My first dog was Big Tony, and he was a huge Saint Bernard. I remember having him when we lived at 38 South High Street, in our house next door to John Herron's Store[4], right smack in the middle of Dublin. Big Tony, I guess, was my first friend. Tony was so big that he just used to stop traffic. The coolest spot in Dublin, temperature wise back then, was just south of the intersection of Dublin Road and Bridge Street, across from Mr. Wirtz's Pharmacy[5]. I can still remember that Mr. Wirtz always kept a close eye on anyone, no matter your age, who might wonder too close to the "girlie magazine" section of the store. Anyway, Big Tony used to lie down there, I guess, to get cool because it was shady; I don't know. I'm not a dog. He would just lie there, and he would not move, and he was big enough so that he did not have to move, and no one could make him move. He would back up traffic right smack in the middle of town. I guess you could say we had traffic jams even back When Dublin Wasn't Doublin', of course nothing

---

4   John Herron's Store was at 32 South High Street. It is now occupied by 'Cullen Art Glass'.

5   Wirtz's Pharmacy was in the building that is now the kitchen at the south end of Donato's Pizza.

like you do nowadays. After a while, I guess, Tony would get tired of people pushing him or coaxing him to move, and he would just pull himself up and lumber over and lie down on our front porch.

Tony had a real mild disposition except, well, except when my parents tried to discipline one of us kids. He didn't like anybody, my parents included, messing with us kids. I can remember that when my parents would come after me with a big wooden spoon to paddle me for something, Big Tony, and he must have weighed around 200 pounds, would just drop his head and growl. He would get right between my parents and me, and he would growl, deep down in his throat; it was the only time he would growl, but it was a mean growl. He never bit anyone; that growl was enough. You knew he meant business.

So as you can see, he was a very possessive and jealous dog. One time at Easter, my mom took us to Graceland to do some Easter shopping. I was really excited because going to Graceland back then was a big adventure. Well, I can't recall all that we bought, but I do remember that I bought two baby Easter chicks, the kind they used to sell every Easter. I was so excited, and had such big plans for them—my own chicken farm. When we got home, I hurriedly took my box of chicks inside and then ran right out to get the other packages. But, when I went back to take another look at my baby chicks, the box was there, but they were not...Big Tony had swallowed them whole. I guess that's the price I had to pay for protection back then. He just stood there sort of smiling. You know how dogs get kind of a smile on their face and let their tongues hang out. Well, I guess Big Tony must have thought he had protected me from something. Anyone who has ever read Stephen King's *Cujo* may get a rough idea of Big Tony's personality, but he didn't act mean—only to people who desired to do bodily harm to my brothers or me.

About the same time we had Big Tony I remember that my mom got me a little kitten—must have reminded her of her days growing up in Burnett County in Texas. She always loved cats; loved to dress them up in little costumes when she was a little girl, as I will tell you about later. Anyway, we had this little kitten, pretty little thing, I think it was a yellow-striped tiger kitten, and Big Tony left it alone. I loved that kitten just like my mama did. Now, what follows is about one of the earliest memories I have; I must have been about two and a half years old, three years old at the most. Like most toddlers, I was fascinated by the toilet. You could float your yellow duckie in the commode; you could watch your little lead soldiers sink to the bottom of the commode; and you could even sail a boat in there, too, just like the ones up at O'Shaughnessy Dam. Anyway, one afternoon I was in the bathroom, and I looked over and saw that kitty cat lying beside Big Tony, real peaceful like. Now, I knew Big Tony could swim because the Scioto River was about a hundred yards behind our house, right behind Flossie Butts' house. He couldn't swim real fast, but he could dog paddle and get back to shore. So, and I don't remember exactly why, I wondered if that kitty cat could swim too. I walked over and picked her up and put her in the toilet. And, you know, she swam pretty good for a little kitty, her little paws going back and forth, keeping her head above the water. Then, and I don't why, it wasn't malicious or anything, I wondered how she could swim against the current if I flushed the toilet. So, I flushed. Well, the whoosh came, and all of a sudden she went spinning around all sides of that commode in a downward death spiral. I thought she was a goner but just when she was about to be sucked down into Davy Jones' Locker, her little head got wedged in the flush hole. I was scared, so I ran and got my mama, and she ran into the bathroom and started screaming when she saw what I had done. When that kitty cat finally floated back up as the water rose in the toilet bowl, my precious mama grabbed her and put her in a towel and rubbed and rubbed and rubbed her dry. She nursed that cat back to good health. She had a way with cats—had good training growing up with them down in Bertram in Burnett County, Texas.

Back to dogs, though. We had another dog when we lived in the middle of Dublin; his name was Jet. He was a black Doberman. He liked to ride around in our Kaiser automobile. He didn't do a whole lot; just hung around the house like most dogs do. He never protected me like Big Tony did. Before I go on to other dogs and other places, I would like to tell you a little about this little house we had in the middle of Dublin. One thing I remember

COLE'S GROCERY

is that Cole's Grocery[6] was beside our house, to the South, and in that store was Mr. Cole, his wife Katy, and Kathryn, their daughter. Kathryn used to go to school with my dad, and my dad said he used to dip her hair in his inkwell. Anyway, I can remember being just tall enough to jump up at the

LEOR COLE

counter and lay my penny on it. You could buy a lot of candy for a penny back then: jaw-breakers, gum, taffy, whatever. For a nickel you could get a candy bar: Zagnut, Hershey's, Butterfinger, Babe Ruth—anything you wanted. I never really had more than a nickel back in those days, but what did you need more than a nickel for anyway? One thing I do remember: Mr. Cole sold me my first set of firearms. They were matching pistols in a big leather holster, and they hung so low that they dragged against the ground. The holsters had fringes on the side, and leggings that you tied. They fired caps, a roll of red caps that you put inside the guns. Well, I just loved those guns; I would pretend that I was the Lone Ranger, or Gene Autry, or some other famous Western figure. I just wore those pistols out, and when I aimed at someone or something, well, I never missed. I think my dad and mom gave me the money for my pistols since I could have never saved up that much by myself.

Another thing I remember about that house was the time I was Super-man. You see, Superman was real popular back in those days, and I just loved Superman. I had a lot of his comic books. I would watch Superman and watch Superman and try to figure out his flying technique. After a long time of study and analysis, I thought that I could fly just like Superman. I had a plan. We had a real high porch in the back of our house that faced Flossy Butts' house. The porch faced to the east, toward the River. It was high off the ground. Now, I wasn't very big back in those days, so what I did was put a horseshoe around my waist, tied a rope to it, and tied the other end of the rope to the back of the porch. Well, I was fearless. I stood on the back of the porch, ran as fast as I could and jumped clean off the end of that porch toward Flossie Butts' house. I did fly—briefly. The end of the rope snapped taught, and there I was swinging back and forth behind

---

6   Cole's Grocery was at 50 S. High Street. It is now 'The Hair Smiths'.

the porch, and my ribs really hurt. I started screaming. My mama ran out the back door, and she started screaming. Jimmy Myers happened to be coming by our house at that moment; there always seemed to be somebody just coming by our house since we lived in the middle of town. He ran over and unharnessed me out of that horseshoe, and started laughing. I guess he had been around Sellses long enough to know not to ask any questions, and that all things are possible. My Mama calmed down, and I don't think she told my dad because I didn't get a spanking or anything. Heck, I didn't need one—my ribs were sore for a month.

Thirty-eight South High was a pretty nice little house to live in. I had an almost endless supply of candy from Mr. Cole's Grocery Store next door, I had a place for adventure, I had my dogs, and when Sue Perry came over to baby sit, well, all the "big" guys in town would just happen to "drop by" to see her, especially Willie and Danny Miller from across the street. Like I said, one of the first TV sets in Dublin was in our house, and even the old man came over the river to watch it. I couldn't tell you if he came over the river in one of his robes or not, but I suppose that he did; he never wore hardly anything else.

We moved to Worthington when I was 5 and lived there for a year, but then moved back to Dublin, to 74 Marion Street. We had just one dog when we lived on Marion Street, and I would rather forget him. My dad kept him up at Mrs. Snouffer's at 7700 Dublin Road, (Donegal Cliffs, now) to guard his business and equipment there, and he could not have picked a better sentry dog. This dog's name was King, and he was a massive German shepherd. He was a very, very mean dog, and he was loyal only to my dad. I don't know where he came from, and I don't know where he finally ended up, and I don't much care. He was "trained," but I don't know who trained him, and I don't know what for. King was a stone cold killer. You could not play with him. He would just sit and watch things and never move a muscle. If someone was smoking, King would walk up to them and eat the cigarette. Up at Mrs. Snouffer's, he would never let the oil man out of the truck. On Marion Street, he once broke a thin wire rope we used to tie him to a clothes line, and went after another dog. If I remember right, he killed a dog down at the Dublin Nite Club when my dad left the back of his station wagon open and King got out. We had to get rid of him. He was too vicious. We gave him to Carl Finkes who ran the Bait Store on Riverside Drive. I bet you that nobody ever broke into that bait store to steal soft craws with King around. When I went around back to see him there, he didn't remember me; he just growled and flashed those big incisors. I knew he wanted a piece of me. I always stayed my distance from that dog. He did have a weakness, though. You could always tell he was around because he would pass the worst gas you ever did smell. At least he could never sneak up on you!

After we had lived on Marion Street for three or four years, we moved down to the house where the Blankenships' had lived, at 6052 Dublin Road. It was at the Blankenships', on the Scioto River, with all of the river front-age that you can imagine, that I had two of my greatest dogs: Their names were Boolie and Chopper. If you think of dogs and you think of the water and you think of a lot of fun, what breed of dog do you think of? Well, for my money (which is limited) I would choose Labrador Retrievers. That's just what I had, two of them: Boolie and Chopper. You know, back when Dublin Wasn't Doublin', I can't remember ever seeing a dog tag on a dog. It seemed that everyone just knew whose dog was whose. They ran free, but at the end of the day they always made it home. Anyway, Boolie was my first Lab, and Chopper was my second. A friend of my dad, Jack Shank, gave them to us. Also, at about that time, Helen Delewese gave my mom a little Spaniel mix, and we called him Toby; he didn't weigh more than 20 pounds. He just loved my Mama. Boolie was jet black, and I never saw a dog that could swim like Boolie. You could throw sticks and balls into the river, even with a pretty good current, and Boolie would jump in and get them, and bring them right back to you. Boolie could play fetch in the river all day long if you wanted him to; he never got tired. I think that's how my arm got so strong for baseball: throwing things out in that river all day for Boolie. Little Toby would just sit there on the bank, watching and barking. She and Boolie got along just fine; matter of fact, Boolie got along with everyone just fine. One day, when I threw a big stick in the River, Boolie jumped in—and Toby jumped in right behind him. I never knew Toby could swim; course, I never asked her. Boolie swam real strongly, but that little Toby kept right up with him with her short, quick little paddles. They reached that stick at almost the same time, and Toby grabbed one end and Boolie grabbed the other end, and they turned around together out there in the middle of the water and just brought it home. I ran up to the house and told my mom, and she didn't believe me until they did it again—and again and again—while she was watching. My mama loved Toby. I think she loved Toby as much as she did her little dogs and cats when she was a child down in Texas.

Now, there was one thing that Boolie did that irritated me. Whenever I went fishing on the African Queen, you just could not keep him off the raft. If you didn't let him on the Queen right away, he would track you up or down the bank, wait till you were anchored, then swim out and around the raft until you let him on. I am sure that he would have followed that raft all the way down to Fishinger Bridge just to get on. And when he started swimming circles around the raft, it messed up the fishing because that scared all the fish away. When he was on the raft, he was OK until you caught a fish, and then he went into some kind of war dance, whooping and hollering. I loved Boolie, but he did have his faults.

Another one of his faults was that he was too good of a retriever. When we lived at 6052 Dublin Road, the house was down a very long gravel driveway. I imagine it took a good ten minutes to walk it. Someone always had to walk up and get the paper. Many times it was Little Brother Kelly who got it. Well, Kelly and Boolie were great friends, of course, and Kelly, I suppose, always being the innovative young man he was, struck upon an idea: if Boolie would retrieve balls and sticks thrown into the river, most certainly he could be taught to retrieve our newspaper. It was a logical enough assumption. So began the newspaper retrieval education of Boolie. Kelly would walk him up to where the paper was; show Boolie how to put it in his mouth, and then the two of them would make their way back down to our front porch. Over and over and over again, repetition being the mother of education. And, may I add, it does not take much to make a retriever "retrieve." Well, I am happy to say that Boolie learned to do his job well. We could count on him, shortly thereafter, to get our paper—no more long walks up the driveway. But, lo and behold, one Sunday morning Boolie, always eager to please, took it upon himself to not only get our newspaper, but most of the newspapers from Marion Street, Longview Street and Grandview Street. Our front porch was a mound of Sunday newspapers, and Kelly had to return them to their rightful owners. After that, Kelly had to rein Boolie in, so to speak: one paper and one house at a time.

I wish that I could tell you that Boolie had a long life, but such was not the case. Not only did he develop some sort of cancer, but he discovered the chickens at the Karrer's house who lived near-by. I have been told that once a dog gets a taste for chicken, it becomes their food of choice. Anyway, Boolie, the great swimmer and retriever, had to be done away with. I hated it, but he was dying anyway.

I grieved for Boolie, but not for long. Soon after, there appeared at our home another great Labrador Retriever in the long list of retrievers around Dublin, When it Wasn't Doublin'. We called him Chopper, and he was just a pup when we got him, and I think it was Toby who taught him how to swim. Anyway, Chopper grew up with Toby at his side, and Toby taught Chopper everything that Boolie had taught him. They fetched sticks thrown in the river together, each swimming back with an end of the stick in their mouth. They ran after balls thrown in the wide green yard. Chopper would lift Toby off the ground when they both got ahold of a rubber ball at the same time. They would both lie out on the front porch when they got tired, which was seldom, and pant and pant, their pink tongues lolling.

Now, like Boolie before him, Chopper loved that raft and everything about it. Like Boolie, you could not keep him off it. You could get up at 5:00 AM to go fishing, and Chopper would be right there. The only consolation was he did not seem to get so excited when you caught a fish; maybe he thought that was what you were there for. Like I said earlier, sometimes I would have friends come down to go fishing, and we usually went at night when the fish bite best. So, one evening I was getting everything ready to go fishing, the bait and tackle and food and such, and I told my mom, "Mom, please keep Chopper in the basement all night. If you don't he'll swim out to the raft and ruin our fishin." She said she would. So, my friends arrived and we headed north for the Riffles. We were having a great time: eating, drinking pop, telling stories, and even catching some pretty nice fish every now and then. Well, about 1:30 AM I was sitting on the couch, watching my line by the light of a shielded lantern, when I got this tremendous strike. To this day, I have never had a hit like that, and I have fished the waters in Lake Erie, Michigan, Canada, North Carolina, Florida, and South America. My pole just about disappeared even though the drag was open, and I held on for dear life. I let the fish run a good sixty or seventy yards, and then I set that hook as hard as I possibly could. My pole doubled over, the drag sang, and then I heard the most sickening sound ever: Ooooh, Ooooh, Ooooh. I didn't have to think twice. It was Chopper. I tightened my reel to snap the line. Somehow he had gotten out of the basement. Well, we fished a little longer, but then came back in. I didn't see Chopper then, but in the morning I saw him lying on the front porch. He was "smiling," and had a hook caught right in the middle of his butt. I got the needle nose pliers and removed the hook. That was the last time I ever went out on the African Queen without Chopper at my side.

So, my brothers and I had our dogs, and my mom had Toby. Whenever my mom left the house, Toby would jump up on this chest of drawers we kept downstairs in the kitchen, and that dog would just howl like a coyote, all the time she was gone. But as soon as she turned into the driveway, way up the hill, she would jump down and run around the kitchen linoleum floor like crazy.

Of course, I liked Boolie and Chopper best, but Toby would prove to be a companion and "confidante" of still one more dog, my favorite of all dogs—Big Otis, another Saint Bernard. When Big Otis came our way, he wasn't big; he was only about six weeks old and he was just a little hand full of fur. In fact, you could hold him in one hand. This was after we had moved from the Blankenships' to our home in River Forest, at 5175 River Forest Road, just off Dublin Road, south of what is now Muirfield Village. He was brown and white, with a big tongue even then, and one thing I can remember about Otis: he had the biggest paws that I had ever seen on a puppy. Another thing I remember about Otis, even when he was a pup, he really loved to eat. He would eat and eat until he couldn't hold any more, and then he would go to sleep, just like a hog does. Well, it got so, in his baby years, that Otis would eat so much that you could just about watch him grow. It was magical; he would just grow right before your very eyes. In fact, I think that dog put on about four or five pounds a week. One week you could hold him in one hand, and the next week you couldn't. One week he could scoot right under Toby (and they were great friends), and the next week, well, Otis would knock him over just trying to get under him. Otis had a wonderful childhood, I would say. We fenced in the back yard for him, about a half of an acre, and like I said, he had plenty to eat. My dad always kept a side of beef in our freezer in the garage, and it was not unusual for Otis to get pieces of steak and steak bones along with his ever-increasing portions of dog food. I loved to go outside and play with Otis, and he could run pretty well for a big dog, but not real fast; he just kind of lumbered. Otis, well, he liked to get you down and wrestle with you. In the beginning this was a lot of fun, but later when he really got to be "Big" Otis, well, he was a load. Of course, he wasn't aware of his great bulk. He just grew and grew, and he grew up big and he grew up strong like an oak tree. Little Otis became Big Otis after eighteen months or so.

If my dad got big Otis to be a watchdog like King was, well he could not have made a bigger mistake. You see, Big Otis never knew a stranger; he just loved people. If you pulled up to the house real quickly and opened the gate to Big Otis's back yard, he might run up to you as fast as he could run, and jump up on your chest (about knock you down) and try to lick you to death. He had that big, old fat pink tongue of his, and he loved to lick on things: Toby, cats, but especially people. You had to be careful when you were dressed up and you tried to slip out of the house in your good clothes because Big Otis would spot you from the far corner of the yard where he stayed and make a mad dash to jump on you and lick you. My dad made Big Otis a really nice doghouse, fit for a king, but he never slept in it. He liked to camp out in the southwestern corner of the back yard where he could take everything in. I remember it was kind of funny when we would get a lot of snow. Big Otis, even in a snow-storm, would still not sleep in that doghouse. In the morning after a big snow, I liked to get up early so that I could watch Big Otis wake up. There would be a big mountain of snow in the back yard—a big mountain. I would stand there staring through the

**BIG OTIS GETTING
COOLED OFF**

window, and eventually Otis would climb out from underneath that mountain of snow. He would just shake it all off (the snow would fly everywhere), and he would act as though nothing unusual had occurred, and come trotting onto the porch for his breakfast.

The snow and the cold and the rain never bothered Big Otis, but it was a little different with the extreme heat. It can get hot in Central Ohio, as I am sure you are aware, and the same fur that protected Big Otis in the cold proved to be a problem to him in the heat. What we would do for Big Otis though, was I thought rather unique and I thought illustrative of Big Otis' adaptive behavior. When it got real hot, Big Otis would come trotting into the middle of the back yard and stand by the water sprinkler. Well, one of us would go over to the water spigot connected to the house, turn it on, and out would come the water, squirting and spiraling around and around. Upon seeing this, Otis would walk (not trot, now), over to the sprinkler, and just stand on top of it. As the water sprinkler would go around and around, you would see Big Otis making his rather large pirouettes exactly in time with the sprinkler. What I found equally fascinating was I never saw any water at all coming out from Big Otis' stomach or chest; that is, his long fur caught every shot of water. It was kind of funny watching him just standing there in the back yard going around in circles, but after what seemed like hours, when he had had enough, he would return to the far corner of the yard, under the shade of the pine trees, well refreshed and invigorated.

He loved to play, and football was his game. We had a large front yard, and many times we would get a bunch of guys together and play football. Now, When Dublin Wasn't Doublin', this was a pretty common occurrence. We played, and we didn't need any adult "supervision," so to speak. Big Otis was not a barker; didn't need to be. But, when he saw us playing football, and he was cooped up in the back yard, he would bark: whoof, whoof, whoof—in a deep baritone. This was a nuisance and a distraction, so for the sake of sanity, I would go up and open the back gate for him. Well, he would come rolling down the hill and onto the field like a freight train, like the *City of New Orleans*. When someone got the ball, Big Otis would chase him and roll on him when he was down and bark and just carry on. He would hit you like a linebacker and then lick you and that football to death—all in fun. He would jump up on his back legs and then jump on top of you, and Big Otis was very, very tall. He especially loved to play football in the snow. He never got tired of playing football. He always seemed disappointed when we had to quit and go home and do homework. I think maybe what he loved the most was that there were so many kids in the front yard to be around. Big Otis loved people and he loved football.

He loved football, but I could never teach him to fetch. Toby would fetch like a son-of-a-gun, but when I threw a ball and told Big Otis to fetch it, why, he just looked up at me like I had lost my mind. "Fetch, Otis, Fetch," I would say. But he would just sit there with that big smile of his and that lolling pink tongue hanging out of the side of his mouth and seem to say: "If you want that darn ball so bad, you go and get it."

I never saw Big Otis fight or even lose his temper. Toby was in the backyard a lot of times, and on rare occasions other bigger, meaner dogs would make their way into the backyard. Toby, a housedog, couldn't fight, and for that matter, neither could Big Otis. But, when one of these stray dogs meandered into the yard, Toby would get scared and make her way for the corner of the back porch. Big Otis, well, he would be taking things in from his sentry post at the southwestern corner. If things got a little tense between Toby and the other dog, Big Otis would get up real slowly, shake himself off, and come trotting over to where this stranger and Toby were. Well now, I can just imagine what this strange dog must have felt like when he looked up and there was this 200 pound mastodon standing beside him. Big Otis didn't do much; he didn't have to. He would sniff the stray just a little bit, maybe enough to remember him, and the stray would quietly meander off, tail between his legs. Big Otis would go back to his corner of the yard. Big Otis would offer safety and security to others, but he would never attack another dog. He did not like to fight; he let his bulk do his barking for him. He was gentle and kind. So, he was no mere dog to me—he was a Saint.

One thing I found unique about Big Otis was how very long he was when he stood on his back feet. He was just tall! What he liked to do was run over to the redwood fence beside our porch, stand up on his back feet, and put his massive head and front paws over the top of the fence. I don't recall how high that redwood fence was, but it had to be at least six feet. We had at the time, due to the danger of pulling in and out on Dublin Road, one of the widest driveways in all of the State. I don't know why Big Otis stood with his front paws on the fence for so long, maybe it was to see the cars and the people in them go by that he enjoyed. I do know this. When passersby saw this huge head, giant tongue, and black nose, it was common for them to pull into our driveway to take a closer look at Big Otis. Maybe this is what Big Otis wanted. And, given the fact that the Columbus Zoo was just a few miles to the north of us, maybe people pulled in because they thought that big Otis was another attraction. Who knows?

Big Otis was not without his faults. He was not allowed in the house. If you were foolish enough to let him in the house (and he loved forbidden territory), well, you paid the price. He came in the house like a freight train: plates broken, chairs upturned, and lamps knocked over. I can remember he was so big he never jumped to get on the couch; he just rolled onto it. He loved little Toby and would lick her to death. After a while, we managed to shoo him out of the house. His visits were always brief but gruesome. His indoor soirees bring up another story and a strange predilection of Big Otis. My dad, as mentioned, was a beer drinker, and he could drink a lot of beer. Many times he would come home late at night, after a long night of drinking, and Big Otis would be there on the back porch to greet him.

"Hello, my little Otto, my little baby. I know how much you miss me. I know how much you love me."

That's how my dad talked to Otis, especially after he had been drinking. My dad's term of endearment for Big Otis was "Otto."

"Otto, do you want to go inside the house with me? You know, Otto, you are one of the best friends I have ever had. But you have to be quiet."

Inside they went, two bosom buddies, but many times my dad could only make it to the couch before he collapsed.

Now, here comes the weird part: Big Otis would lie down beside my dad on the couch—and eat up my dad's glasses, whole. I don't know what prompted this behavior; the only thing I can figure is that Big Otis was attracted to the salt on my dad's glasses. It happened more than once. My dad would awaken in the morning, and there would be Big Otis beside him, but there would be no glasses anywhere.

"Darline, I can't find my glasses," my dad would yell.

"Dog probably ate 'em," she would reply.

Big Otis pulled a similar trick on me one time. I came in from a date once, around 1:30 AM or so, and I was really hungry. Big Otis was lying on the back porch. "Hi, Otis," I said, "You want to come inside for a little bit." He looked especially harmless that early morning. "Be quiet, though." Well, like I told you earlier, we kept a half side of beef in the garage, and there were always steaks thawing out in the refrigerator. Tonight was my lucky night. There were two T-Bones, or they could have been Porterhouses, already to be broiled in the oven. When Dublin Wasn't Doublin', there were no microwave ovens. Anyway, I broiled those big, fat juicy steaks, buttered up a couple pieces of bread, and got two sodas out of the refrigerator. Big Otis was quiet, like he wasn't payin' attention to what I was doin'. I put everything on a big plate, but then had to run to the bathroom first for just a split second before I could sit down to eat in complete comfort. When I got back, there was nothing. There was no steak, no bones, no butter, no bread, not even a drop of steak juice on the plate. Frankly, I was surprised that there was even a plate left. Now you see it, and now you don't. And Otis, well, he was just lying on the floor as if he had absolutely no idea of what had happened. I don't know; maybe he thought I had invited him in to feed him, certainly not my intention. The only thing he left me were those two soda pops, understandably, because Big Otis would go on to become one of the great beer drinkers in the annals of Dublin history.

It started innocently enough; doesn't it always? We held a wedding reception for my big brother Mike at our home, and of course, Big Otis was in all of his glory with all those people around, patting him on the head, and he licking them. Anyway, someone poured a beer into Big Otis' water bowl. It was probably my dad, though no one knew for sure except Otis, and he took that to the grave. With that big, heavy pink tongue, he must have just lapped it right up: slurp, slurp. Maybe someone else caught on, maybe they didn't, or maybe it was my dad that poured him a few more. The reception was long, and I am sure that Otis had his share of beer, but he held his own. He never made a spectacle of himself; he would just lie down after a few hours and go to sleep, which was to become a familiar pattern. After that, whenever my dad would come home from work, well, let's just say he always had a drinking buddy. We had a refrigerator out in the garage, and my dad would have a beer for himself, and then give Otis one. Big Otis would drink as much beer as you would give him until he got sleepy and passed out. Needless to say, in the evenings Big Otis, or "Otto" as he was so affectionately called, would anxiously await my Dad.

After a while they became such close "drinking buddies" that my dad bought a new Mercury Station Wagon to haul Otis around. For those of you in Dublin, this was well before the multi-purpose vehicles that popu-late the highways now days. My dad sat in the front seat and Otis in the back fold-down portion of the wagon. Their destinations were predict-able: the Wyandotte Inn, the White Cottage, or the Zoo Bar (Hut, Dam Site, Bogey Inn, etc.). My dad, of course, knew all of the owners quite well, and they had no reservations about letting him bring Otis inside. My dad would ask the owner for two beers, and a bucket or a bowl if he had one on hand. They would oblige. My dad would drink his beer and pour the other into Otis' bowl. Otis would just make the liquid evaporate. Soon, I would guess, there were others in the bar who would befriend Otis , with a beer or two (hail hearty fellow!), and who wouldn't. After a while, after my dad and Otis had gotten their swill, they would head home, none the worse for wear.

Well, the above arrangement was all very good for the two chums, except when, sometimes my dad would go to one of his other destinations after work and not come directly home. I am sure my reader is aware that alcohol can be quite addictive, even for a dog. Big Otis loved his nightly pint(s), and when occasions arose that my dad was working late or was otherwise engaged, and thus not able to feed his habit, well, Big Otis would just ven-ture out on his own, solo, so to speak. Otis knew the pubs and the patrons there. It is my suspicion that the patrons of the various pubs knew Otis and had grown quite fond of him. After all, he had not a mean bone in his body, and his bowl was already there. Well, as I said, Big Otis would drink and drink and drink until he couldn't drink anymore, and then he would pass out on the floor. Now, this presented quite a problem for the owner and for my dad. Most bars back in those days closed at 2:30 AM, and there would be Big Otis, passed out on the floor. So, my dad would get a call from the owner of the bar, and he would have to go up and get Otis and bring him home. This happened more than once. Big Otis would sleep it off, and in the morning, though he doubtless arose a little bit later, he would be none the worse from last night's foray.

We really tried to keep Big Otis home. The back yard was fenced with barbed wire, but he was just so massive and with such long, thick hair that he could lie on the fence and make it collapse. I don't know if my dad asked the bar owners not to let him come in anymore, but even if they refused him entrance, I can just imagine Otis standing outside their establishment, barking and scaring patrons away until they let him in. Such was his lust for alcohol. Otis coming home on his own after a bout of drinking was dangerous. Dublin Road is a very hazardous highway.

In the end, we had no choice. What began as an innocent act ended in a full-blown addiction. We gave Big Otis away to an electrician who lived way up in Jerome, Ohio, and who had a lot of land and things to do to help him dry out. I will never forget Otis. Every time I see another Saint Bernard, I always think of him. He never knew a stranger, and he was my friend. And he wasn't just a dog, he was a "Saint."

CHAPTER 7

PEOPLE AND PLACES

I t had always been my desire to have Big Otis sit up front with me in the car, but first I had to learn how to drive. I learned how to drive, and took my first driver's examination in a brand new Rambler that my dad had bought. He had the entire interior covered in clear plastic; my dad loved anything that would stay "clean": "Cleanliness Is Next to Godliness," he would always say, "It's in the Bible; you can look it up," but I haven't been able to find it yet. Anyway, the Rambler was a real nice car; it was nice, but it would get hot with those plastic covers—but the seats they protected never got dirty. When you took your driver's examination, you had to know how to parallel park; that is, pull up parallel to a car on your right, and then back into the space behind by cutting the steering wheel exactly right. It took a lot of practice, and was the downfall of many an examinee. I took the Rambler down in the quarry at the Snouffer's, set up my practice poles, and practiced, and practiced. I practiced so much that I would overheat the engine, but I never told my dad that. Anyway, I felt real confident about my driving and parallel parking, so I scheduled my test. I was doing real well on the driving part until the instructor told me to take a left on the road after the next. I got confused, and tried to take an immediate left—right in front of a big dump truck. The instructor reached over and grabbed the steering wheel, and let loose with a couple of obscenities. So I flunked the driving portion of the examination—but I did pass parallel parking—no dump trucks there!

Eventually I got my driver's license, and soon thereafter I inherited my first car from my brother Mike, a 1962 Ford Falcon, 3-Speed Manual on-the-Column. I liked it, and it wasn't too bad on gas. I learned to drive a car with a manual transmission in my Falcon, which is rapidly becoming a lost art these days. After the Falcon, my dad would let me drive the Rambler around. Once, I was coming north up Dublin Road toward home in February in the Rambler, and I hit what must have been a patch of black ice. It was just below where the new bridge runs over Dublin road. Anyway, I lost control of the vehicle, and it turned a complete circle right in the middle of the road. I was lucky because there was nowhere to run off Dublin Road without hitting a telephone pole or a tree. I always lived in fear of Dublin Road after that. Anyway, I had a lot of fun with the Rambler. It had a car phone which was a big deal in the days before cell phones.

After the Rambler, my dad got my favorite car of all, whose "purchase" I will describe a little bit later. It was a 1966 Lincoln Continental, beige, with a black top, and suicide doors. It had the greatest sound system of any car I had been in up to that point. I loved to go out on dates in the Lincoln, and I liked to wash her and wax her before I went. Sometimes at night I would go out and put some of my Beatle eight-track tapes in, and just lie down and listen and listen. The Lincoln was huge, and it reminded me a little of driving the African Queen—big as a boat. After the Lincoln, I inherited my Brother Mike's 1967 Ford Mustang: metallic green, fastback, 3-speed on the floor, with a small six-cylinder engine. I loved that car, too; it ran like a son of a gun, and I don't think I ever had to put any oil in it. It just ran and ran. That Mustang saw me all the way through college and through my tour of duty at Fort Knox, Kentucky.

I have a very early memory about cars that still sticks with me. I also remember about cars, even before girls. When I was real little, my dad bought my mom a Pontiac convertible, and all of the truck drivers would whistle at her as she drove by when her dress accidentally crept up. I don't really know if my mom ever figured out why the truck drivers would whistle at her. She always was a little oblivious to her surroundings. I suppose, now days, you would say that she was a little naïve. Also, as you will hear, she used to drive our Kaiser around town with our dog Jet in the back seat for "protection."

I used to love to watch Flippo the Clown on TV, so one day my mom decided to take my Brother Mike and me downtown to the studio to see

Flippo—live. Most shows were "live" back then. Anyway, the main sponsor of Flippo's Show was Wonder Bread. From time to time during the show, Flippo would ask the audience of little boys and girls, "And what bread do you eat at your house, boys and girls?" And everyone was supposed to jump up and shout, "Wonder Bread!" Well, after two or three times of this, I'd had just about enough, so after everyone had jumped up and shouted "Wonder Bread" and then sat back down, I stood up by myself, as the camera panned over: "Flippo, in my house we eat Tip-Top Bread." That didn't go over too well, but I have always associated that Kaiser with Flippo the Clown.

When we lived down at the Blankenships', my dad bought a jet black Chrysler Imperial with fins as high as a sailfish. It was really deluxe, as my mama used to say. We had a character in Dublin; his name was "Him Frank Kelly." Whenever you would see someone walking up or down Dublin Road, another person would ask, "Who is that?" "Him? Frank Kelly," would invariably come the reply. So Frank Kelly just came to be known as "Him Frank Kelly." Him Frank Kelly lived up in Shawnee Hills in Lucy Depp Park north of Dublin. Him Frank Kelly did not have a car or a bicycle, nor would he accept rides from anyone. Him Frank Kelly just preferred to walk, no matter how far. Moreover, Him Frank Kelly had the reputation of being the hardest working man in Dublin. Him Frank Kelly was the John Henry Johnson of Dublin, When Dublin Wasn't Doublin'. Him Frank Kelly could dig and lift and swing a sledgehammer, and chip away with a spud bar all day long and then walk fifteen miles or so back home. Whenever my dad had a big heavy job to do, he always got Him Frank Kelly to do it. Him Frank got to be a regular for my Dad, and after a while Him Frank would let my dad take him home in my dad's big Imperial. I don't know if Him Frank Kelly ever went to school, but there wasn't anyone in Dublin who didn't like and respect Him Frank Kelly. At the very least, he was in better shape than about 99.9% of the population. You could hardly understand Him Frank, though, when he spoke; I think he chewed a lot of tobacco, but you sure could see the results of his work. Anyway, in the Imperial, which had just about every luxury item there was in that day, there was a button on the floorboard, and if you pushed it with your toe, the station on the radio would change. Like I said, after my dad had gained Him Frank Kelly's confidence, Him Frank would let dad drive him home after a hard day's work. Him Frank would sit right up front in the car beside my dad, like the dignitary he was. My dad would turn the radio on, and the two would go "cruising" up Dublin Road.

"You like music, Frank?" my dad asked Him Frank.

"MmmHuh," Him Frank replied. "MmmHuh" was about the extent of Him Frank's vocabulary. I never really ever heard him say any more than that phrase, but maybe he did when I wasn't around. It was just a nod of the head and an "MmmHuh."

"I like music," my dad told Him Frank.

"MmmHuh."

"I like Frank Sinatra."

"MmmHuh."

"I like Bobby Darin when he sings 'Mack the Knife'."

"MmmHuh."

"Do you like cowboy songs and country songs, Frank, like Gene Autry and Roy Rogers?"

"MmmHuh, MmmHuh!"

"Do you want to hear that kind of music?"

"MmmHuh, MmmHuh!"

"OK, Frank, just watch that dial move real slow across the radio. I ain't goin' to touch the radio. It's magic, and when you hear something you like, just let me know."

"MmmHuh."

My dad gently pressed down on the button on the floorboard that controlled the radio station and let it up when it found a station. Slowly, as Him Frank watched in amazement, the dial hit one station after another until it found a country station; my dad took his toe off the button. Frank looked over at my dad and smiled; it was a big smile.

"Well, I guess we found us a pretty good station. We'll just leave that dial there for whenever I take you home again. Personally, I like Buck Owens and the Buckaroos. You like Buck, Frank?"

"MmmHuh!" Frank said, and he was almost laughing now.

It's downright strange how you associate girls, other people, and even dogs with cars. I told you how my dad had to buy a brand new Mercury station wagon just to haul Big Otis around in when they would go out and drink beer together. The back of the station wagon door would swing open sideways and Otis would run and jump into the back of the wagon. He about wore out the rear end shocks of that car. My dad would crack the rear station wagon window down just far enough for that mastodon to get his head out, and Otis would fly merrily down the road, anxiously awaiting his arrival at the White Cottage or Zoo Bar, gulping big heaps of air as he went, his big pink tongue lolling and goggling back and forth.

I have a lot of memories of when I was a little boy in Dublin; some of them are unusual. One of the first things I remember is lying on my back on the sidewalk in front of our house in the middle of Dublin with my Saint Bernard, Big Tony. Big Tony would be lying right beside me. People would walk by and stop and start talking, maybe talking to my mom, I suppose, or say hello to Big Tony. Seems like people always took the time to stop and talk back then. It was like the Louie Armstrong's song: "I see skies of blue and clouds of white/The bright blessed day, the dark sacred night/And I think to myself what a wonderful world." Sometimes the people would come up on the porch and sit on the swing and talk in the shade while I just lay down on my back watching the flies get stuck in the sticky paper. Sometimes I would take my pair of six shooters with me that I got from Cole's Grocery and walk up and down the sidewalk pretending that I was Roy Rogers. The sidewalk was always real warm. There were always people walking by our house, so it gave me a feeling of security. I remember one time, though, I was ridin' on the back of a big tricycle that my dad had bought my big brother Mike and me, and my big brother started going really fast down the sidewalk. I kept yellin' for him to slow down, but he didn't, so I just jumped off—right in front of Mose Myers' Barber Shop. I hit real funny like, and I couldn't get up. They took me to our house just down the sidewalk, and my mom started screamin'. It was Dinky Daugherty who carried me down to Dr. Karrer's. I remember tryin' to stand on that leg, but I couldn't. It never really hurt that bad, but it felt like Jello. It was broken, so they took me down to Grant Hospital, put it in a cast, suspended it way up in the air (traction, they called it), and gave me a room to share with a kid about my age. I was only three or four when all this happened. Anyway, this other kid's name was Sherman, and he was the first African-American who I had ever seen. We sure had a lot of fun together. Back then, they kept you in the hospital for a long time when you broke something. Anyway, I would tell Sherman scary stories at night until he begged me to stop. Now, my readers may find this hard to believe, but back then we didn't have that much plastic, or any plastic at all, so the straws Sherman and I drank out of were made of glass. As an aside, Homer Lynn, Virginia Geese's brother and David Geese's Uncle, was the one who I believe invented the plastic straw and plastic extrusion machine.

Anyway, I really don't know what got into me, maybe I just wanted to scare Sherman some more, but I told him one afternoon, "Sherman, when they feed us dinner tonight, I'm going to eat my straw."

"You can't eat that straw!" Sherman yelled, "That straw's made of glass!"

"Well," I said, "I don't care; I'm going to eat it anyway and swallow it." So, true to my word, after dinner, I just chomped up that glass straw and ate it. When the attendant came in, I guess he noticed that I didn't have a straw.

"Where's your straw, son?" he asked.

Before I could get out a word, Sherman shouted at the top of his lungs, "Mister, he ate that straw; Mister, he chewed it up and ate it and swallowed it whole, and I saw him do it!"

I was caught by an eyewitness. For the next three days I was on a diet of bread and water, but I never had any complications. I guess Sherman had a pretty good story to tell for the rest of his life. And strange thing, for what seemed like forever after that, the nurses at Dr. Karrer's always used a rectal thermometer on me when they took my temperature. I suppose my reputation preceded me.

There was another temptation that I succumbed to at an early age, one, may I add, that lured many young boys and even older ones. It was Mr. Cole's Grocery Store and inside, the Luckyball Machine. Mr. Cole was a nice fellow and his store was where all the candy was. For no bigger than that store was, Mr. Cole had it stocked with about every kind of candy you could think of, and of course my favorites were candy bars: Baby Ruths, Zagnuts, O'Henry Bars, Hersheys, Three Musketeers, Snickers—just an endless array. I really loved candy bars; I loved the sugar and the nuts and the chocolate and the texture and the aroma when you unwrapped them. They would just about knock you out. They make my mouth water to this day. The only trouble was I never had a nickel to buy one, or at least it seemed that way. Oh, I may have had a penny or two in my pocket, but a big candy bar cost a nickel.

And there arose the dilemma: Mr. Cole had, up front in the corner of the store, something that, without doubt, led the lesser willed children of Dublin to a life of chance: the Luckyball Machine. It worked like this: you put your penny in (instead of buying good penny candy), cranked the handle, and prayed that you got a Luckyball and not just a regular gumball. Because, you see, a Luckyball was indeed lucky; a Luckyball was worth a nickel, and thus a candy bar. The question you always had to ask yourself when you went into Mr. Cole's was: "How lucky do I feel today?" Did you feel like putting two or three cents in the machine and forsaking a bunch of penny candy, jaw breakers and suckers if you lost? What if you had a nickel? Would you let everything ride on the LuckyBall Machine on a nickel with the hope of hitting two Luckyballs? A nickel gave you five cranks on the LuckyBall Machine. Imagine that! Or were you conservative?: "I have a nickel Mr. Cole and I want a Clark bar." I think the most I ever saw were two Luckyballs come out of the shoot on a nickel's worth of spins, though there may have been more that I didn't know about, but I am pretty sure that I would have heard about it. The LuckyBall Machine was the center of attraction and fascination for us kids growin up in Dublin.

I used to love to stand back and watch how different people would open the gumball shoot after they took their cranks. Some kids would pry it open real slowly and barely take a peek at their gumballs, like they were playin' poker or somethin', just turnin' over the edges of their cards. Others would almost rip the gumball shoot open and slam it closed. Getting a Luckyball, well, that almost made up for losing a little league game—almost. On a few occasions, I wouldn't shout or slam my Luckyball down on Mr. Cole's counter, I would just quietly take it home and put it on my dresser. When Dublin Wasn't Doublin', little girls had their dolls; and little boys had their Luckyballs.

Speaking of the Coles, I do have a pretty good story to share with you. Once upon a time, not so very long ago, people did not go to banks, especially people who had lived through the Great Depression. Mr. Cole, Katy and Kathryn were such people. If I remember correctly, the Coles hailed from Tennessee, and they kept all the money that they made from the store upstairs where they lived. They saved practically all of their money, and very seldom did any of them ever leave the store. Now, saving money is a good practice and we would all do better doing it in order to make it through future recessions. I don't know what we can do about the huge national debt that we have incurred, but I'm no economist, so I won't go on.

Let's just say that Mr. Cole was frugal and saved his money, and after many, many years in the grocery business (and his was one of the few in Dublin at that time), he was, to employ an understatement, "well off." There are basically only two problems with storing your money in your home. Your money could be stolen, or could be destroyed. The latter, unfortunately, befell the Coles. I am unsure of the details, but it seems as though a fire struck Cole's store on the first floor. While I am sure that the near-by volunteer fire department, headed by Harold Shriver, reacted quickly enough, all the Coles ran upstairs and sought out the hiding places of their currency. I am told that Sears and Roebuck catalogs were used by the Coles as their depository. That is, they would insert different denominations of bills between the pages of the Sears and Roebuck catalogues. In the "heat" of the moment, during the fire, they ran upstairs and started throwing the catalogs with their money inside out of the windows into the streets below. I suppose it seemed that the Leprechauns were finally out in full force. For the first time in the history of Dublin, it was literally raining money in the streets. Out it came, in a never ending stream of denominations—5's, 10's, 20's, a few 50's, possibly some 100's—from between the pages of the Sears and Roebuck catalogues. Can you imagine the reaction of the Dubliners? Money raining down from heaven! Manna from heaven! However, this moment of largesse was brief. The fire was put out, the Coles were saved from injury, and I am sure that the good people of Dublin returned all of the Coles' money to them.

After running coon dogs for Bobby Joe Bailey and Willie Miller in the Dublin Cemetery, my next job was in Mose Myers' Barbershop[7]. I think that I was only about seven or eight years old. You see, my dad tried to instill the work ethic in me at an early age. What he did was buy me a little wooden shoe shine kit that the customer could rest his foot on while Mose cut his hair, and I gave him a shine. Inside my wooden shoeshine kit were cans of different colors of Kiwi shoe polish, shoe brushes, cotton buffer rags, and bottles of liquid sole treatment for the soles of the shoes. I loved my work at Mose's. I loved to just sit in one of the big green chairs around the wall and listen to Mose answer the telephone when someone called to make an appointment for a haircut: "Yeaaah... yeaaah... yeaaah." That's all he would

---

7   Mose Myers Barber Shop was renamed 'The Dublin Barber Shoppe' but
          is still at the same location, 24 South High Street.

say as he wrote down the time for the haircut. He couldn't say too much more because he was in the middle of a haircut, and he was also in the middle of smoking that big cigar he always had in his mouth. I loved to just hear

the clip, clip, clip of the shears as Mose went about his business, and the buzz of the electric trimmer as Mose would taper the hair up a customer's neck. I really liked it when he would strap that straight razor of his, lather up the customer around his ears and neck, and then cut in a perfect sideburn. Of course, I should have been working, but it's a malady I've always suffered from: I would rather watch a true artist at work than work myself. When I first started out as the shine boy there, I suppose a typical afternoon might go something like this:

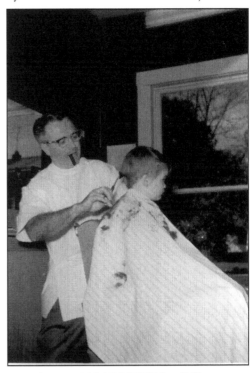

MOSE MYERS – 1958

"Shine, Mister?" I would ask when someone sat down in the barber's chair. Now, you have to remember that I knew very few of my "customers," but just about all of them knew me because my dad, and my family, had lived in Dublin for over one hundred and fifty years.

"Shine, Mister?" I would ask.

"How much do you charge, boy?" A customer would ask.

"Quarter, Sir," I would respond.

"Don't you think a quarter's too much money, son?"

"My dad told me to ask for a quarter, Mister."

"Well, what you're asking for and what you're going to get may be two different things, sonny."

"Quarter, Sir."

"Well, who is your dad anyway?"

"Bob Sells, Sir."

"Bob Sells isn't your dad."

"He sure is, Sir."

"No he isn't."

"He is."

"No, Dan Sells is your dad."

"No, Sir; he's my uncle. Lives across the river."

"Well, now, you're a pretty smart young man after all. You know a Dick Sells?"

"Yes, Sir. Got quite a few of them. Got an Uncle Dick; got a Cousin Dick I believe from my Uncle Joe and Aunt Inez, and I got a Cousin Dick from my Uncle Jab and my Aunt Lucy. I got another cousin Dick lives down in Lancaster, Ohio. I may have some other Cousin Dicks I don't know anything about."

"That a fact? Well, tell me, son, how many aunts and uncles and cousins do you think you have all together?"

"Mister, I can't really say. Got aunts and uncles I always thought were my cousins, and cousins who turned out to be my aunts and uncles. Got an Aunt John D. and an Uncle Dolly—couldn't ever figure that one out. Even got an aunt turned out to be my step-grandma. There's just so many of them."

Then Mose would jump in, "Harold, just get your shoes shined and give that boy a quarter. Can't you tell he's already mixed up enough as it is? You know what the Sellses are like."

I would get this routine a lot. After a while, when someone would start asking me Sells' questions, I would just play dumb, which wasn't too hard to do, and say I didn't know, which usually was the truth. I was there to shine shoes, and I liked doing it. The colors were black, brown, cordovan, or neutral. I would apply the polish very lightly with a soft cotton cloth and then brush the shoes. I remember that I had real good, soft brushes. The trick was not to apply too much polish. I would then apply the liquid sole treatment and let it dry. Then, I would take a little spit from my tongue and rub it on the toes of the shoes. I would then go back and forth, very quickly, with a very soft cotton cloth, and try to make the cloth crack over the shoe. Sometimes it did, and sometimes it didn't. If it did make a little crack, I was pretty sure I would get a pretty good tip. In regards to tips, I would usually get a nickel or a dime. I think once I actually got a half dollar. The people in Dublin back then, didn't really tip a lot. A lot of times I didn't get a tip at all, but that really never bothered me. I couldn't understand why people wanted their shoes shined in the first place; they just got 'em dirty again. One time I spilled a bottle of my shoe sole treatment all over the floor in the barber shop, but Mose never even batted an eye; he just pointed to where he kept the cleaning rags, and kept on smoking his cigar.

I never worked real hard in the Dublin Barber Shop, just hard enough. Fact is, I never really worked real hard any place. I just enjoyed being with people. I liked to sit in the green chairs against the walls and listen and watch the customers. Lots of the old farmers would go to sleep while Mose was cutting their hair; that clip, clip, clip seemed to lull them into a deep sleep. When they woke up, their haircut was over. I liked the farmers a lot because I didn't have to leave my chair when they came in; they mostly just wore work boots. Sometimes they would talk, but not often. Their conversations were mostly about corn and wheat and beans and crows, and of course, the weather. They always were concerned about the weather. When the teen-agers came in, it was different. They all seemed to be real fussy about their hair, reminded me of Virginia Geese's beauty salon. They wanted their flat tops and crew cuts just right. Mose never got rattled; he just clipped and trimmed away, put a little butch wax on their heads, cut in their side burns with his straight razor, and sent them on their way. The teenagers would slink out the door kind of like James Dean, still glimpsing at themselves in the mirrors as they left, their blue jeans hung real low on their hips. I never had many teenagers for customers; they mostly wore black sneakers anyway. I guess most of my customers were people who lived in Dublin, but who worked downtown in Columbus. These were people who appreciated a good shine, and I tried my best to please them. They all seemed to have beautiful leather shoes, soft leather shoes; some were made of calfskin. I liked it that they would come to me for a shine because I knew that they could get a much better shine at the airport, the Southern Hotel, the Neil House, or places like that downtown. Heck, those were professional shoe shiners down there; they didn't even use a cloth to apply the wax; they just used the inside of their palms and their fingers—and they could make that cloth pop anytime they wanted!

You are probably wondering what I did with "all" the money I made at the Dublin Barber Shop. Well, I gambled away a lot of it in Cole's Grocery Store on the LuckyBall Machine. I started suffering from addictions and compulsive behaviors at an early age. I bought a lot of baseball cards, and I ate a lot of candy, mostly Snickers Candy Bars or Mars Bars. I bought a lot of comic books; Superman was my favorite. When my mom took us to Graceland, I would go to Hobbyland sometimes and buy models, mostly model cars. I liked to buy balls of any kind: tennis balls, rubber balls, footballs, basketballs. Don't get the idea that I became rich from working at the Dublin Barber Shop because I mostly just worked there on Saturdays. Ever since then, though, barbershops have held a strange fascination for me (even though I now have little hair). I can remember even then that people would tell Mose things that I am sure they would tell no other human being. It would be personal stuff, which I didn't really understand. Mose would just listen, clip away, smoke his cigar, and then say "Yeaaah."

You might be wondering what the nightlife for Dublin was back in those days, When Dublin Wasn't Doublin'. We had the Dublin Nite Club, and that was just about it. "The Nite Club," or just "The Club" as it was usually referred to, sat at the intersection of Route 33 and Route 161, and people would come from all over to eat and have a drink or two there. I used to love to call up the Dublin Nite Club to hear Eber Neds answer the phone: "Dublin." That was all he ever said; he didn't need to say anything more. I really liked Eber; he reminded me of Sidney Greenstreet, the character actor in all of those Humphrey Bogart movies. Calling Eber Neds was just like calling up Mose Myers at the barber shop: "Yeaah," that was all Mose ever said. Anyway, the Nite Club was owned by the Deleweses, and it was famous for miles around for its Italian food. I used to love to go in there and eat, and since Bobby Beiriger was one of my best friends at that time, and his mother was a Delewese, I even got to go there and eat during lunch time at school, unbeknownst to my teachers. Mrs. Delewese would have submarine sandwiches and milkshakes made for us, and we would eat in one of the "back" rooms, and there were a lot of them. What a treat. Don Delewese, the dough ball maker, was always around, of course. And then there were Nardine and Al Delewese, kind of the patriarchs of the Delewese family. Anyway, Al was always in there; it seemed to me that he pretty much ran the place. There were lots of Deleweses running around!

Congratulations Dublin

Dublin Nite Club & Restaurant

1930   19–

WE CATER TO SMALL PARTIES
AMERICAN AND ITALIAN FOOD

The Dublin Nite Club was established on Labor Day, 1930, by Ben Delewese on a 20 by 60 site. Ben died July 28, 1942, and his youngest son, Albert, took over. Albert died October 17, 1956, and another son, Leonard (Nardine) became manager on September 2. Nardine died in 1959. Virginia, wife of the first owner, now has the club. The Nite Club is operated by Mrs. Al (Erma) Marchi, Mrs. Dominic (Mary) Christopher and Mrs. Helen Beiriger all daughters of Ben. Benny, grandson of Ben and son of Leonard and Nancy, is also associated.

6478 Riverside Drive   TU-9-8381

**THIS IS AN ADVERTISEMENT THAT APPEARED IN THE 1960
SESQUICENTENNIAL PROGRAM**

And there were a lot of Delewese women: Irma, Helen, Bobby's Mom, and so on and so on. There seemed to be as many Deleweses as Sellses, and Headlees. Anyway, for fine Italian food, a few drinks, and, at times, some extracurricular activities (I heard that gamblers came in from all around

Central Ohio and held high stakes card games in the back, secluded rooms), there just wasn't anyplace to rival the Nite Club in Dublin.

I swear, I was at the Club one night with my family when someone brought in a big, brown bear for anyone to wrestle. It did, at least, have a muzzle on. Things were different When Dublin Wasn't Doublin'. Can you imagine trying to bring a big bear into one of those fancy restaurants they have in Dublin now? Probably have PETA, the National Guard, and the State Highway Patrol in there all at the same time. Well, the Club was just a magical place to go. I remember having dinner at the club with my 3rd grade teacher, Mrs. Coffman. I think she was about the nicest teacher I ever did have. I was there with my Mom and Dad and she was there with her husband, Clark Coffman. I loved Mrs. Coffman. So, the Club was a watering hole for all of Dublin, and, like I said, folks used to come down from Marysville, Marion, Delaware, and other parts of Central Ohio.

Remember when I mentioned Al Delewese, Nardine's brother? He was the epitome of everything an Italian embodied. He looked Italian and he acted Italian. He had an Italian temper and he worked hard like an Italian. He would get mad and yell at you one minute, and the next minute he would have his arm around you with a big smile on his face. I think that Al talked more with his arms and hands than he did with his mouth. My dad used to tell me that when you want something done right, go get an Italian to do the job. I never fully understood what he meant by that, but he used to tell me that quite often. Al was my dad's best friend. My dad flat out loved Al, and the feelings were mutual. Whenever my dad needed any money, cash money, Al was there for my dad, and vice versa. People didn't have credit cards back then; they used cash, and it seemed as though Al always had plenty of it on him, a big wad of cash in his pocket, just like my dad did. They did business together, cash business, and it seemed like they were always together. I don't know if Al was ever in the Army or not, but if not, it didn't seem to bother my dad. Like I said, back in those days, business was done in cash or checks.

Dad owned a small plumbing company. I remember he gave turkeys and hams to his workers when Thanksgiving rolled around. My dad was a generous man. Anyway, he worked with a lot of contractors and homebuilders, and he had a payroll to meet. He did business with this one contractor, whose name I won't mention, and when it came time for my dad to be paid his first of three payments for the job, he didn't get paid by this contractor, and so my dad didn't have the money to pay his men. He called up the contractor's house. The man's wife answered the phone, and, as my dad related it, he asked to speak to "John," the contractor. "Well, Bob, John's not here." she responded, "He flew down to Florida to go fishing. "Oh," my dad said, "do you know when he is coming back and what gate he will be arriving at?" "Sure," she said, and she gave my dad the arrival time of his flight and the gate number. When the contractor came strolling down the corridor in his tropical shirt, dad walked up to him real casual like, grabbed him by the collar of his shirt, and lifted him up about three inches off the ground, and slammed him against the wall. "Listen to me, you S.O.B.; if you ever take another vacation on my workers' money, I am going to beat the s— out of you so bad that you'll be eating through a straw for the next six months!" Well, needless to say, my dad received his money shortly thereafter. My dad knew violence; he grew up with his fists. He was very good with his fists, and he was never afraid to use them. Looking back at it now, considering all of the combat he must have seen in France and Germany, and growing up as the last born of fifteen kids, he had to fight to survive.

My dad could have gotten the money to make his payroll from Al Delewese. All he had to do was ask, but I guess it was the principle of the thing with my dad. Back then people seemed to live by a very strong moral code. My dad was a man of principles and fierce loyalty, and maybe that's what got him through the War. My dad hated liars. He always told me, "If someone will lie to you, they will steal from you." I think that's one of the reasons my dad loved Al so much; Al used to work by the same code of ethics. My dad wasn't a religious person, but for some reason he really liked the Catholic Church—maybe

MY DAD IS AT THE FAR RIGHT BY THE TREE. AL DELEWESE IS STANDING - 3RD FROM THE RIGHT

because most Italians went there Al Delewese was closer to my dad than most of his brothers.

The only time I ever saw my dad cry was on the morning when he got a phone call and heard that Al had been killed in a car accident. I guess Al and some other men were on their way back from a fishing trip and there was a terrible car crash, somewhere in Indiana. I never saw my dad cry again, even when we got word through the State Department that my big brother Mike had been killed in a car crash outside Sidney, Australia. My dad just didn't cry. He didn't cry when my mom died. He loved Al Delewese, and broke down when he got the terrible news that morning.

As I mentioned, I loved the Dublin Nite Club, as everybody else did in Dublin. It had a little something for everybody: you could eat, drink, if you were an adult, see all kinds of people, see all kinds of critters, and gamble in the back if you were so inclined. Everybody loved the club, and the Deleweses who owned and ran it. So, it was also a very sad day when early one morning my dad received a telephone call: the Dublin Night Club had burned down. I guess they tried to pump water on it from the Scioto River to quench the flames, but my dad summed it up best when he said: "Thirty years of grease went up in that fire." It had a lot of false ceilings in it too, and there may have been electrical problems. When the Dublin Nite Club burned down we lost our favorite restaurant and the most famous place in Dublin. Now, since Dublin Is Doublin', they replaced the Nite Club with a Wendy's—go in there and try to wrestle with a bear.

I asked my dad once, besides money flying out of Leor Cole's Store and the Nite Club burning down, what were some of the most unusual things that he had ever seen in Dublin. "'Course, you have to remember, I grew up on the Farm, and just watching the old man walking around on the front porch in one of his robes in the middle of a summer day was always pretty unusual. The old man never cared who came over; he just stayed in that robe. I do remember pretty well something out of the ordinary. It was the day they brought the John Dillinger gang down from the Mansfield Reformatory, on Route 161 right through the middle of Dublin. They brought them down to the Ohio State Penitentiary. It was a funny thing because I remember they dismissed school and let all of us kids go out and stand by the road to see the John Dillinger Gang's motorcade go by. You would have thought it was the President."

Personally, I was always quite fascinated by the Ohio State Penitentiary back in those days. When I was eleven years old, I got to go on a "tour" of the penitentiary with a friend of mine. I don't know the exact purpose of this tour. Maybe it was to serve as a deterrent from crime. If it was, it worked. I got to see the electric chair. To this day, I can still see "Old Sparky" as they called it: the big wide oak arm rests, the high hardwood back, all the cuffs, and straps. It was very foreboding, to say the least.

I have read some books about electric chairs. Most electric chairs, I guess, are made right in the prison in which they are used. There is no such thing as an electric chair factory. When they first invented electricity and, of course, saw the myriad applications for its use, someone thought of the "bright" idea of humanely executing people with it. However, unsure of its reliability, they had to first perform some "tests." The executioners would travel around like carnival people with their electric chairs and a small menagerie of orangutans. They would charge their audience a fee to view the shows when they electrocuted the orangutans. Orangutans proved to be better subjects for the show than human beings, which would come later. But, enough of that gruesome tale; at least it did not happen in Dublin.

Please allow me to share with you a story about another notorious criminal, Willie Sutton, whose career was at about the same time as John Dillinger's and whose logic was more or less like that of my Uncle Ted's. Sutton was interviewed by a reporter and was asked:

"Mr. Sutton, why do you rob banks?"

"Because that's where the money is," he replied.

My Uncle Ted would have said the same, I am sure.

Oh, sure, we had our fires and we were aware of notorious criminals, but we also had really fun things to do, like the Dublin Jubilee. Now the Dublin Jubilee was not exactly like the Biblical Jubilees where all past debts were canceled and forgiven, but it was an exciting time. A big Ferris wheel was set up right in front of our house in the middle of Dublin, and we had cotton candy and ice cream and popcorn. We even had a "dunk 'em." That's where you throw a ball at a levered target, and if you hit it, the person sitting on the chair fell in a tank of water. Louie Geese was one of those guys who sat on that chair; he would do anything for a laugh. Now, our Jubilees were not like the "Festivals" I've heard about down in Rio De Janeiro, or the Mardi Gras that they have in New Orleans, but we always looked upon our Dublin Jubilees with great anticipation. And don't forget the Dublin Sesquicentennial, 1810 to 1960, that was quite an event for us. We had all kinds of things to do: a parade, floats, a queen, and the history of Dublin and all kinds of plays and such. That was when I got my picture in the <u>Columbus Sunday Dispatch</u> section along with Becky Eberly; I can still remember her in that pretty little red dress with a bouquet of flowers.

Besides historic landmarks and figures like Indian Run, Leatherlips, Indian Bill, Mr. Cole and the Luckyball Machine, the Dublin Nite Club, and the spring beneath the west side of the Dublin Bridge, and notorious criminals coming through town, in January of 1959, we had the big Scioto River flood. I remember the flood of 1959 very well for three reasons: Van Blankenship who lived on the River came up to our house on Marion Street; my dad who was in the plumbing/water well drilling business at the time kept driving back and forth to Dayton, Ohio, to get submersible pumps for his customers so their basements wouldn't flood; and there must have been literally a billion night crawlers all over the roads. Along Dublin Road west of the River, and Riverside Drive east of the River, you could just stop your car and scoop handfuls of night crawlers right off the asphalt. If you could have found some way to keep them alive for the spring and summer, you would have been a millionaire, but we weren't prepared for such a slimy onslaught of crawlers! Well, my dad wasn't afraid; he just kept on driving in that big old black truck of his back and forth to Dayton for pumps. He just couldn't get enough pumps. And I think that was the first time I ever saw Mr. Blankenship at our house. I don't know how high the water rose at his place, but it must have gotten really close to the house (the house we moved to later that year). Mr. Blankenship was a World War II Veteran out of the Navy, and he didn't scare easily.

The only houses that I am aware of in the Dublin area that were flooded by the 1959 flood were a few on the east side of the river, north of Butler's Swimming Pool, near the dam, that were built very close to the river. Carl, Barbara and Carol Finkes' house was one of them. They had a ranch style house and had water in it right up to their ceilings. A little north of the Finkes' house, another friend of mine, Bill Baer, had just started building his house and the river took away what he had built. After the flood, Bill built his house on top of telephone poles. When asked how it was living in a house on top of stilts, he said it was OK, but when his wife did the laundry the whole house got to rocking and rolling in time with the washing machine. Bill Butler's ticket booth for his swimming pool was washed down the river about a quarter of a mile and ended up in Moon's backyard. The only house on the west side of the river that might have had water in it during the flood was the Clyde Phillips' house which sat very close to the river between Indian Run and where the new bridge is.

Though not nearly so dramatic, we had annual minor spring floods when we were living at the Blankenships' house right on the Scioto River, and the river got kind of close to the house. That's why I think that during the Flood 0f '59 it must have really gotten awful doggone close to it. Anyway, every spring the ice would break on the Scioto River and we would have our spring rains to go along with it and the river would rise. Now, this brought about a really enjoyable pastime for me. When Dublin Wasn't Doublin', it seemed as though you just entertained yourself with the simple things in life. At least, that was the case for me. When the ice broke and the rains came, the waters of the Scioto would creep right up over our big front lawn making a lake. And, invariably, with this great encroachment of waters, we would see various types of fish and other wildlife. Low and behold, I had my own little (or big!) wetlands, far before the term came into vogue. There would be ducks and geese in the front yard and some cranes and giant blue herons, but what I had the most fun with were the shad and carp that would wash up with the high water. I would pretend that I was the great white hunter, and would make myself a spear out of a broom handle with a big nail driven into the tip. Shad and carp, beware! All day long, well, at least after school, I would seek my prey. The shad were not hard to spear; there were millions of them, big too. But those doggone carp gave me fits. You could try to bury your spear into carp hide, but they had scales on them like silver dollars, and they swam right away. I never minded, though; that was just one more for me to catch in the summer. To see a nice spawn of shad, though, was always a good sign because that meant there would be plenty of big catfish later to eat. Catfish just love to eat shad!

Before we leave stories about life during the high waters in Dublin and some of the other uncommon things I witnessed growing up, I would like to take my reader back to the Scioto River one final time and share a fishing story. Now, I am aware I told you "no more fish stories," but I do have a rather obsessive personality, and this is a rather unique story, which involves *The Creature from the Black Lagoon*, so to speak.

Jug fishing is when you take a whole bunch of Clorox jugs and tie nylon line to the handles, set big turtle hooks about 18 inches deep from the handles, and hook big live chub minnows either through the lips or under the dorsal fin so you don't kill them. You jug fish when the water is rising and high, after or during a good, hard rain. My dad and I set our jugs out at the Riffles and let the current carry them downstream to about Hayden Run Bridge. After a couple of hours of fishing and waiting upstream, we chased after our jugs downstream on the African Queen. With a strong light, you could see your jugs pretty easily. If a jug was lying flat, chances were there was nothing on it, but, when you saw that jug doing the Scioto River Hop, well, that's when the good times rolled. As the jug bounced up and down, you just gently eased a corner of the Queen to where it was, got down on your belly, and, with the gaff, pulled the fish right out of the water. Just slick as silk, my dad and I caught some beautiful 7, 8, and 9 pound channel cats. They were great to eat, and a beautiful fish to behold.

The advantages of jug fishing were that no fish can hold a Clorox jug completely under the water for a very long time, and it was easy to tell when you have a fish on. However, sometimes we would get a surprise. We would see the jug bouncing a little and rolling back and forth over by the bank. Well, I would ease the Queen over, get down on my belly, get out the gaff, and…a huge snapping turtle. Now, you talk about a critter with a poor disposition! They say snappers are good to eat if you know how to clean 'em, and maybe they are, but if you got down and dirty with 'em about 3:00 AM on a rainy morning, a few inches away from that prehistoric beak of theirs, I think you would just do what I always did—cut the line.

But wait; there were uglier and scarier things you could bring up from the murky depths. Sometimes, the jug would roll and bounce a little by the bank or close to it, so we would follow the same procedure: ease the raft in, and I would lie down on my stomach, get out the gaff, and slowly pull up the nylon cord on the jug—A DOGFISH. Now, I don't know what the ugliest, most hideous thing you have ever seen is, but I would not be surprised if a dogfish would not give you a case of the frights. They just scared the livin' daylights out of me, and made me think of every monster that I had ever seen—real or imaginary. I couldn't cut that line quick enough. I once caught an eel in the Muskingum River, but it looked like a beauty queen compared to a dogfish.

Speaking of those night crawlers a while back, while I was talking about the great flood of 1959, made me think about something else we used to have a lot of all over the place, When Dublin Wasn't Doublin'—crows. We always had a lot of crows, because we had a lot of cornfields. Well, I am happy to say that it seems as though all those crows who used to live in Dublin are coming back home to roost. Yes! I've been noticing that the crow population in Dublin is on the increase. When just about everybody in Dublin had a cornfield, we had more crows than we knew what to do with. I think a lot of those crows have come back because of all the French Fries and food particles and whatever lying outside the many restaurants in Dublin, and they have adapted to their new surroundings. Maybe those crows think French Fries and such is kind of like a new hybrid form of corn. I don't know; I'm not a crow, but I have always had a great respect for crows because I grew up with them. Like I said, when all the old Dublin clans— the Tullers, the Tuttles, the Frantzes, the McCoys, McKitricks, etc.—had their corn fields, there were so many cornfields that the Freshwaters up on Dublin Road would give you 25 cents as a bounty for every crow you brought in. There was a bounty on crows, just like you got 2 cents for a pop bottle. I understand that there is a piece of modern art now in Dublin of an artificial cornfield. Needless to say, the last thing we needed When Dublin Wasn't Doublin' was an artificial cornfield. Sometimes I wonder what those crows must think when they fly over that artificial cornfield, which is a nice work of art. Maybe they don't think of anything, maybe they think of the good old days. I don't know; I'm not a crow.

When I was growing up, like I said, I had a strange fascination for crows. I always wanted to open the side door of our house at the Blankenships', and blaze away at a bunch of them roosting in a big tree in the morning. I had a Mossberg, 12 gauge, bolt-action shotgun, with a three shot clip. Heck, I never did it though; it would have scared my mom to death. I couldn't hit any of them anyway. I am a terrible shot. But, boy, I would have liked to see them all take off, and nobody would have complained down at the Blankenships', it was so isolated. But, can you imagine blasting off three rounds at 7:00 AM in Muirfield Village or Donegal Cliffs nowadays? They would empty out the Beightler Armory. I once went crow hunting with my friend Jim Terrell. It was really neat. You use a blind to hide behind, the call of a wounded owl on a tape recorder, and a stuffed owl. Crows hate owls. As they fly over, even way way up in the sky, a pack of crows can hear the tape-recorded cry of the stuffed owl. They will circle a little while, and then come in like a dive bomber for the kill. You have to wait and let them get in range, about thirty or forty yards, I guess, and then you jump up and fire away. I don't think I ever hit one, but Jim Terrell could knock them right out of the sky, one after another—bang, bang, bang. It may sound cruel, but remember that a bunch of crows can reek havoc in a farmer's cornfield, and anyway, 25 cents is 25 cents.

Now, that old stuffed owl ended up getting me in a whole lot of trouble with the law, and here is the way it happened. Jim Terrell and I were fishing up in the Riffles one night/morning, and I think we were using his little aluminum boat. We had parked his station wagon beside Joe Dixon's house, below the red barn, and below Dr. Karrer's house—on Riverview Street. We slid the boat in a little bay that Joe had below his house. Well, we were catching a whole bunch of beautiful channel cats, and we had pretty much filled up our metal stringer with five and six pounders. Before I go any further, I wonder if my reader knows just how good a channel cat tastes. Back then, to clean them, I would just gut them, put them on a board, cut around their head, and peel their skin back with a pair of pliers. I always liked them best deep fat fried and served with coleslaw and bread and butter and plenty of iced tea to drink. Of course, down South, you'd probably get them with hush puppies and French Fries. I would fry up some home French Fries on occasion. You couldn't beat those cats for eating. They would come out of that deep fat fryer piping hot, and all you had to do was slide your fork down their middle and the backbone would just fall out. Clean as a whistle—no bones. It was like in the cartoons when you see a cat eating a fish and he drops the fish down into his mouth and just pulls out the skeleton of the fish. That is the way we would eat those big channel cats. They certainly were succulent. Now, on occasion we would catch blue cats and some shovel heads, but I was always a connoisseur of the channel cat. Well, we had filled up our metal stringer, always to be used instead of a rope stringer, when we started hearing these strange, loud noises on the west bank of the Scioto. It was about 3:00 AM in the morning by then, and the noises startled me.

"Did you hear that, Jim?" I asked.

"Yeah, I heard it," he said.

"Must be a big coon," I said.

"Must be a real big coon to make that much noise," he said.

We waited, and waited. Then, a kind of rustling, crashing sound came again.

"There must be a pack of wild dogs running through the bank," I said.

"If they're dogs, they're big dogs," he said.

Quiet. Then a loud tumbling noise came again.

"Jim?" I asked, "Do we have any bears around here?"

"Not that I know of, but you never can tell."

Well, that certainly didn't reassure me. I don't mind telling you that I was really frightened. For all I knew, it could have been Big Foot over there rambling through the trees and brush. Finally, it was quiet. It got quiet, and it stayed quiet.

"Jim," I whispered.

"Yeah," he said.

"Do you think it's OK?"

"OK for what?"

"Well, OK for us to bring the boat into shore?"

"I suppose so. The fish have quit hittin'."

So, Jim rowed the little boat toward shore. I was sitting on the front seat. Just as he slid her into the cove, I heard the most awful rustle of trees breaking and limbs snapping. I grabbed an oar and just prayed that my swing as a ballplayer from Dublin High School was still with me. Then, all of a sudden, a light flashed and almost blinded me.

"Hello, boys; catch any fish?"

It was worse than Big Foot. It was my most dreaded of all enemies. It was the game warden. There were two game wardens! No wonder they made so much noise coming down the side of the bank.

"Well, we caught a pretty good stringer of channel cats," Jim said.

"Nice to hear," he said. And then he followed with some of the worst words I have ever heard, "hope you got your fishing licenses."

"I got mine," Jim said.

I remained silent, kinda hoping he would overlook me, hoping I would just blend into the woods.

"Son," he said, "you got a license?"

"Well, Sir," I said, "It's kind of complicated."

"How old are you, son?" he asked.

"I'm 19, Sir," I said.

"Well, son, don't you know that in this State, as soon as you turn 18, you need a fishing license? That's the law."

"Well, Sir; it's a matter of economics," I tried to explain. "You see, Sir, I'm a student, and I don't really have any money, and every time I go into the bait store to buy soft craws, I never have enough money left over to buy a fishing license."

He didn't say anything. He just wrote me out a ticket. I figured if that fellow would have been from Dublin, he would have just let things slide, but he didn't. I didn't mind, though, really. I did some quick calculations in my mind: I didn't get a license the year before; I didn't get one that year, so if I didn't get one in the next year, which I didn't plan to do, I and the State would be just about even. I never told him that though. Some things are better left unsaid.

The other game warden jumped forward, "What we really want to know is who has that stuffed owl in the car. Possessing a stuffed owl in this State is a very serious offense. Whose is it?"

Jim just looked at him with those cold blue eyes and said, "That's my owl you're talking about, Mister. I use him to go crow hunting."

"Well, son," the game warden said, "That's how we come to be here. Someone reported a vehicle parked up above the river, and when we shined the light in your station wagon, we saw that owl in the back. I don't mind telling you that you're in a whole heap of trouble."

Terrell never flinched, "Mister, what you're a saying is true, but I never shot that owl in Ohio, and I never stuffed him in Ohio. That's an Indiana owl, pure and simple, and there's no law against transporting an owl across State lines for crow shooting purposes. And I got proof if you need to see it."

Well, the game wardens scratched their heads and hemm-hawed a little. There just wasn't anything they could do to Jim. I guess you could say that he had "out owled" the game wardens…and I didn't buy a fishing license the next year either.

When Dublin Wasn't Doublin', the zoo wasn't as big an attraction as it is now. We didn't have any Zamboozie Bay, and we didn't have all that traffic running back and forth between Powell and the dam, like we do now. However, the zoo did have a great impact on our little village. Many of my readers probably do not know that Colo, the first gorilla ever born in captivity, was born at the Columbus Zoo. One of my friend's mom, Mrs. Larcamp, well, she took little Colo home and brought her up like she was one of her own. If my friend Joe Larcamp ever got jealous of Colo, he didn't show it. I think Colo was born in the late 50's, it was about the same time that Fidel Castro took over Cuba, and from the last report I heard, Colo's doing better than most of the people down in Cuba. But, talking about the zoo brings me to another story I am not real pleased to relate to you. It may be apocryphal (now isn't that a university word if I ever heard one), but I have heard the story more than once. It seems as though I had a few friends who liked to go up to the Zoo Bar, get liquored up a little bit, and after they had had their swill, and gotten a false sense of bravado, they would walk east across the O'Shaughnessy Bridge to the Zoo—with a BB pistol in hand. Now, the polar bears were always kept at the west end of the zoo; they were always easy to spot from your car going east. The elephants were kept off toward the center and back, and there was a moat for them. I believe that the gorillas were kept east of the elephants, but I don't recollect for sure. Anyway, for "sport," my friends, in their inebriated state, would walk down around the outside enclosure of the zoo, and the gorillas would be out there. Taking a wobbly, but as close an aim as possible, one of them would shoot a BB at the chest of one of the great apes. Now, I do not condone such cruelty in any way, but the hide of a great ape, so I have been told, is pretty darn thick, and I suppose that their skin is so leathery that the BB shot would not have felt like anything more than a pinch or mosquito bite. However, I was told that as soon as one gorilla was "pinched" with a BB shot, he would immediately turn around, and looking for the culprit, crack the next gorilla beside him upside the head, and then that offended gorilla would, in turn, crack another gorilla upside the head, and then a free-for-all amongst all the gorillas would break out. I guess it was a cheap source of entertainment for my drunken friends, but I certainly didn't condone it.

Dublin has always had its drinkers. In the late 1800s there were numerous saloons in Dublin and the town had a reputation for rowdiness. Fights were commonplace. Men were advised to approach Dublin cautiously with a rock in each hand. The following was a popular refrain:

"Dublin, Dublin, city of beautiful roses,
Gouged-out eyes and bloody noses
If it weren't for the solid rock foundation
It'd be gone to hell and damnation."

Considering it to be sort of the "Tombstone, Arizona," of central Ohio, some folks even avoided going into Dublin unless it was absolutely necessary. The situation got so bad that in 1881 a group of people in Dublin decided to attempt to incorporate the town as a municipal corporation so ordinances could be passed in order to establish some semblance of law and order. They were successful in becoming an incorporated village, and the village council did pass numerous ordinances outlawing disorderly and rowdy behavior and imposing penalties. Conduct outlawed by council included the following: intoxication, quarreling, gambling, running horses, shooting at targets in town, rock throwing, and disturbing religious meetings. The village council hired a marshall and two deputies to enforce the ordinances, and in 1883 they built a jail. Notwithstanding their efforts, the disorderly behavior continued until, in 1888, council passed an ordinance forbidding the sale of alcohol at the taverns.

My grandfather Amiziah, the old man, was born in 1867 and grew up in Dublin. He was 14 when the town was incorporated; he was 16 when the jail was built; and 21 when the bars were closed down. I don't know exactly what part he played in the disorderly days of Dublin, but I do know he had a reputation as a fighter.

After several years, council repealed the 1888 ordinance and allowed the sale of alcohol in the taverns, but by then the rowdiness had calmed down. The sale of alcohol in Dublin stopped again because of prohibition and resumed when prohibition was repealed. But, by the time I was growing up, the voters had voted the town dry and all of the bars in Dublin had been closed down. The Dublin Nite Club was outside the corporate limits of Dublin and therefore remained in business after the vote, but it burned down about 1961. After that the drinkers headed north for their refreshments. The "watering holes" were up around the Zoo. In fact, I would say that the White Cottage and the Zoo Bar on the west side of the Zoo, and the Wyandot Inn on the east side, formed a Bermuda, or at least, an "O'Shaughnessey" Triangle, for lost souls who temporarily wanted to drown their sorrows. We had fellows who would frequent one of these establishments to get just a pint or two, and then head on home. On the other hand, we had the heavy beer guzzlers who would put a tremendous strain on their bladders, kidneys, and elbows as they propped themselves up at the bar. I don't think there was a heavier beer drinker than my Uncle Ted who could drink and drink and seemingly never get drunk—unless it was Big Otis, and he just went to sleep at the end of the bar.

So, we had some real, heavy weight beer drinkers (in more ways than one) When Dublin Wasn't Doublin'. But, there was one who was a light-weight both in pounds and in his drinking, and yet who stands out as a legend in the annals of Dublin's beer drinking history. He looked more like a choir boy than a barley and hops man. He was kind and soft-spoken and tender of heart. Beloved by all who knew him, he had a warm Irish smile for anyone who happened to glance his way. He was slight of build, and certainly did not fit the beer guzzler profile. In short, he was the type of gentleman who you would invite into your kitchen for iced tea and chocolate chip cookies. But, on some occasions, it was not iced tea that he would get a taste for; it was for a brew or two, and poor Billy had a very low tolerance, so once Billy had downed just a couple of mugs of draft, he was done for.

Here's how Billy Headlee made it into the Dublin Beer Drinker's Hall of Fame. One night he came rolling up to Eddie Merrit's Wyandotte Inn and true to form, Billy knocked down a couple of beers, smiling and happy, entirely within his element. And then, in view of what happened, I think he must have downed a couple more. I wasn't there, but I can imagine that at closing time there came a conversation something like this:

"Bill, it's 2:30 AM, and I've got to close, and I think you went over your limit tonight. I don't think you should drive home. I'll call you a cab," said Eddie Merrit, owner of the Wyandot Inn, one of Billy's favorite watering holes when he was tempted with the taste.

"I'm not drunk."

"I'm calling you a cab."

"Maybe I should have one more beer Eddie, to sober me up."

"The bar's closed, Bill; I'm calling a cab."

"I don't need a cab."

Eddie picked up the phone, but Billy made it off his stool and out the door, and managed to make it to his car and start it....

The next morning Billy and his car were found in the elephant moat in the zoo, and the elephants were spraying water on him, from what I was told, to bid him a good morning. I guess that the elephants had never seen a car and driver in their moat before. It seems as though Billy, once he started his car, put it in reverse and gunned the engine. Now, if you are familiar with the Wyandotte Inn and the zoo, you know that they sit back to back; that is, the Wyandotte Inn is just across the highway from the zoo. Billy's car, just like a rocket ship with the pedal to the metal, had zoomed backward out of the parking lot of the Wyandotte Inn, crossed over the two lanes that run north, up and over the grass median, across the other two lanes running south, and then backed up and over the cyclone fence that encloses the zoo, backed another couple of hundred feet and landed in the elephant moat. Billy, Dublin's first "astronaut," survived this space shot with no major injuries. Luck of the Irish (or the intoxicated). I am also told that this air-borne escapade, elephants and all, was covered by the *Columbus Dispatch*, complete with a photo. Maybe Billy thought that he was the re-incarnation of Cannonball George Richards, the percussive specialist of the Sells Brothers Circus, who would shoot himself out of a cannon on a daily basis. Hard to say; life is strange. But, by the grace of God, I am happy to say that this incident not only sobered Billy up, it kept him sober. He never drank again. The ornery Leprechauns of Dublin left him alone; they let him be the Billy Headlee we all loved, back When Dublin Wasn't Doublin'.

So, When Dublin Wasn't Doublin', the zoo had a great impact on our lives. Colo, the polar bears at the end of the bridge, the gorillas, the elephants (there always seemed to be talk of elephants in Dublin history (maybe it originated from the circus)—we always loved the zoo. Sometimes, though, someone would start a rumor, like: Did you hear that an alligator escaped from the zoo?; watch out when you go fishing. For a long, long time, When Dublin Wasn't Dublin', when people asked me where I lived, I would just say, "By the Zoo." That seemed to say it all.

One of the most fantastic things that I have ever seen involved my friend Rennie Smith. Now, I told my readers right at the beginning that I have this illness called a bipolar disorder, which is a fancy name for manic depression. It just gives you tremendous bursts of energy, so much so that you cannot eat or sleep or think straight. You can even become truly paranoid and delusional, which I have been before. It is terrible to go through this manic phase, but it is just as bad to experience the depression that follows. Anyway, the energy it takes to found a town, or start a circus, or to be like the old man and just wear bathrobes—well, was that manic energy and depression? Who knows?

Anyway, one time I was right in the middle of a manic attack, and I was driving my Pontiac Astre, on the east side of Columbus down McNaughten Road. And just as my reader is sure he or she is reading this book, I was just as sure that my Pontiac Astre was a fighter airplane and I was flying over enemy territory. Funny thing, though, I wasn't a very good pilot because I had that thing floored, and I was trying to see how fast I could fly it in second gear. Well, I remember that engine whining and whining, and I was hoping that I wouldn't get shot down. But all of a sudden, I did. I got hit by a big piece of flak. I coasted, or landed, in someone's airfield (or driveway), and I jumped out. As a matter of fact, I think I may have had on an old jump suit from the Air Force Reserve, given to me by a friend—to make things more authentic. It was quite a flight, but my aircraft was destroyed. Anyway, I ended up in the VA Chillicothe Hospital where I convalesced, and eventually came home to live with my big brother Mike. This is where Rennie comes into the scene.

You see, Rennie Smith was about the greatest automobile mechanic that there ever was, and he lived just down from my brother's on Route 161. In those days, after I had gotten sick, I was feeling pretty depressed, and I spent a lot of time down at Rennie's house. I didn't know the first thing about cars, and that was the only thing Rennie, and Peanut and Darren, his sons, seemed to talk about. But it didn't make any difference to me; just listening to them talk was all I cared about. They were all Ford men, and I got a real education, through osmosis, about Fords. Rennie always reminded me of Willie Nelson; he had this real soft voice and beard, and it seemed like he never got too excited about anything. Rennie never asked me what was wrong with me. He didn't care that I didn't know anything or say anything about cars. We did like to go fishing together. I owe my getting better then, quite a bit, to Rennie Smith. He would just talk and tell car stories to me, a lot of which I didn't understand. But he made me feel like I did. Anyway, back to that "flack" attack and what I wanted to tell you about, what I saw Rennie do. The car was over at my brother's, and I told Rennie all the circumstances of me getting "shot down."

"It's a Pontiac?" he asked.

"Pontiac Astre," I said.

"Well, that's your problem."

"What do you mean?"

"You should have got a Ford."

"What causes that clanking noise?"

"A rod."

"A rod?"

"Yep, a rod. You blowed a rod."

"What does that mean?"

"Gotta get another engine."

"A new engine?"

"What do you want a new engine for? Your car ain't new."

"A used engine?"

"Yep."

"Where do I get a used engine?"

"Junkyard."

"Rennie, have you ever put a used engine in a car?"

"Oh, just a few times," was all he said. Now, I didn't mean to insult him, but this was the same man who had put 450,000 miles on an old Ford Station Wagon; this was the man who probably owned the fastest car, a jet black '67 Ford Mustang which he and Peanut raced all the time, not only in Dublin, but probably all of Columbus; and this was the man who probably had a wrench in his hand at the age of three.

Now, I want to pause and tell you something. When I was down at the university, I took an art appreciation course. It wasn't particularly the best time of the day to take the course because it was right after lunch. Remember me telling you about the Dublin Nite Club? Well, Mrs. Beiriger had moved her kitchen down to the student union, and of course her being famous for her submarine sandwiches, that's what I would feast upon every day for lunch—with a big milk shake to wash it down and some French Fries. And that being the case, when I went into Art Appreciation 101 right after lunch, and they turned the lights out in the room so that you could see the pictures on the big screen, I swear, I couldn't keep my eyes open. Oh, I heard words, like High Renaissance, and Baroque, and Rococo, and Titian, and Caravaggio, and Michelangelo and such. But it was just too hard to stay awake, especially not seeing them actually at their work. What I mean to say is, there weren't any action figures to watch.

Well, Rennie Smith gave me a real life course in Art Appreciation 101 when he fixed my car, when he set that engine in it. He came over to our house, to the garage where the car was, where the engine was, and where we had rented a hoist. He came over about 9:00 AM or so; he didn't seem in a big hurry; he never was. He walked up to that car like, I suppose Rembrandt used to just stroll up to a blank canvass. What impressed me most about that whole process was there was absolutely no hesitation or wasted motion in him. I guess Rennie could see the end of everything before he ever got started, and maybe that's the way Rembrandt worked: maybe artists can see the end of things before they get started and they just fill in the details when they're painting (or fixing a car). I don't know. I'm not an artist. Anyway, I just watched Rennie work. He never got rattled. The thing about Rennie, he wasn't just a "remove and install" mechanic. No, if Rennie ran into a road-block, and he didn't have the right part, he would make the right part with his own hands and tools and machines. He pulled the old engine and set the new, used engine: There were wires, gaskets, nuts, bolts, and what have you all over that garage. But, he knew where everything was; he never stopped working, very methodical. I guess that's what a painter does, just one stroke after another. For Rennie, it was one twist of the wrench after another. Well, I figured it would take him at least all weekend to put that engine in; I had never seen an engine put in a car before; I didn't know how long it took. But, about 4:00 pm, (having started at 9:00 am) he looked my way and said, "Start it up."

"You think it will start, Rennie?" I asked.

"Should," he said.

I turned the key and that baby purred like a Masserrati. I couldn't believe how Rennie had made order out of such chaos, and at the same time, I think I understood, for the first time, what it takes to be a real artist. I will never forget that afternoon with Rennie, When Dublin Wasn't Doublin'.

There were other characters back then who I will never forget. One of them was my cousin, Danny Lee Sells. Danny used to work for my dad's plumbing company, AAA Plumbing, and he was a lot of fun to be around and also a great plumber. When Danny Lee laughed, everyone in the whole room laughed. He has the most infectious laugh I have ever heard. He has the greatest sense of humor I have ever seen. My dad's plumbing company did a lot of work for the Department of Housing and Urban Development, doing the rehabilitation work and the plumbing work on the older houses. On the front door of every "HUD" house there was a lock and a sign that said: "Warning, this House Is Protected by the FBI: a Theft from the Government Is a Theft from You." One morning Danny Lee and I were approaching a HUD house to do some work; and he had a toolbox in each hand, and I was carrying one, too. However, on the doorstep to the house sat a little African-American boy of about 8 or 9 years of age. As we came toward the house, the boy stood up and said to Danny Lee:

"Mister, you can't go in that house."

"Why not?" asked Danny Lee.

"'Cause that's an FBI house," the boy said loudly.

"Have you ever seen an FBI man before, son?" Danny Lee asked

"No, Sir," replied the boy.

"Well, now you know what they look like," chuckled Danny Lee, and in we went.

When I was working for my dad, I always wanted to be with Danny Lee. I can remember how strong he was. He was always breaking the heads off bolts because he twisted them so hard. And those big old cast iron tubs? Well, he picked them up like they were plastic. And dig? No one could dig a hole in the ground like Danny Lee. They were always perfectly symmetrical. They were such beautiful holes that it was just a crying shame that they had to be covered up. And neat? No one could sweat copper pipe like Danny Lee. I loved to watch him work, but my favorite time was when he said:

"Well, Cousin, I think it's about time for you and me to go get something to eat." The two of us would walk up to the food counter together.

"Four Big Macs, three orders of fries, two milkshakes, and a Seven Up," he would say. The waitress would turn around to get our order. "Excuse me, ma'am," I would say, "I haven't ordered yet."

The waitress would go about her business, shaking her head in disbelief. Danny Lee could eat. In fact, I was told that Danny Lee, Jeff Mathers (another employee of my dad's plumbing company), and my big brother

Mike once ate one hundred White Castles at the White Castle at Central Point in Columbus, plus fries and drinks. They just rolled down the windows of one of the black trucks and flipped the boxes back in the bed of the truck after they had finished off a White Castle.

I always liked Jeff Mathers, too; he was a special guy. In a way he was a role model for me, only much closer. When I got out of high school, I went to a university far away from Dublin, Louisiana State University. My Aunt Blanche lived there along with my Uncle Jimmy Geideman, the assistant band director of the LSU Tiger Marching Band. I had not been there for more than a month when I got real sick; very, very depressed. I had to come home because I just broke down there. I couldn't function. I had tried to run away and join the Navy while I was down there, but I couldn't pass their entrance test, and remember, this was when the Vietnam War was going pretty hot and heavy. Anyway, I came home, and Chi Weber gave me my old job back—no questions asked. I will be forever grateful to Chi for that. Anyway, I would work at the savings and loan, and come home and study this book about how to pass the Navy's entrance examination. However, having absolutely no sense of spatial relationships, it was really a lost cause. I would study and study, but just couldn't figure out how this block opened up this way, or why this gear turned that way. It was frustrating and I was a real mess. One day Jeff asked me why I kept studying the Navy book. "Jeff," I said, "I don't want to go to Vietnam."

Now, let me describe Jeff Mathers to you. He was tall, about 6'2', dark hair, a mischievous grin, and looked a lot like Paul McCartney. To say that Jeff had no problems with the ladies was a gross understatement. He grew up racing motorcycles, and later I am told, worked for an engineering company

JEFF MATHERS WITH EVEL KNIEVEL'S ROCKET MOTORCYCLE JEFF IS THIRD FROM THE LEFT

that helped design the motorcycle that Evel Knievel used to jump the Snake River Canyon. He also raced cars in Kansas, driving an Austin Healy Sprite.

Jeff had studied mechanical engineering technology and earned an AAS degree, and anything mechanical posed little difficulty for him. He always had a calm, composed demeanor.

Speaking of motorcycles, as an aside, we once had a high school kid in our neighborhood up in River Forest who took it upon himself one day to go riding his motorcycle through Dublin—*au natural*. He was our male counterpart to Lady Godiva, so to speak. I don't know whether he was ever caught by our constable, our beloved "Rosey the Cop," and maybe Rosey didn't want to catch him. Anyway, I don't think this kind of behavior would have shocked the old man any. He drove his machine around in one of his robes. But, back to Jeff Mathers...

"Vietnam! You're not going to Vietnam," he said. "You need to go to school," he said.

"Jeff, I don't think I'm smart enough," I said.

"Smart enough? I'm down there!" he said.

"You're different, Jeff," I said.

"Listen," Jeff said, "I knew a lot of the guys in your class, and girls, of course. Believe me when I tell you that you can go to the university, and do well. Just trust me." I didn't have anybody else to trust at the time, so I trusted Jeff Mathers, and that's how I ended up at the university. I don't know how Jeff came to work for my dad, but he was a very special and charismatic person who influenced me greatly. He was very grieved when I told him about my big brother's death in an auto accident in Sydney, Australia. Jeff went and visited my big brother Mike's gravesite in Springfield, Missouri. Jeff and his beautiful wife Cathy are living now in Texas not too far from Burnet County where my mama grew up. Small world

Well, I guess this part wouldn't be complete unless I told you about Jim Abbot and the 409; that's right, the same Chevrolet Belair 409 that the Beach Boys sang about When we lived down at Blankenships', Jim used to be a frequent late, late night visitor. He would be out drag racing his Chevrolet 409, and it seemed like he always won. I remember that car was really light, and it had a big engine in it—409 cubic centimeters. It wasn't too impressive to look at, but it could really fly. The Beach Boys made a song about the 409: "She's real fine, my 409/she's real fine, my 409/...a 4 speed, dual quad positraction 409." Anyway, Jim used to drop in and tell us about the races (and dates) he had been on. All of the drag racers used to go to Sawmill Road; seems kind of impossible now, doesn't it? Anyway, I remember one night Jim rumbled in and he was kind of serious like. Jim was a real good-looking kind of guy; he looked a lot like Paul Newman. He just said, "I finally decided who I'm going to marry. She's one of the prettiest girls I've ever dated: she's really fine, and to top it off, her dad is Wayne Brown, who happens to own Big Bear Stores." Well, Jim married her, but his racing days were over. The last I heard he and his beautiful wife were living up in Muirfield Village. I don't know whatever became of that 409…

Well, by now I hope you know how Dublin and its people and places were, When It Wasn't Doublin'. But, there is one more story I'd like to tell. I can't help myself; I'm a storyteller. One summer I worked for Perry Township doing roadwork. We put in driveway aprons in Worthington Estates around McVey Boulevard, and I had the greatest boss ever—Jim McCoy. We had quite a crew—Jim McCoy, Jim Weaver, myself and a guy by the name of Ovay (I never knew his last name). We used a big hot tar truck and a big dump truck full of small pebbles to make the aprons for the driveways.

We worked out of the Perry Township shop, and at the shop there was a constable who we called "Festus" after the character in Gunsmoke. I don't know what prompted Festus to go into law enforcement because, although he was a nice fellow and smart enough, he seemed to have an inordinate fear of his sidearm. Whenever he would clean his gun, it was like a doctor performing surgery. His little desk faced to the

JIM AND NAOMI MCCOY

north of our shop, and Jim's faced to the east, and when he was cleaning his gun, Festus couldn't see Jim. Well, Jim was a McCoy, and McCoys, like the Sellses, could never pass up an opportunity for a good laugh. One afternoon Festus was deep in silence, intricately cleaning his weapon and counting his bullets, and Jim nonchalantly pulled a firecracker out of his desk drawer, lit it, and tossed it over onto Festus' desk. Well, a closed room makes for a loud explosion, and that's what there was. When that thing went off, the whole room was just deafening. Festus started yelling at McCoy, and the more he yelled, the louder McCoy laughed. I don't know if McCoy laughed so loud that he wet his pants, or if Festus got so scared and mad that he wet his, but we all laughed just like the Sells boys did when they finally got that big old bull strung up over the barn beam and watched him swing back and forth.

I loved Jim McCoy and I enjoyed going over to his farm and driving his tractor for him, working the fields. I particularly liked his wife, Naomi; she was a great cook. When we worked at Perry Township, a lot of days, we would have lunch at the Worthington Inn. We walked right in there in our tar-stained work clothes, sat down, and ate to our stomach's content. That's before it became "The" Worthington Inn.

I remember that summer well, because when the end of my work time came, I needed more money to help pay for my apartment on campus. I walked up to Jim one afternoon after work and asked him if I could stay on and work two or three more weeks. Jim always reminded me of the actor, Jimmy Stewart; he was tall and tan and soft-spoken with this big Irish gleam in his blue eyes. He was sitting at his desk, and he swiveled around and stared at me. He had his glasses on.

"When you gonna start?" he asked.

"Start what, Jim?" I asked.

"Well, start workin'," he responded.

"What do you mean, Jim?" I asked.

"Well I haven't never seen you work yet," he replied. "All I see you do is lean on that shovel against the gravel truck."

"Aw, Jim; you know I work hard," I said.

"Well, I know Ovey and the Weaver kid work hard, but I don't know about you," he replied.

"Aw, Jim…" and I just started shuffling my feet, my head down.

"He held me like that, for about thirty seconds, and then he just leaned back in that swiveling chair of his and burst out in the biggest and loudest laugh I have ever heard. He laughed so hard that his eyes watered, and he had to take his glasses off and dry his eyes. He had been teasing me all along.

"Well, the township building needs to be painted; I'll talk to the trustees," he said.

"Jim, I could even run the mosquito fogging truck if you wanted me to."

"Well, that's not a bad idea, either. Kid running that thing now, laziest son of a gun I ever did see. Every time he passes a little gas he's got to sit down and rest for fifteen minutes. Just promise me this, during the next three weeks or so, whenever you see a trustee's car come rolling down the driveway, grab that push broom and act like your cleanin' the garage floor.

CHAPTER 8

MY FRIENDS

I had friends who weren't dogs When Dublin Wasn't Doublin'. My best friend when I lived on Marion Street was David Geese: he lived a few houses up the street at 89 Marion Street. David would later become known as the "Wild Man," and that is quite an epithet for anyone who has ever lived in Dublin. I guess we became friends as soon as I moved to Marion Street. Like I said, we had lived one year in Worthington when I was five, when my little brother Kelly was born, but the allure of Dublin, I suppose, was just too strong for my dad, and we returned when I was six years old. Anyway, David Geese and I became close friends, really like brothers, right off the bat (and we still are). Now, I know there are a lot of definitions out there about what a friend is: someone who knows all about you and loves you anyway, or someone you share your secrets with. These are pretty good definitions. But, for me, a

**MY SECOND FAMILY
SEATED: VIRGINIA AND
LOUIE GEESE
STANDING: BONNIE
AND DAVID
INSERTED: JOYCE**

friend is someone who will let you come into their kitchen and open their refrigerator—and eat from it. That's friendship. That's the way it was at the Geese house for me. I felt like I was another son there. Of course, having Louie Geese as David's dad certainly was a great bonus for our friendship. Louie was always playing some kind of game with us and teasing us and just being Louie. He was like a second father to me. Louie would get Dave and me down on the carpet in the front room and tickle both of us so much we would almost wet our pants. We would just laugh and laugh and so would he. I remember Louie took us swimming down at the Ohio State University, and I recall going to see Louie's dad with him when he lived over on Martin Road. I guess you can tell that it was hard for me to separate the bond between Louie, David, and me. David and I did a lot of things together: We picked night crawlers together; played in the creek which ran parallel and just north of Marion Street; and played basketball on a hoop that Louie put up for us in the back yard. We would also pester the ferrets that Louie kept in a cage outside the house. Have any of you out there ever seen what rats do when you turn ferrets loose on them in an old barn? Also, whenever Mike Ryan and Gary Headlee or Gary Hatcher came over to see David, David would let me tag along, even though they were all three years older than me. But, they never let me go up in the tree house they had built in the woods; that was a mysterious place for me. I always liked Gary Headlee, and all of the Headlees for that matter. It was just kind of hard for me to understand Gary most of the time. He sounded like an old Dublin farmer at a young age. It seemed like everything he said was funny, even when he tried to be serious. It was kind of like the way Yogi Berra talks now, I guess. I remember that Gary always got "asthma" when hunting season rolled around and he "had" to miss school. Like the Sellses, and the Geeses, and the McCoys, and the McKitricks, and a lot of the other clans in Dublin, for the life of me, I just could not keep the Headlees straight. I think Mike Ryan was about the only person I knew of who really knew who all the Headlees were, but I think that was just because he could understand Gary when Gary talked about them. Anyway, Dave Geese and Mike Ryan would let me tag along whenever Gary came over.

So, David and I were pretty close, brothers really. I had a lot of meals in the Geese home with Virginia, the mother; Joyce and Bonnie, sisters, David and Louie. I always liked the way David ate. When he wanted some orange juice, for example, he would go over to the refrigerator, open it, grab the orange juice container, and drain it—no glass, straight from the container. I guess no one else drank orange juice at the Geese's. It looked cool, though, the way David did it, kind of like the way James Dean would do it. You know how James Dean would just walk into a room, take off his leather jacket, and throw it on the floor. That was kind of the way the "Wild Man" did things. If there ever was a kinder lady than Virginia Geese, Dave's mother, I never saw one. She operated a beauty salon in the back of the house, and all the women in Dublin came to Virginia to get their hair done. She must have been pretty successful because she was in business for a long time, and all the women kept coming back. She was such a sweet lady; I just liked to hear her talk; and it didn't make any difference to me what she talked about.

Well, as David got a little bit older and wilder, Louie got a whole lot more respectable. Louie became the manager of a Bank in Dublin, and one of the great, great mayors of Dublin. Between Joe Dixon and Louie Geese, as to who was the better Mayor, well, that's like asking: who was better, Mantle or Mays? Dublin was very fortunate to have had these two when they did. David, well, he became a pretty fair country football player, an all-county linebacker at 135 pounds. He was athletic and always played with a lot of heart, played to win, as they say. I understand that his dad played the same way, when he played on Dub-

**MAYOR LOUIE GEESE
BANK MANAGER TURNED
LEPRECHAUN
COLLECTING FINES FOR NOT
WEARIN' THE GREEN
ON SAINT PATRICK'S DAY**

lin's Dirty Dozen Baseball Team, and was quite an athlete in his day.

I remember the day Louie drove up Marion Street real slowly because he had a sixteen-point buck deer tied on the hood of his car. I remember going to his house and seeing that monster. Louie was just carrying on and laughing, telling us how he shot it. I think it was in 1959 when he shot that big buck. Louie could, and would, do anything. David followed in his foot-steps.

After high school David joined the United States Marine Corps. He got sent to Vietnam, as just about everybody else did back in those days. Dublin had three kids who got killed in that War who I knew: Kenny Carr, Larry Strayer, and Norm Tarpley. They were all great guys. Norm was an All-State football player. Little kids would run up to him and ask him for his autograph, and he would just write an "x" on their hand. He would quickly laugh with that big 'white' smile he had, and then autograph whatever they wanted. I believe that Kenny was a helicopter pilot. Anyway, for some rea-son, I knew that David would make it back home from Vietnam, and he did, though he did get hurt pretty bad—his back. I just felt that the "Wild Man" was too tough for those Vietcongs. He was our midnight rambler.

We kind of lost touch after he got home, but I did hear stories about him. Heard that he was alive and well, and reconnoitering the bars on both sides of the O'Shaughnessey Dam: the Zoo Bar, the White Cottage and the Wyandotte Inn. David could drink a lot of beer. He did not inherit this trait from the Geeses or from his mother's family, the Holders. Perhaps he was trying to establish a precedent. He liked to drink beer with my dad, and, I thought, just like in my Cousin Danny Lee's case, he would have made my dad a great son, a chip off the old block, so they say. Anyway, it was not uncommon for David to get juiced up, walk out of the bar, get in his car, and peel out, hell-bent for adventure. I don't know how many encounters he had with the law, but it was reported that he once woke up in the middle of a cornfield outside of Dublin. An appearance before the Dublin Mayor ensued and from what I am told, David was given the option of doing some "time," or doing some community service—in the Peace Corps, by Mayor Catherine Headlee. Being the fine patriot and altruist he was and is to this day, David chose the latter, and was on his way to El Salvador. Well, from what I heard, conditions in El Salvador at the time were no more tranquil than they had been in Vietnam. I guess David let it be known that if he was going to have to fight down there, the least they could do was issue him an M-16 to defend himself. I suppose that the "powers that be" found this request a little extreme, and eventually, as time slipped by, David made his way back to the USA. So, what do we make of the "Wild Man" of Dublin? Dublin wasn't big enough for him; Vietnam wasn't big enough for him, and neither was Central America. And, I guess the police cars they had back then weren't fast enough to catch him. As Miller Huggins, the great Manager of the New York Yankees once asked rhetorically about another legendary figure, Babe Ruth: "What are you goin' to do with a big bugger like that?" There was only one Louie and one David Geese, and I loved them both.

My other great friend whose refrigerator I could walk right into was a David of a different kind—David Wolfe. Dave was my best friend while we lived on the Scioto River, and then later when we moved to River Forest. He was three years older than I was, but it never seemed to affect our friendship. Oh sure, he would call me up while he was at work and tell me to go mow the grass on one of the bloop ball diamonds (we had two, one designed after Yankee Stadium, and the other after Fenway Park), but I never minded that. That just meant we were going to play bloop ball that night. Outside of that, we were equals. He did get to play right field on our runner-up State Baseball Championship team, but, playing right field with David Bakenhaster pitching…give me a break. Bakenhaster signed with the St. Louis Cardinals, and as long as he was pitching, I don't know if there ever was a ball hit Dave's way. I loved Dave even though he was a Dodger fan. Back then, when your team was in the World Series, it was just assumed you would not be in school. I remember in 1963 when the Dodgers were playing my beloved Yankees and Dave came down to my house to watch the game. Anyway, in the first inning, Yankee pitcher Al Downing, a left-hander, picked Maury Wills off first, but Wills beat the first baseman's throw down to second, and was safe. I knew at that very instant that New York was in trouble. It was a defining moment for me when I figured out what speed and pitching (Koufax and Drysdale) can do for any ball club. I always enjoyed watching baseball games with Dave; he was so knowledgeable and could see things I had trouble seeing.

He was a solid baseball player; he was not afraid of a fastball high and tight. He is in the Bloop Ball Hall of Fame. I remember that our mutual friend, Jim Weaver, a left hander, would try to get him out on curve balls low and away, and Dave would just hit rocket shots deep to right center, just like Al Kaline used to hit them for the Detroit Tigers. We would play bloop ball for blood; I guess we played everything for blood back then. Dave was never better than when the game was on the line. I always wanted him on my team. He could flat out hit. We would hit buckeyes all morning long at his house, and then come down to my house in the afternoon and try to hit them across the river using my split wooden bat. It was Dave who was umpiring when I was catching, and I caught a pop up behind the plate. I pivoted around to throw the runner out who had tagged up and was headed for third base. However, my front toe spike got caught in the infield drag that we kept in front of the backstop. I fell straight down on my left arm, and it snapped in two places like a dry stick. Dave looked at me, and I thought he was going to throw up. I will never forget the look on his face. But with that broken arm, I learned how to play cribbage that summer, and I think that it was then that I taught Dave how to play cribbage also. No matter what, even to this day, cribbage is a vehicle for our friendship. I did really get mad at him once though. Never a power hitter, I hit a shot way way down the left field foul line one day that almost made it into Indian Run for a home run. Dave called it foul, but to this day, I swear that it was a fair ball. Oh well, I'll make him pay for that on the cribbage board.

It wasn't baseball, and it wasn't bloop ball, and it wasn't just fishing that held our friendship together—it was also eating. We loved to eat! We would go down to the river and catch rock bass and clean them and eat them. We would get ahold of green tomatoes and okra, fry them up and eat them. We were very eclectic in our tastes. On some Sunday mornings Dave's Mom, Sally, a nicer and more saintly woman never lived, would make us mounds of grits, bacon, sausage, eggs, pancakes, syrup, and butter. We would eat and eat and eat until we just couldn't move. The food just kept coming. Then, there were the Sunday afternoons when Dave and I would be watching professional basketball in the TV room; we both loved the Philadelphia 76ers and Wilt Chamberlain. Mrs. Wolfe would come back to the TV room around half time and ask us if we happened to be hungry. Well, I don't remember a time when we weren't hungry, especially when we had a pretty good idea of what might be on the menu. "I thought I might go down to the Nite Club and pick you two up some submarine sandwiches and some strawberry pie," she would reply casually. Nobody could make submarine sandwiches like the Dublin Nite Club, and their strawberry pie was succulent. Mrs. Wolfe would bring back the eats, and we would gobble 'em right down. We would forget about the game, and just roll around the TV set like hogs in front of a trough. I loved that front television room, and one of the things

I really liked about it, beside all of the vast quantities of food that were consumed in there, was the fact that Dave's dad was always in there reading the paper, supine in his contour chair in the corner of the room. Mr. Wolfe was the founder of Little League Baseball in Dublin, and therefore, a man of great esteem in my book. He was also a really good golfer, and Mrs. Wolfe once told us that she had been a golf "widow" for many years. However, another thing I admired about Mr. Wolfe, besides his founding of our little league baseball organization and his golfing talent, was his ability to fall asleep so quickly. You could be carrying on a conversation with him one instant, then after the very briefest of interludes, he would be asleep. His face would be hidden behind a layer of newspapers, just dreaming away. No one could fall asleep like Bill Wolfe.

By now, I hope that my reader is aware of the fact that, back when Dublin Wasn't Doublin', we did not have the problems with drugs or teenage drinking or just outright disrespect of our elders that seems to be so prevalent in our society today. No, we were much more into the simple pleasures of life: baseball, fishing, eating, and especially sleeping. During our vacations, during the

FROM LEFT TO RIGHT – JIM WEAVER, A STRINGER OF SCIOTO RIVER CATFISH, AND ME

summers, we all loved to sleep just as long as we could. Maybe we were all guilty of the sin of sloth, but I believe that if you are going to practice a sin, well, that one, besides gluttony, is probably the best to have. The only trouble about the summer is that it could get downright hot at night, thus making it difficult not only to fall asleep, but to stay sleep. And if you can't sleep, you can't dream. I used to always dream of big fish and hitting home runs. I don't know what Dave Wolfe or Jim Weaver had dreams about; they never told me—

maybe girls (ugh). Anyway, our parents solved our problem about hot sleepless nights for us when we all got air conditioners in our houses about the same time. Jim and I got central air conditioning, which was pretty good, no complaints, but Dave got the best air conditioner—his own private room air conditioner. After that, we would swap stories about how long we had slept, and of course, Dave won most of them. He was a tremendous sleeper, though I think some of that was inherited from his dad. I would crank our air conditioner down in our house and run and jump under the covers; it was the best time of the day, just jumping in bed between those cold sheets. Then I went off to la-la land. I hated to wake up in the morning; those covers were sooo heavy!

Anyway, if my reader thinks the gluttony which we used to practice when we would devour strawberry pies was something, witness the greatest of all our delights: the grape pie, as prepared by the one and only, Sally Wolfe. Every now and then, every blue moon let's say, Mrs. Wolfe would take it upon herself to make for us by her delicate hands a truly delectable treat, the grape pie. I never knew exactly when they were coming; it didn't have to be any special occasion, they just came from the great goodness of her heart. It was by her grace, like manna from heaven. I will not attempt to describe to you the richness of that Concord Cornucopia and the heavenly grape sauce that enveloped the grapes. The metaphor of nectar of the Gods does her grape pies no justice. That first bite with a glass of milk or iced tea at your side was heavenly, and then it just got better and better. That flaky, lard crust was light enough to float off the table. Sometimes, miraculously, I would open the refrigerator door, and there, lo and behold, would be one piece left over. No greater treasure was enjoyed by any scavenger or pirate on the hunt. I would quickly jam it down my throat, and wash it through with iced tea. I often wondered why Mrs. Wolfe never entered her *piece de resistance* in the Ohio State Fairs, but after all, she was a humble lady, and maybe she didn't want the other ladies to feel embarrassed.

I also had the privilege of growing up with Mike Ryan. He lived at 250 Franklin Street, and I lived near-by up on Marion Street. He had a beautiful family and still does: Joe, Margaret, and brothers Casey, Johnny, and sister Laura. To put it succinctly, pound for pound, Mike Ryan was the greatest all-around athlete I have ever known, and that I have ever seen come out of Dublin, even to this day. He was thought of as magnificent by those who played sports with him, or against him.

We played baseball just about every afternoon after school on the field next to the Sidle's house (265 Franklin St.): Greg and Stan Davis, Mike Cooke, Tom Thomas, Greg Peck, my brother Mike, Jim Weaver, Dave Geese, maybe Gary Headlee, maybe some others, and me. We all played hard, and we all played to win; there was just no other way to play back then. But Mike Ryan, Mike Ryan was in a league of his own. He was so good that he could will his team to win, no matter who he had on his side. I loved to watch him play. And even then, when he was about thirteen or fourteen, I never saw him make a mistake. I always tried to tailor my game after Mike's, but I was no Mike Ryan. Up on Sidle's field, we had no adults for "supervision," we just played, and Mike Ryan ruled the diamond. At an early age, he could hit, he could hit with power, he knew by instinct how to run the bases, and he could field anything hit his way; he could backhand balls at an early age. It came as no surprise to me that he had such great success when he moved on to high school.

When Dublin Wasn't Doublin', although baseball wasn't the only sport that was played competitively, there was football and basketball too, but baseball seemed to be the sport where Dublin excelled the most. Whereas baseball has been played at Dublin schools since the beginning, Dublin didn't have a basketball team until 1911 and its first football team was in 1947.

Mike Ryan played with David Bakenhaster, who signed a major league contract with the St. Louis Cardinals as a pitcher, but Ryan, who could always back up what he might brag about, was never in Bakenhaster's shadow. It was Mike Ryan who pitched in Dublin's State Championship game against Powhatan. So, he could pitch, he could play the outfield, any infield position; and he could catch if he wanted to. He could do just about anything on a baseball diamond.

I remember one game he pitched against a pony league team from Columbus West. Back then, the city schools, not the suburban schools, reigned supreme in sports: Columbus West, Columbus East, Columbus South, Columbus North, and Columbus South were all power houses for sports. If my readers will recollect, Frank Howard, the great basketball player and later major league baseball player, came from Columbus Central. And there is a long, long list of many other great athletes that Columbus City Schools produced. When Dublin wasn't Doublin', we were just a little hick school out in the country. We had a diamond behind the high school that

Baseball

1964

Mike throws another great pitch.

MIKE RYAN – ONE OF DUBLIN'S BEST EVER ALL ROUND ATHLETES

consisted of telephone poles and wire for a backstop, and a left field that was left behind by the Wyandot Indians called Indian Run. Any ball hit in Indian Run, and it was a poke, was a sure home run because you could never find the ball in the high, woody grass. The rest of the diamond was, well, it was just field. Anyway, Columbus West came to Dublin for a Pony League Game, and Mike Ryan must have been right around fourteen. Even then, he had pinpoint control, almost a major league fastball, and the most beautiful overhand curveball, or "drop" that was ever seen. It actually reminded me of Sandy Koufax's overhand curve. His curve ball would buckle even the most ferocious hitter's knees. I will never forget the comments that some of West's city slickers made when they got off the bus in their fancy uniforms (we had hats and tee shirts and blue jeans to wear for uniforms, but nothing more) and took a gander at our "diamond": "Boy, is this the sticks or what! Wonder if they have Coca-Cola out here yet? Where are all the cows?" Well, we may not have had the fanciest diamond or uniforms, but we did have Mike Ryan on the mound and a bunch of guys behind him who would play their hearts out. I don't know how many Columbus West hitters Ryan struck out that day; but probably about fourteen or fifteen. They did manage a couple of bloop hits, but mostly, they spent their at-bats just walking up to the plate and then walking right back to the bench, shaking their heads. Ryan looked like a matador out there on the mound; fearless and totally in control. In the top of the last inning, with Dublin way ahead and Mike throwing a shutout, a Columbus West hitter did something that I thought was odd after Ryan had thrown a strike right by him. The batter asked the umpire to check the ball. Now, this is not an unusual occurrence, but you would have thought that it would have happened a lot earlier in the game when Mike was just mowing Columbus West hitters down one right after another. Anyway, the umpire got the ball from the catcher, and checked it over real good. Ryan, in the meantime, walked halfway to the plate and yelled at the umpire so everyone could hear him: "Give me that ball back, ump; I gotta get home and milk me a bunch of cows!" I never played organized ball with Mike, but I always wished that I had.

Mike Ryan was good at everything he did. He was only about 5'10" or 5'11", but he could dunk a basketball. In fact, he was a great basketball player for Dublin High School. He was never shy about shooting. He always wanted the ball in his hands when the game was on the line. He could punt a football almost 60 to 70 yards, though I do not remember him playing on the team. He was always the fastest runner, and could probably have made a career in track. He had the quickest hands that I have ever seen, and could probably have become a great boxer given different circumstances. And I never saw him back down from a fight. He was cocky and arrogant, but he could always back up his words with his deeds. I used to love to watch him take infield practice when he played shortstop. He would field about every ball hit to him backhanded. He was that quick, cat quick, and then he would laugh and throw all kinds of junk over to the first baseman who would have trouble catching his stuff. He truly had a cannon for an arm, and he could go in the hole and up the middle, field the ball without any apparent effort, and then throw a rocket shot to first base.

I could go on and on about Mike Ryan. Let me conclude with this: He signed a major league contract with the Chicago White Sox. Unfortunately, he was cut down in the prime of his life. Playing second in the Florida Instructional League, Mike was going into a pivot on a slowly hit double-play ball when he was roll blocked by the on-coming base runner. He broke both bones in his leg. They were very serious breaks and he was never the same after that. To this day, many times when I am watching ball games or listening to them on the radio or reading about them, I think of Mike Ryan. I have followed baseball for a long, long time, and there is no doubt in my mind, that Mike Ryan would have been a major league ball player. He had all the tools and the attitude to play second base for any team in the "Show," because he was a show.

SHERMAN SHELDON AND HIS WIFE CLARA

I had other friends when I lived on Marion Street and later down on the Scioto. I particularly liked going up to Rodney Sheldon's house because he had a real nice basement and he always had all the latest Beatles and Rolling Stones 45s. We would listen to the Beatles all evening long. But what I liked even more was when his dad, Sherm, would come out and play basketball with us. Sherm put up this portable basketball hoop at the end of the driveway, and I think he enjoyed playing more than we did. Rodney was good, and he later developed into a pretty good high school ballplayer, but it was Sherm I really enjoyed playing with. Seems like we could always find another ballplayer to make it two versus two, and I always wanted Sherm on my side. He knew how to rebound, and he had this funky little left-handed jump shot that, if you let him inside, he always made. He always played to win, too. Seems like back then, When Dublin Wasn't Doublin', they didn't hand out any good sportsmanship awards or anything like that at the "banquets" to help improve your self-esteem; you just won or lost, so you always played to win. Sherm was really funny, too; he was one of those guys you loved to be around. I know that I am right in my assessment of him because he was so very instrumental in the later development of Dublin.

Speaking of the later development of Dublin, I would be remiss right here and now if I didn't mention a great figure in Dublin's history, Chi Weber. His real name is Charles, but everybody just calls him "Chi." Back before the days of "mentors," he was a man who took it upon himself to guardian many of the youth of Dublin, and there were a lot of us that needed his helping hand. He was my Sunday school teacher, my boss, and my friend, and practically half raised me up. I first met Chi at Dublin Community Church where he was my Sunday school teacher, and right off, to know him was to love him. He was so doggone smart and had this tremendous sense of humor and was such a great role model for us kids to follow. Truth be known, he wasn't much more than a big kid himself in many respects. But he had a lot of wisdom and compassion even as a man at a relatively young age. I think wisdom and caring for others kind of blew off the high banks of the Scioto River and onto the farms and fields in Dublin back then, and I think a lot of the farmers just breathed it in as they sat out front on their porches on hot summer nights, rocking back and forth, back and forth, taking the wisdom, the patience, and the kindness of the soil deep into their lungs. Anyway, Chi was the President of Ohio Federal Savings and Loan at a very young age, and you could talk to him naturally, just like he was the janitor at your high school, or your fishing buddy. He was a great listener; would make some observations every now and then; and then maybe ask you a question or two—heck, he was like some doctors I have had. I worked for Chi Weber downtown at Ohio Federal Savings and Loan, and Mr. President, Chi himself, used to come up to my house, out of his way, to pick me up, take me to work, and then take me home again.

I remember the conversations we had in the car; you couldn't put a price tag on them. I remember he had a real soft voice. We were heading south on Riverside Drive to work one morning in the summer of 1967 and were just north of Fishinger Bridge when Chi said:

"Tim, I want you to look over at those buildings to your left. You see them?"

"Yes, Chi," I said. "I see them."

"Well," he said," those buildings are going to be the first condominiums around here."

Now, I didn't want to appear altogether stupid. I didn't have any business background like Dave Wolfe or Jim Weaver did. I had no idea of what one of those "condominiums" were. The word sounded to me like those big snakes they have down in the Amazon Jungle. I never had heard of such things before. I wouldn't have felt so ignorant if it hadn't been my boss with me. Of course, I knew he would never intentionally try to embarrass me. At heart, Chi was a teacher. So, I just resorted to a typical "When Dublin

Wasn't Doublin" phrase that the farmers used. I hoped it would get him to change the subject.

CHI WEBER – 2004 GRAND LEPRECHAUN

"That a fact?" I replied

Chi was kind. He knew that I had no idea of what he was talking about. "Tim," he asked, "Do you have any idea of what a condominium is?"

There was no way out for me now. I could never lie to the one who nearly raised me up. "Well, Sir, now that you have brought up the question, I can't say that I have." He looked over at me and had that wonderful smile on his face. I thought he was going to laugh there for a moment.

"A condominium is like an apartment, only you buy it and eventually you own it. You pay a fee to have your grass cut and your driveway shoveled when it snows. Most of them have swimming pools."

Well, being a young man of leisure and extremely averse to hard work of any kind, what Chi was describing to me sounded like heaven on earth. "Why Mr. Weber," I replied in my most business-like tone of voice, "could you please expound more in depth about the advantages of the condominium style of living?" Chi just smiled. He had a great smile....

Another morning we were making our way to work on Riverside Drive. I was rambling on about baseball. Chi was quiet. I could never tell what he was thinking about, but I knew he was always thinking about something.

"Tim," he said solemnly, I knew he was preparing me for something important, but I didn't know what, "in the future, we will not use money as you know it now; we will use plastic, or credit cards when we want to purchase something."

Well, I glanced over at him real quick like; he seemed to be in control of his faculties. On the other hand, I had to roll my window down real quick to catch my breath. I liked it when he talked about those condominiums, but using a piece of plastic to buy a baseball glove, or something, well, that was impossible! Honestly, I thought he must have fallen in his strawberry patch the night before and hit his head on a rock, or maybe he got hit upside the head too many times with those hard handballs he was always playing around with. I didn't think he ever got hit too hard on the head playing basketball for my Uncle Jim Geideman at Dublin, or surely it would have showed up before now. And, I was not aware of any serious war injuries.

He looked my way. Like I said, he seemed normal. He was serious. He wasn't joking with me. He knew more about this kind of stuff than I ever would. I trusted him. What in the heck could I say? I took a deep breath, exhaled, and looked at him: "That a fact?"

He liked to eat cheeseburgers for lunch up in his office. Chi Weber may have had a lot of money in that bank of his, but I believe his real treasures were already laid up for him in heaven. He "mentored" not only me, but many other kids: Jim Weaver, Dave Wolfe, and John Prout, to name a few. He was a captain in the United States Marine Corps in China, but a Boy Scout leader back in the United States.

There's this story about Chi that I have to share with you. Like I said, Chi gave me my first job—literally. I was a teller at Ohio Federal Savings and Loan, at 90 North High Street, in Columbus. The first afternoon that I balanced out, I was $1,400.00 short. Well, needless to say, I got a little concerned. I looked and looked for that money, but I just couldn't find it. Finally, all of the other tellers came over and helped me find $1,300.00 of it. We never did find that other $100.00. Strangest thing, though, after that, all of the other tellers would have me close my window first so that I could balance out early and then they wouldn't have to stay late helping me. I worked in the deposit section, and I took people's money, and Ohio Federal kept paying them money in interest on their savings accounts and Certificates of Deposits. For the life of me, I couldn't understand how that savings and loan stayed in business, paying out money all of the time. Eventually, though, I found out that there was another side to the savings and loan business. I told you, my readers, that I never was too long on smarts. Chi didn't say much when I lost that $100.00, maybe something like, "you balance better when you're in a rhythm," maybe something like that. And that's the way he was.

Now, I don't want to disappoint you, but that wasn't the story that I promised to tell you. I hadn't been working at Ohio Federal very long at all when I looked out the window one day—and I loved to look out that corner window at 90 N. High Street—when I saw these two fellows working on something on the granite pillar at the north-west corner entrance to the savings and loan. It was early in the morning, and it was in June, and it can get hot in June in downtown Columbus—and it was hot that day. I was standing behind my teller's window, not doing anything, just waiting for a customer, when this man I knew as Charlie, all dressed up in a fine suit, walked by. He looked at me, and he looked at the workers through the window, and he said, "Tim, looks like they could use some help outside." Well, it did look like they could use some help outside. They were trying to drill holes in this granite pillar, which might have even been marble. They were attempting to drill these holes so that they could install a new marquis, which would be used to post the interest rates at Ohio Federal. Now, I know this to be true from being in the United States Army: when you first go in the Army, when you arrive at the reception station, you don't know a sergeant from a general. And, as far as I knew, this Charlie fellow was a vice-president who worked up on the second floor. Heck, you know how many vice-presidents there are in a bank! Even I knew that. Anyway, he looked important enough to me in that suit of his. So, I left my teller's window and ran outside and asked the two workers—I think that they were both on break, smoking cigarettes— "You guys need any help out here?" I asked. Well, I suppose, knowing a real rube when they saw one, they first looked at one another, and then they looked at me, and they replied, almost in unison, "Sure, son." Well, to make a long, hot, dirty story short, I ended up drilling four holes in that granite pillar to mount that marquis, and they are still there, to this day!. I remember running back and forth to a hardware store down on Naughten Street to get new drill bits because they burnt out so quickly. Every now and then one of the "workers" would put a level on top of the sign and say, "Looks pretty good." I worked all day on that marquis, and when Chi came downstairs from his office at closing time, he took one look at me and asked, "What the heck happened to you today?" "Chi," I said, "I did what Charlie told me to do. I put that marquis up for Ohio Federal; I drilled all four holes in that granite pillar to mount it." Chi just shook his head. It turned out that Charlie was the maintenance man for Ohio Federal—although I never did figure out why he wore a suit, and Charlie was also the official office prankster. I think I can remember Chi laughing a little on the way home: "You know, Tim, you don't get paid to drill holes."

Again, along this same vein of "mentoring," there was a phenomenon in Dublin, which I think bears mentioning. Our neighborhood was bounded by the creek to the north, cornfields to the west, Grandview Street to the south, and Blankenships', or the Scioto River, to the east. There were a lot of kids in the neighborhood, and all were about the same age. Now, no matter what kind of outlets you have for your kids—baseball, football, basketball, fishing, eating, sleeping, Sunday school—you are going to have your pranksters, or in Dublin, your little Leprechauns. Some of the pranks would be harmless by Dublin standards, burning manure during Halloween on a front porch, knocking over outhouses, or lining exhaust pipes with limburger cheese, but some pranks would cross over the line. I remember two of my friends who took it upon themselves one night to knock down a whole bunch of mailboxes with a baseball bat; both of them must have been in slumps on the baseball team. Anyway, word got out, and they were apprehended. Now, in Dublin, When It Wasn't Doublin', we didn't have all these fancy correctional and sociological and penology terms that they use today to justify what they call "diversion" programs, which, I understand, are an attempt to keep a juvenile offender out of the criminal justice system, in order to keep him or her from getting stigmatized. This, I believe, is a good thing. No, if you grew up in Dublin back then, and you did something really bad, you didn't have to worry about being "stigmatized" by going downtown to the Franklin County Juvenile Detention Center at 50 East Mound Street, and having your "criminal record" started. If you messed up, we had our own little "diversion program," and it was simply called "Judge Rose's House." Simply stated, when someone was guilty of some particularly "heinous" act, you and your family simply visited Judge Rose's house; it was at the end of Franklin Street. Judge Rose was the Juvenile Judge and of the highest repute; in fact, he even had his own TV show, along with a friend of mine, Bob Harden, then the Director of the Juvenile Detention Center. So, in the evening, along of course with your parents, you paid the Judge a visit, and he gave you a few words of wisdom, and possibly some "community service." Suffice it to say, with the Judge in the neighborhood, I never saw one of my friends go "downtown" to the Juvenile Detention Center.

One thing I did like to do when I was with my friends, and we spent the night together, was call people up on the telephone and play tricks on them. I can remember that we always called this one guy in the telephone book called Jesse Pancake, and when he answered, one of us would say, "Hey, Jesse, don't you think it's time to turn over?" We thought that things like that were tremendously funny, and that was back in the day when everyone had their number in the telephone book, and back in the day when Dublin's prefix was "Tuxedo 9." We would call up tobacco shops and ask, "Do you have Prince Albert in a can?" "Sure do," would be the reply. "Better let him out; he's suffocating in there."

I remember one night at Mike Coriell's house on Monterrey Drive we called up OSU Coach Woody Hayes' house. Imagine "The Coach's" number was in the book!

"Is Coach Hayes there," one of us asked, with all of us gathered around the phone.

"Well, no, he isn't," came the reply. "Who is this calling?"

"Oh, we're just Buckeye fans from Dublin; that's all."

"Well, I'm Mrs. Hayes; is there something I can help you with?"

"Mrs. Hayes!" we all yelled at the same time, "Mrs. Hayes!"

"Yes, boys," (doubtless she could tell by the immaturity in our voices) "I'm Mrs. Hayes, Woody's wife. What can I do for you?"

"Mrs. Hayes, do you think the Buckeyes are going to win tomorrow?"

"Well, boys, Purdue has a pretty good team this year; we'll just have to play hard."

"Mrs. Hayes, do you think Bob Ferguson will get 200 yards rushing?"

"Well, boys, I don't know; he's capable of it."

Mrs. Hayes, do you think Coach Hayes is going to throw many passes?"

"Well, you know what the Coach thinks about passing the football, but we'll just have to wait and see."

That's the kindness and grace that Anne Hayes extended toward a bunch of pre-teenage boys way back in the simpler days, When Dublin Wasn't Doublin'.

CHAPTER 9

THE LOVELY
LASSIES OF DUBLIN

Speaking of friends, I guess I would be forgetful if I didn't mention some of the lovely lassies of Dublin with whom I had the pleasure to be acquainted. I don't know why, but I always thought that the girls from Dublin were prettier than other girls from the surrounding areas: Upper Arlington, Worthington, Hilliard, Plain City, and Westerville. It might have been the water they drank, or it might have been the way the wind from the high banks of the Scioto caught and flushed their cheeks to a light, rosy hue. But those girls, well, they sure enough were lovely and so pleasing to the eye, fine examples of God's handiwork.

It was kind of funny the way I got introduced to the wiles and ways of the female world. Growing up, I never liked girls or anything that they did. All I wanted to do was fish and play baseball. I was sitting behind a girl in Mrs. Dulin's fifth grade class one day trying to pay attention to what was happening. Mrs. Dulin asked a question and she raised her arm to answer. She had a sleeveless blouse on and I just couldn't believe what I then saw! She had hair under her arms, which she had shaved. I was speechless. As soon as school was out, I ran straight from the bus stop at the end of Marion Street to Virginia Geese's beauty salon. "Virginia, Virginia!" I cried, "This girl in my class has hair under her arms!" Virginia started laughing just a little bit, and then all the other ladies whose heads were encased in hair dryers and looked like aliens from outer space, all burst out laughing. I didn't see anything funny at all about what I had just said. Virginia was always so kind and understanding. She looked at me and said, "Timmy, that young lady is growing up, and one of these days you'll have hair under your arms too just like she does. You are growing up to be a nice young man, and she is growing up to be a nice young lady." Well, I kept looking and looking to see hair grow under my arms for a long time. It finally showed up after a long wait.

Anyway, I just thought that Dublin girls were prettier, and I still do. Growing up, though, I stayed away from girls until the end of my sophomore year in high school. Oh, I would hear them chattering and snickering in the hallways; they were always talking about the latest fashions, or who broke up with who, or who was going steady. That stuff never interested me. I was more concerned about how our baseball team would do, or what kind of season the Yankees would be having. So, I suppose my reader will not be surprised when I share that I felt like I had been hit in the head with a Mike Ryan fastball when a girl asked me to be her "escort" to the basketball homecoming. She had been picked to be the sophomore attendant to the homecoming queen. Her name was Vicki, and I guess she just felt sorry for me. I was awkward around girls, but Vicki, and I don't know why, well, she just took a shine toward me. We had always been friends, and we would talk when we weren't supposed to in study hall. Funny thing, she really liked the Beatles, and I did too, and she even looked like a particular Beatle, John Lennon, in a very, very feminine way—even our English teacher said so. Of course, Vicki's brown hair was quite a bit longer than her Beatle counterpart, and she sure enough was beautiful with deep brown eyes that twinkled when she teased me, which was quite often. It seemed like she always knew so much more about things than I did, and I could never figure out how. Like I said, I didn't pick up on things real quickly, but she was really smart, and all the teachers in Dublin High School really liked her a lot.

So, for whatever reason, she chose me to escort her to the basketball homecoming dance, and this presented three major difficulties: I didn't have a suit of clothes, I didn't know how to dance, and I didn't have a driver's license. Much later in life, I would commiserate with Leon Spinks, the Heavyweight Champion of the World, after he had just fought Muhammad Ali, when he was pulled over by the police for some infraction while driving. Leon was reported to have said to the arresting officer: "I ain't got no driver's license, I ain't got no money, and I ain't got no teeth!" Anyway, I had a lot of "ain't gots" to deal with before the homecoming dance. However, my dad took me to Northland Shopping Center, and we picked out a pretty nice suit for me to wear. As far as dancing went back in those days, well, I figured I could fake it; you just pretended that you had grabbed hold of a live electric wire. I practiced the monkey, the mashed potato, the Bristol stomp, the jerk, and even the twist. As for transportation, well, a friend of mine, Dean, was dating Vicki's older sister, so we could hitch a ride back to Vicki's home with them after the homecoming dance. I met Vicki at the homecoming at school, right before I escorted her down the aisle. We all lined up in procession right before they called out our names on the loud-speaker, and Vicki looked at me and smiled, and reached down, and took my hand...and that was the first time that I had ever held a girl's hand. I knew, right away, what the Beatles meant when they sang "I Wanna' Hold Your Hand." It was quite a sensation. I remember that Vicki's hand was real cool and dry, and her fingers were long and slender, like she played the piano or something. I remember having a great time that night with Vicki, and we were girlfriend and boyfriend for a long time afterwards. I recall sitting beside her in study hall, just holding her hand. Occasionally she would look over my way and smile, or smirk; it was kind of a mix between the two, and she had it down just right. She had a little twist in the upper corner of her lips when she smiled, like the *Mona Lisa,* which made it look like she knew a whole lot more than she was letting on, which was like most females, I later discovered.

Of course, my first kiss followed shortly thereafter. Dean and Vicki's sister were in the front seat of Dean's car one night as we were driving home after going to a dance or movie or something, and they were sitting pretty close together. Vicki and I were sitting close together on the passenger side of the backseat, and we were holding hands. From up front we could hear the music playing, and it was always AM music back then, When Dublin Wasn't Doublin', and it seemed that it was always George, Paul, John, and Ringo who were on the air. They say you never forget the music you were hearing when you have your first kiss, but I don't recall exactly; "Just Seventeen" comes to mind, and seems appropriate. Anyway, Vicki was staring outside the window, her head turned away from mine, but I was looking at her. I was always looking at her. Suddenly she turned my way, but just as quickly dropped her chin. I could just make out that smile on her face. Then, quickly, she raised her face, and almost defiantly looked right into my eyes. She tilted her neck ever so slightly, parted her lips, leaned forward, and closed her eyes. I really didn't know what to do right away; I felt almost frozen in time, but I got the idea soon enough. And then I kissed her. It was the most amazing sensation, even better than holding hands. The kiss was warm and tender and moist and everything that a first kiss should be. I kissed her again, and it was even better than the first one. Suddenly, I stopped and looked at Vicki, "Vicki, is this making out?" I asked. She stared me straight in the eyes with her lips upturned in that smile. "Come here and bring your face close to mine," she said. I did as she asked. She rubbed her nose back and forth, very quickly, against mine, "That's an Eskimo kiss," she said. Then she put her hands behind my head and pressed forward, placing her eyes right into mine. She fluttered her eyelids very quickly, very quickly up and down. "That's a butterfly kiss," she said. Then, she took the sides of my head with her long fingers and pulled my face hard against her's so that our lips were pressed tightly together for quite a long time. She released me and stared straight into my eyes again. "And that is the way I would kiss you if you had been gone in the Army for a long, long time and come back home to me," she said. She snuggled up against me and, holding my hand, whispered in my ear, as the radio played on ("Do You Want to Know a Secret," The Beatles):

> "Listen, do you want to know a secret?
> Do you promise not to tell?
> Closer, let me whisper in your ear
> Say the words you long to hear
> I'm in love with you.
> I've known a secret for a week or two;
> Nobody knows; just we two...."

My second girlfriend was just as pretty as Vicki, and she had the biggest, most beautiful brown eyes and cherry red lips that I have ever seen. There was a song written in those days, which suited her well: *The Brown Eyed Girl*. Her name was Mary, a common name for an uncommonly beautiful girl. I remember that my mother would drive over and pick up Mary where she lived, and take us to the swimming pool in Shawnee Hills. Mary and I would lay our towels beside one another in the grass, and then we would proceed to just lie there together, getting a tan, and kiss one another all day long—a *Splendor in the Grass*. And, boy, Mary sure knew how to kiss you. She would just look up at you, roll those huge, liquid brown eyes, and you couldn't help but lean down and kiss her. Then, after all day up at Shawnee Hills, my mom would appear and take Mary and me back to her home. I will never forget Mary and those lazy summer days at Shawnee Hills Swimming Pool. It later came to my understanding that Mary became an attorney. She could defend me from anything—anytime.

My next girlfriend was Sally, and she lived in a big house up on Riverside Drive, on the east side of the Scioto, and south of the Sells Farm. Sally was an only child; she didn't have the brothers and sisters that Vicki and Mary did. I remember that Sally had wonderful, nice parents, and that she had a horse. When we wanted to be alone together, we would go to this little television room out front and watch TV. In the winter, I remember there was a little space heater there. I will never forget Sally. She was quiet and reserved, with big, brown eyes too; and she had the longest, straightest, blond hair that I had ever seen. I remember that she went away to college, but came back home, and ended up dating one of my best friends, Mike Coriell.

My next girlfriend was anything but quiet. Her name was Kay. She was short, saucy, and sanguine. She had pretty blue eyes, and wore her hair short, which was a bit unusual during the late sixties. And, of course, with her personality she was a cheerleader. With all of the energy that she had, I think she actually willed the basketball team to a few wins by herself. I loved to go swimming with her up at Butler's Swimming Pool (now Dublin Scioto Park), and I really enjoyed being with her family. Her brother Tom was a classmate of mine, and Kay's dad (Kay was a "PK", preacher's kid) was a swell fellow. He was an associate minister at First Community Church in Columbus. Kay was just so much fun. My dad had a radio phone in his car (remember, this was decades before the age of cell phones) and I would call Kay up and tell her I would be over in just a minute to pick her up. I'd then walk up her driveway seconds later, and there she would be. Kay was the last Dublin girl I dated before I left Dublin for Louisiana State University, and I used to think of her all the time when I was down there, just pined over her.

When I came back from LSU and finally got settled at Ohio State University, I started dating a girl from Dublin who I had once taken to a prom.

Her name was Barbara, and she lived just above the Geese's on Marion Street. I went with Barbara for four years, from my freshman year in college until I graduated. If ever there were a Dublin girl who I wanted to marry, it was Barbara, but I never even asked her. I knew even then that deep down inside of me I lacked the foundation to make her happy as a wife, that something was "wrong" with me inside. She sure was pretty enough, though, and my mama said she used to love to hear Barbara's voice over the telephone. She spoke so softly and sweetly, almost like in a whisper. One year her dad sent her abroad on a long cruise around the world to study fine arts, World College Afloat, I think they called it. I think her dad was afraid Barbara and I were getting too serious about one another. I really missed Barbara that year, and I waited for every letter that she would send me. Once I got a photo of her coming down the steps of the Coliseum in Rome. She was so pretty in that picture, so sophisticated; she looked much better than any movie star I had ever seen. What was an added attraction about Barbara's house, also, was the swimming pool in the back yard. A bunch of us guys in the neighborhood would play pick-up games of basketball on her driveway, get all sweaty, and then go run and jump in the pool. Barbara was about five feet two or three inches tall, with brown eyes and light brown hair, and she had a beautiful figure. When she got back from traveling abroad, we reunited and picked up where we had left off. Barbara did have a temper, though. Once, when I took a liberty with her, she just slapped me hard right across the face. I never did forget that. She hit me harder than any man ever has. She was the only girl who ever hit me. I understand that she is a dental hygienist now, practicing out in Gahanna, with a beautiful family of her own. I wish her and hers the very best.

Now, all that I have told you before, all about these Dublin girls, well, they were not exactly the only girls I dated. You see, in the summer of 1970, at the height of the Hippie movement here in the United States, I spent a summer down in Colombia, South America, under the auspices of the International YMCA and the First Community Church here in Columbus. Well, the organization picked seven of us from Ohio State to go down to Barrio Suba in Bogota and do community outreach work. The seven of us got to know one another at a retreat before we left for Colombia, at First Community Church's Camp Akita. It was there where Janine and I first laid eyes upon one another. Well, we were both smitten, as they say, even though we were very much the opposite. During my first three years of college, I was pretty much of a straight arrow: go to school, study, and then, hopefully, be with Barbara. But things changed after I met Janine; she was a real, honest-to-goodness hippie. She looked like a hippie, she talked like a hippie, and she thought like a hippie. And, to top it all off, she was knock-down gorgeous. She was tall, maybe about five feet, ten inches, and had beautiful, long, straight, golden brown hair, which she parted, of course, right in the middle. I can remember looking up into her deep blue eyes, with her hair cascading down, covering half of her face (and half of mine), and she gave me a kind of smirk and grin rather than a big smile. I guess you could say that she had a Mona Lisa smile too. She was almost like an alien to me, but I really adored her and all of her strange ways. When everyone else was listening to the Beatles, Janine was listening to Leon Russell. When everyone else lived in dormitories or apartments, Janine lived in the Spanish House down on campus. She always wore bell-bottom jeans (embroidered on the bottoms and sides), a loose fitting blouse or T-shirt, beads around her neck and wrists, and sometimes, if she was in the mood, a red headband. I don't think I ever saw her with a flower in her hair, but she didn't really need one. She was a flower child, and she didn't need to go to San Francisco to prove it. She came from a pretty neat family too; both of her parents were electronic engineers. She talked about strange places like Ithaca and Cornell and Lake George. Maybe that's where she really wanted to be. To make a long story short, Janine and I toured Colombia together that summer of 1970, and she made me care less about what was happening back in Dublin. To keep up with her, I grew a mustache and let my hair grow long. We worked together, we would sit down together up in the Andes Mountains while we were in Campamento Bochica and listen to the roar of the Tequendama Falls, we would play basketball with the kids from Barrio Suba, we would laugh and listen to the Dominican Friars who were our hosts in Suba. First Community Church had arranged it so all the girls slept in a near-by convent, and my friend Andy and I stayed at a monastery. We worked hard, but we played hard too. Janine and I and the rest of the group would get lost together on all the buses running throughout Bogota. At the end of our time in Bogota, the team took the Espreso Del Sol, a twenty-five hour train trip, for Santa Marta down on the northern coast of Colombia. Santa Marta is the oldest town in South America, I believe, and it has gorgeous beaches, both in old

Santa Marta and in El Rodadero, the newer part of Santa Marta. Every one of us had a great time down there, but Janine and I in particular: swimming, getting tanned and drinking ice-cold beer and eating oysters on the beach. In the evenings, little bands would come up and down the sidewalks to serenade our group us as we sat in a little cafe on the shore of the Caribbean. If we felt really adventuresome, we would drink a little aguardiente, Colombian liquor that tastes a lot like the Greek's ouzo. Sorry to say, though, that all things must pass, and when the summer ended and we returned to the States, I just saw Janine a few times. She dropped into my apartment to say hello, but I knew, deep down in my heart, that she was out of my league and life style. She was in a world of her own, and she lived life to the fullest. The last I heard of Janine was that she had left school and was working as a beekeeper down in Virginia somewhere. Sounded like a perfect job for her. Funny thing, every time that I think of that summer of 1970 and Janine, I think of John Lennon's "#9 Dream":

> "So long ago was it in a dream
> Was it just a dream?
> I know, yes, I know
> Seemed so very real.
> It seemed so real to me."

After Janine, Barbara and I got back together, and I spent my whole senior year down on campus with my two roommates, Phil Hill and Steve Munson. Phil was a life-long friend; I had known him since I was born, and Steve Munson, from East Greenwich, Rhode Island, was the perfect roommate. Steve paid his share of all the bills, but hardly ever set foot in the apartment. Both Phil and Steve were very active in their fraternity, the ATOs, or *Alpha Tau Omegas*. Barbara and I were really close my senior year as Dublin just kept on Doublin' every day, or so it seemed. We were more or less oblivious to the changes taking place in our little village, which was rapidly becoming a city.

Graduation came for me in June of 1971, and I high-tailed it back to Colombia as soon as I could. I spent the summer there with the Alvarado Family, and worked at La Calle Cien, an adult YMCA center. I got a leave from the center, and flew down to Cali to catch the Pan American Games. I became the unofficial interpreter for the United States Pan American Basketball Team. Many of the players there eventually ended up playing in the National Basketball Association: Paul Westphall, Jim Chones, and Bob McAdoo, among others. Henry Wilmore, an All-American from Michigan, was about my favorite. I introduced myself to Luke Witte who was there; Luke was from Ohio State. I told Luke that I was going to be a teaching assistant at OSU in the fall, and that he should try to get into my Spanish class if he could. He did, and he was a great student. I believe, now, that Luke has a ministry somewhere in northeast Ohio. The name of Mentor, Ohio, rings a bell.

Unfortunately, it was down in Cali, Colombia, that I was first stricken with a bout of mania. My mind was constantly racing, I couldn't sleep, and I had minor delusions of grandeur. It seemed like the intense pressure of having to speak Spanish so quickly, interpret and translate simultaneously much of the time, seared even the little nuances of the language into my mind forever. It was a very, very intense time of learning the language for me. The pressure of being a lone "gringo" in a Spanish-speaking country during a time of high excitement forced me into speaking just about like a native. I would write to Barbara back home, and she detected that something was wrong with me because she asked in her letters if I had been drinking. Well, I was drinking, hoping that the alcohol would put me to sleep, but my bizarre writings to her were caused by mania.

After the games, I made it back to Bogota, finished out my stint with the International YMCA, and then headed for home. I had a teaching assistant position waiting for me. I started coming down from my first manic high very slowly, and got about halfway through the quarter when I was hit by a full-fledged depression. One of the worst I had ever had. But, let me backtrack for just a second; I did have a wonderful surprise when I finally made it home. Back when I was in high school, there was this girl in my algebra class named Pamela. She was always real nice, and well mannered, but I never thought she was anything to rave about. In fact, I used to tease her a lot. She sat behind me in class, and I would take my pencil eraser behind my back and poke her in the legs. It wasn't too hard, just enough to irritate her. She did come from a great family, though. Her dad, Cy, was the owner of a printing company, and he and his wife, Kay, who always reminded me of Kathryn Hepburn, lived on Ashford Road in River Forest, not too far from our house. Anyway, after I started dating and going to school and going back and forth to South America, I forgot about any Pamela. But, lo and behold, when I got back to the States the second time, when I started graduate school, Pamela and I happened to cross tracks. I don't know exactly how and when, maybe it was kismet. I think she had been dating a friend of mine, Bill Corwin, who was in medical school, but when I saw her after all those years, she literally looked like a movie star. She was taller than I was (most of them were) with thick long brown hair that she parted in the middle, and she had blue eyes, deep blue eyes. She had long white shiny legs and a funny little smile, a grin. She was always smiling, it seemed. She lived in an apartment off Route 161 in the northern part of Columbus, and she was an elementary school teacher in the Olentangy School System. She drove a little Volkswagen. She had attended a private college in West Virginia, and I suppose that's where the metamorphosis had taken place: from a gangly blond headed willow to a breath-taking beauty. Or, to quote from a song by the Beach Boys, I would say to myself: "She's not the little girl I once knew." I had heard that her beauty had captured the attention of *Women's Wear Daily Magazine*, but I did not know that for a fact. If not, it should have. What was more special about Pam, though, was that her inner beauty far surpassed anything exterior. She was the kindest, sweetest, and most compassionate of all the girls who I had known. I felt totally unworthy of her, and entirely awe-struck in her presence. She was brilliant, like her mother and father and two sisters. I really liked her dad, Cy, who once took all of us to the Cleveland Museum of Art to see Caravaggio's *The Conversion of Saint Paul*. I became really depressed halfway during my first quarter of teaching, and Pamela, God bless her, did her best to nurse me back to health. I just didn't have the energy to write, to read, to teach, or to do anything. It seemed like the only time that I felt halfway secure during this life and death struggle was when Pamela was around. She was the only thing that I had. I did manage to complete the quarter, thanks to Pam's inspiration, but I then had to go into the Army. I literally went from the frying pan into the fire as far as depression goes. I had drawn number #14 in the national lottery draft. I enlisted in the Army mainly because I didn't want my studies to be interrupted mid-way through the next quarter. I remember the night before I had to report at Fort Hayes for my trip to Fort Knox. I spent a sleepless night on the couch in the basement of our home at the Snouffer's. I was really depressed from this bi-polar depression, and now I had to go into the Army. Pamela picked me up early the next morning in her little Volkswagen "bug," and off we went to Fort Hayes. I can remember looking out the window of the bus at Pam. She was smiling and waving to me, of course, but it was raining outside, and it was "Raining in my Heart" as Buddy Holly once sang.

Bi-polar depressions do wear off after, it seems like forever. I made it through basic training, and all during basic, Pamela would write of course and send me down ginger snap cookies. One morning Pamela drove her little "bug" down to Louisville to see me, and it really helped to spend the afternoon with her. It was so nice to actually see and talk to the girl that I was dreaming of every night, but that's just the kind of girl she was. That's when I came to understand what the Eberly Brothers must have meant: "When I want you/In the night/When I want you/To hold me tight/Whenever I want you/All I have to do/Is dream/Dream, dream, dream/Dream, dream/dream...." I got better, and on the weekends, when I was working at Fort Knox as an interviewer in the reception station, I would drive home from Louisville to see my family and Pamela. I loved that girl so much. But, my mania struck again in the late summer of 1972, and my bizarre behavior and irrational thought patterns really affected the relationship between Pamela and me. We stopped seeing one another. But I will always be grateful to her for her love and support. Bi-polar disorders can literally be killers, and this one killed our relationship.

Well, that about does it concerning Dublin girls who I have known and loved. They say old men dream dreams, and many times I will dream of Vicki, Mary, Sally, Barbara, Janine, and Pamela. I think my experiences with those Dublin girls could best be summed up by the lyrics in a song by the Lovin' Spoonfuls, *Younger Girl*. To paraphrase:

> "Those Dublin girls keep rollin'
> Past my mind.
> No matter how hard I try
> I can't seem to leave their memory behind.
> I remember their eyes,
> Soft dark and brown,
> Said they'd never been in trouble,
> Not even in town.
> Those Dublin girls keep rollin'
> Past my mind...."

CHAPTER 10

THE BEGINNING OF DUBLIN

N ow I want to tell you about the real "Old Man" of the Sells family, Ludwick Sells, and how Dublin began. **Ludwick Sells, my great-great-great-great grandfather**, was born February 15, 1743 in Pennsylvania and died October 13, 1823, a resident of Dublin, Ohio. His father, Anthony Sells, was also born in Pennsylvania, the son of Hendrick Sellen who had immigrated to America from Germany. In 1770, Ludwick married **Catherine Deardorff, my great-great-great-great grandmother**. Catherine was born March 5, 1749 and died December 1, 1828. Ludwick and Catherine had six sons; Samuel (1771-?); **John (1774-1841)**; Benjamin (1777-1837); Peter (1780-1832); William (1790-1872); and George (1792-?). They also had four daughters; Mary (1782-1814); Susanna (1783-?); Sophia (1785-1847); and Margaret (1786-1869). Ludwick, Catherine and their family lived in Huntingdon County, Pennsylvania where they kept a tavern. Huntingdon County is in south central Pennsylvania, about 20 miles east of Altoona. In 1800, at age 57, Ludwick traveled to the Central Ohio town of Franklinton located on the west bank of the Scioto River, at the confluence of the Olentangy and Scioto Rivers. Franklinton is now the part of Columbus that is called the Bottoms. Ludwick came to Ohio from his home in Huntingdon County by way of Pittsburgh, where he purchased a flat boat and floated down the Ohio River to Portsmouth, and from there he came up the Scioto River to Franklinton. Ludwick set out from there to find land to buy and on which to establish a new home for his family. About 12 miles up the Scioto, on the west side, he found what he was looking for. It was on the river which would provide a means of transportation, north and south. It sat high above the river (thus eliminating the worry of flooding); it had a good spring, and fertile soil. It also had lots of limestone, sand and gravel, as well as clay for bricks, and lots of trees; all of the materials needed for building houses. Afterwards, his son, Peter bought the land that Ludwick had chosen, and it was on a portion of that land that the town of Dublin was established.

Now, you need to know a few things in order to try to understand what life was like in the Dublin area at that time. First of all, there were only a few settlers living in the area. Most of them were living in log cabins near the Scioto River or near streams that emptied into the river. Also, there were still quite a few Indians living in the area, and other Indians passing through on their way to other places. Ohio had not even become a state. It

THE GREENVILLE TREATY LINE

didn't become a state until 1803. Settlement in the area had only recently become possible. That was a result of the Greenville Treaty which was entered into between the United States Government and the Indians in 1795 following the defeat of the Indians, by U. S. forces, under the command of General "Mad" Anthony Wayne, at the Battle of Fallen Timbers. The treaty allowed for pioneers to settle in Ohio, south of a certain line, referred to as the Greenville Treaty Line, which was a complex line running in a generally east-west direction roughly 30 miles north of Dublin (a few miles south of Marion). Article VII of the treaty allowed the Indians to continue to hunt on the lands south of the line.

The United States had just become a country. The Revolutionary War had ended less than 20 years before Ludwick came to Franklinton. Money wasn't available in the federal treasury or in the state treasuries to pay the people who had fought for independence from England. Pay for the soldiers was given in various ways—eventually. One of the ways was through land grants in the Virginia Military District. Congress established the Virginia Military District out of land in the Ohio Territory and granted the land to Virginia for its use in paying their soldiers for fighting in the Revolutionary War. The district included the land that Ludwick had

picked out (and all of the land in present day Dublin, lying west of the Scioto River), and much, much more— 4.2 million acres in all[8]. The land in the district was surveyed and divided into parcels and the rights to these parcels were given to soldiers from Virginia as compensation for their services in the war. The land the Sells bought, described

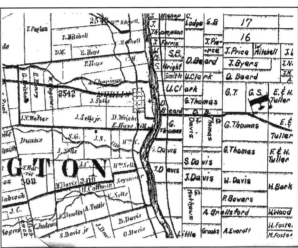

1842 MAP SHOWING THE OUTLINE OF SURVEY 2542 WHICH WAS DEEDED TO PETER SELLS BY JOHN GRAHAM

by "Survey 2542," had been granted as consideration for John Holt's service as a Lieutenant in the Continental Army during the Revolutionary War. Most of the soldiers who were entitled to receive land as compensation, weren't interested in uprooting their families and moving to the Ohio territory, and so they sold their right to the land (directly or indirectly) to people who were. And there were plenty of people who were excited about going to the Ohio territory. It was considered a very desirable place – a modern day "promised land," with lots of game and fertile soil. Ludwick Sells and his sons were among those who were interested in "going west" to settle and start a new life in Ohio.

The Sells actually bought the land from John Graham. John Holt had assigned his right to the land to William Chamberlayne and Lyne Shackelford who in turn assigned it to John Graham. The "patent" (which is

---

8 All of the land on the east side of the Scioto which is in present day Dublin was also granted to individuals for their service in the revolutionary war, but under a different Act of Congress. Those lands are referred to as "U. S. Military Lands."

essentially a deed from the government) was from President Thomas Jefferson to John Graham. John Graham then deeded it to Peter Sells, who in turn deeded portions to his family members.

In the spring of 1809, Ludwick and Catherine's son, John Sells, (March 4, 1774 – June 20, 1841) and his wife, Elizabeth Stroup Sells, (September 23, 1777 - April 24, 1852) and their children, arrived at the "Sells Settlement" as it was called at the time. Elizabeth was pregnant with their seventh child, Fletcher, who was born later that year. John and Elizabeth were married in Pennsylvania in 1793. The family of **John and Elizabeth, my great-great-great-grandparents**, including their children born after their move to Dublin, consisted of Charles (1794-1833); Eliud (1796-1849); Matilda (1799-1870); **John, Jr. (1802-1879)**; Samuel (1804-?); Catherine (1806-?); Fletcher (August 16, 1809-1881); Caroline (1812-1816); Lucy (1814-1896) and Caroline (1817-1890). That's ten children in all. So, my Grandfather John and Grandmother Elizabeth Sells and their children, 15 year old Charles, 13 year old Eliud, 10 year old Matilda, 7 year old John, Jr., 5 year old Samuel, and 3 year old Catherine, made the trip to Dublin. John also brought with him to Ohio a black horse, a Kentucky bred stallion. Matilda and John, Jr. were born in Kentucky, which means the family was living there in 1799 and in 1802. So, apparently they moved from Pennsylvania to Kentucky and then from Kentucky to Ohio.

John bought several hundred acres from his brother, Peter[9]. He built a log house and tavern. He named the tavern for his horse, calling it the Black Horse Tavern. The house and tavern were built at the location which is now known as

9   Sometimes it isn't possible to determine exactly when certain events took place in Dublin, because fire at the Franklin County Courthouse destroyed many of the records. However, there are some old real estate abstracts still around that give some helpful information. Among other things, they contain information concerning property transfers and wills. Information in abstracts is normally accurate because the people who produced them were very careful to give correct information since abstracts were used to determine whether the sellers of real estate had good title to the property. I looked at a couple of old real estate abstracts for properties in Dublin, and they indicate the following concerning the property described by "Survey 2542," on which John Sells established Dublin:
1. The property was conveyed to John Graham by a patent (which is like a deed from the government) from President Thomas Jefferson. The patent was signed August 5, 1803.
2. The property was conveyed by John Graham to Peter Sells by a deed signed on March 31, 1810, for a consideration of $2,675.00.

25 South Riverview Street, just south of where the Dublin Bridge presently stands and near the spring where Becky Eberly and I had our picture taken, which I told

you about in CHAP-TER 1 – THE SCI-OTO RIVER. Going into the tavern business was a natural thing for John since that was the family business in Pennsylvania. John apparently decided that the spring was good for more than just a cold drink of water. Within a year or two after building the tavern, he built a distillery near the spring.

**BLACK HORSE TAVERN AND JOHN SELLS
HOME LOG HOUSE BUILT IN 1809
LATER COVERED WITH SIDING
PICTURE TAKEN IN 1880S**

Dublin's Sells Middle School is named for John Sells. When I went to school at Dublin that was our high school building.

Another thing you need to realize is that when the Sells family settled on their land, there was no "Route 161" and there was no "Riverside Drive," but there were Indian trails which were along what would become Route 161 and Riverside Drive. Indian Trails followed animal trails, and the early roads followed the Indian trails. Riverside Drive followed an important Indian trail, known as the "Scioto Trial" that ran north and south between the Ohio River and Lake Erie. It began at the mouth of the Scioto River at Portsmouth, and ran north along the Scioto River to near the headwaters of the Scioto, and then across to the headwaters of the Sandusky River and on to Lake Erie, following the Sandusky River downstream. There were also trails that connected Dublin

3. The deed from John Graham to Peter Sells states that the parcel of land being conveyed and described by "Survey 2542," that was originally thought to contain 889 acres, had been resurveyed and found to actually contain 1,070 acres and that all 1,070 acres was conveyed to Peter by the deed from Graham.

4. Out of the 1070 acres, Peter Sells deeded to John Sells, "450 acres (excepting ½ grist and saw mill yard water and mill privileges)." The deed was signed on January 3, 1811. The consideration was $2,000.00.

to places east and west of Dublin. If you had been traveling from someplace east of Dublin, let's say Worthington, and were heading to a place west of Dublin you would have pretty much followed along where "Route 161" is now until you reached a point just east of Sawmill Place Blvd (the street that goes to The Anderson Store). There is a curve to the right on 161 at that point which wasn't there during the early days. The trail/road continued straight, instead of curving to the right, and went just south of where the Barnes and Noble Book Store and Panera sit at this time, and then followed approximately along what is now Martin Road. There was no bridge across the Scioto River and so travelers had to ford the river. The best place to ford the river was near where Martin Road intersects with Riverside Drive. So you would have gone down what is now Martin Road, crossing the Scioto Trail near the river. Then you would have worked your way down to the river and forded it to the west side—after hitching up your britches, of course. On the west side you would have climbed the riverbank to where Riverview Street now is and proceeded north along Riverview Street to the present location of the Dublin Bridge and then turned west and gone along what became Bridge Street, on "Route 161" once again. On your trip you would have passed the Black Horse Tavern. Likewise if you had been traveling from the Columbus area and heading to that same place west of Dublin, or vice versa, you would have followed the "Scioto Trail" and you would have forded the river at "Martin Road" and once again you would have passed the Black Horse Tavern. The east-west trails between Fort Duquesne (Pittsburgh), Granville, and Greenville in western Ohio, and passing through Dublin, developed into a main east-west travel route across Ohio, with stage coaches using that route. Until the first bridge was constructed across the Scioto at Dublin, travelers forded the river at the end of Martin Road and therefore continued to pass the Black Horse Tavern. The Scioto Trail continued north of Dublin on the east side of the river and there was also a trail on the west side following along where Dublin Road is now, going north from Dublin. So, some of the people traveling to and from places north of Dublin would also have passed the tavern depending on where they were headed to or coming from. Now you can see that Grandpa John had his wits about him when he built that tavern where he did. Just think how thirsty and tired those folks must have been after climbing that high riverbank. In the early years, Riverview Street was the main street of Dublin. That's why the oldest houses in Dublin are located there. Riverview Street was originally called Water Street.

The "Scioto Trail" and the "Duquesne to Greenville Road" were both well-traveled; they were so well-traveled that eventually a bridge was built so as to avoid having to ford the river. The first bridge across the Scioto at Dublin was built in 1840.

John decided to establish a town on part of the land he acquired from Peter. Why and when he made that decision are not known. Maybe his customers at the tavern told him they liked the area and that gave him the idea, or maybe he had that idea even before he bought the land. Maybe he thought it would help convince the Ohio General Assembly to move the capital there. Who knows? We do know that an Irish surveyor, and lay preacher, by the name of John Shields, drew up a plan which divided some of his land into lots, complete with streets and alleys, and it was John Shields who named the town Dublin. There is information that indicates Shields had become familiar with the area in about 1800, while surveying in the vicinity and that he thought it would be a good place for a community and, even at that time, he had the idea that Dublin would be a good name for it. It is said that in 1800, or thereabouts, he marked the spot by writing "Dublin" on a map. Maybe John Shields convinced Grandpa John that he should do it, or maybe Shields had convinced Ludwick that it should be done and Ludwick decided he was too old and talked to John, and maybe John said, "Heck, sign me up, I'll move to Ohio, I'll buy the land, and I'll do it myself!" Lots of "maybes" makes for a good mystery, doesn't it?" Who knows? I've even read an article that refers to Shields as Grandpa John's partner. Maybe Shields at least gave him a break on the price of drawing up the plan if John would name the town Dublin. I have been told that Grandpa John was a good businessman. The information I have says that the plan of the lots was done in 1810[10], so it didn't take Grandpa John long to make the decision and when it came time to give his new town a name, he named it after Shield's hometown of Dublin, Ireland. Some people dress up the story of naming it, by having John Shields use some fancy words when he told John that he thought he should name the town Dublin, but dress it up or not, it's clear that an Irish surveyor gave the name of Dublin to a town founded by Germans. Dublin's history records that John

---

10   In view of the fact that John didn't obtain title to the property until 1811, John's brother, Peter, had apparently agreed to sell the land to John, and John had hired Shields to plan the town, confident that he would get title to the land from Peter.

Shields built a home in Dublin, and in 1811 he founded the Dublin Christian Church, which evolved into the Dublin Community Church now located on West Bridge Street. I can just imagine John Shields and Grandpa John drinking a beer or two at the tavern, now and then, talkin' about the future of their Dublin. Maybe I shouldn't speculate, but it's kind of fun. We will probably never know the answers to these questions, and they will always be mysteries.

The north boundary of the lots that were laid out in 1810 for this new town called Dublin was just north of where the library sits, on the north side of North Street. The south boundary was just south of Short Street. The Scioto River was its east boundary and the west boundary was near present day Franklin Street. The original town measured about 3,000 feet north and south, and about 1,200 feet east and west. So, according to my calculation, it only contained about 85 acres[11]. In 1820 the population of all of Washington Township was counted at 137. Most of these people lived along Indian Run.

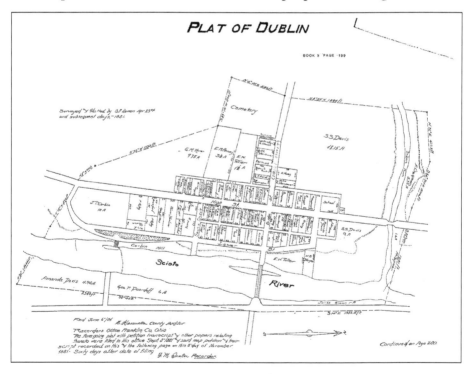

1881 PLAT
SUBMITTED TO THE FRANKLINCOUNTY COMMISSIONERS

---

11   Fire has destroyed any early plats of Dublin that may have been filed at the courthouse. The first recorded plat that exists is the plat that was filed when Dublin became an incorporated village in 1881.

In 1881, a group of Dublin electors filed a petition with the Franklin County Board of Commissioners seeking to incorporate Dublin, as laid out on a plat which was filed with the petition. The plat covered 150 acres and included the river adjacent to the town and the east riverbank. The petition was granted, and so at that time Dublin became a municipal village[12].

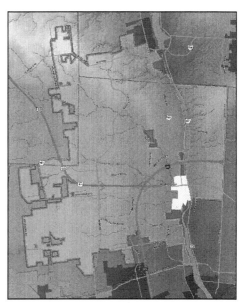

DUBLIN IN 1960
COMPARED TO DUBLIN
AT THE PRESENT

By the time of the Sesqui-centennial Celebration in 1960, the Village of Dublin had grown a little. Shortly after the end of World War II, Franklin Street was extended and lots were laid out along it, and in the mid-fifties, the developments that include Marion St., Longview Dr. and Grandview Dr. were added. In 1960 the area inside Dublin's boundaries was 236 acres and the population was 552.

Almost all of Dublin's growth has occurred since the Sesquicen-tennial. Since then, Dublin has grown to 15,811 acres (24.7 square miles) and now has about 41,325 residents. How's that for "Doublin'?"

There were probably no more than 30 people working in Dublin in 1960. We had three small grocery stores: Carl and Thelma Hill's store where "Tuc-ci's" patio dining area is now; John Herron's "Dublin Food Market" where "Cullen Art Glass" is (across from "The Dublin Village Tavern"); and "Leor Cole's," at 50 S. High, which is now "The Hair Smiths." There were two gas stations: Martine Karrer had a gas station on the northeast corner of Bridge and High Streets; and there was a "Pure Oil" station on the northwest cor-ner where "Mezzo's Restaurant" is. There was a radio and television sales and service business, originally owned by Madge and Harold Shriver, at the southwest corner of Bridge and High. The Shriver building was torn down

---

12   This was the second time Dublin was incorporated. It was first incorporated in 1855, but after a year of municipal rule, the voters of Dublin decided to go back to being controlled by the Washington Township officials.

and replaced by a 3rd gas station at about that time. There was a small restaurant, originally called the "Dublin Sandwich Shop," where "Bridge Street Pizza" is now located. We had Mose Myers' barber shop, now called "The Dublin Barber Shoppe," at 24 S. High. (By 1960 I had retired from shining shoes). There were a couple of beauty shops, including Dortha May Moffitt's shop on S. High St., about where the "Dublin Visitor & Information Center" is now located and Virginia Geese's shop at her home. The post office was where the "The Dublin Village Tavern" is now; Ruthella Termeer was the postmistress and I think she had one helper. Dr. Karrer had an office on South High Street and employed a nurse and receptionist. My dad had his business, "Sells Wells and Water," at our home on Marion Street. I may have forgotten a couple of other places of employment, but that was about all we had within the corporate limits of Dublin at that time.

Now a number of large companies are either headquartered or have large work forces in Dublin, including Wendy's International, Ashland, Inc., Cardinal Health, Online Computer Library Center (OCLC), Nationwide Insurance, and Verizon Wireless. According to Dublin officials, Dublin's present working population is estimated to be 60,000.

When I was growing up in Dublin, the big source of entertainment was the zoo, feeding the carp popcorn off the Monkey Island Bridge, and playing miniature golf at Tricky Trails at the Zoo Amusement Park. Dublin has come a long way since then in regards to entertainment. Golf enthusiasts know of the annual Memorial Golf Tournament which is hosted by Jack Nicklaus and is played in Dublin. This tournament attracts the greatest golfers on the Professional Golf Association Tour. Of course, we claim Mr. Nicklaus to be "one of our own," and will always consider him to be the greatest golfer ever. Also, the country's second largest Irish festival is celebrated in August of every year in Dublin; that's when everyone wears "the green," and "kiss me I'm Irish" badges are frequently seen. The Irish festival attracts approximately one hundred thousand visitors to Dublin each year. I am also proud to say that, under the tutelage of Mr. Jack Hanna (a television fixture and special guest on late-night talk shows) the Columbus Zoo and Aquarium has now achieved international fame.

Another thing you need to know about Dublin in 1810 is that there were many Indians who were opposed to the provisions of the Greenville Treaty. A well-known and highly respected Shawnee warrior by the name of Tecumseh was one of them, and he became their leader. He wanted the Indians of all the various tribes in America to set aside their intertribal squabbles and join together in an alliance to drive the white settlers out of the Ohio territory (and clear out of the country, if possible). He was an eloquent speaker and spent several years traveling to various Indian villages across the country to recruit them to join his alliance.

The Indians living in the Dublin area were mostly Wyandot. Their chief's name was "Shateyaronyah," but the settler's called him "Leatherlips." I think they probably called him Leatherlips because they had a hard time remember-

ing how to pronounce "Sha-té-ya-ron-yah." The Wyandot's main encampment was near where the post office on Shaun Falls now sits. Leatherlips was one of the chiefs who had signed the Greenville Treaty and thereby agreed to pioneers set-tling in the Ohio Terri-

THE EXECUTION OF LEATERLIPS – JUNE 2, 1810 – ARTIST-HAL SHERMAN

tory. He had pledged to fight no more against the whites and was determined to keep his word. When settlers arrived he established friendships with some, including the Sells family. It must have been comforting to the settlers that the chief of the Indians in their area was a man they considered as a friend. It's unknown why the settlers chose the name Leatherlips for him, but it may have had something to do with his determination not to go back on his word to be peaceful toward the settlers.

Tecumseh was embittered against Leatherlips for his unwillingness to join the alliance, and because of the effect that his refusal had on other Indians Tecumseh was trying to recruit. Some Wyandot Indians supported Tecumseh's plans. Roundhead was another Wyandot Chief and a strong believer in Tecumseh's plans, and he too was frustrated at Leatherlips' posi-tion. He became convinced that the only way to get the Wyandot Nation to join the alliance and fight against the Americans was to get Leatherlips to join, or get rid of him.

The headquarters of Tecumseh's movement was at a village on the Tippecanoe River in what is now Indiana. Tecumseh's brother, who was called "The Prophet," was in charge of the headquarters when Tecumseh wasn't there. At the Tippecanoe village a decision was made that Leatherlips should be convinced to join the Alliance, or be executed. It isn't known whether it was "The Prophet," or Tecumseh, who made the decision.

In the spring of 1810 Chief Roundhead and five Wyandot warriors traveled from the Tippecanoe village to Dublin to carry out this decision. They inquired at Benjamin Sells' cabin where they could find Leatherlips. They were told that he was at a camp located about 3 miles north on the east side of the river. Chief Roundhead and the other Indians went there and confronted Leatherlips. It is believed that they tried again to convince Leatherlips to join their cause, but he refused. Then they tried him for being a witch, blaming the misfortune of some Indians on his witchcraft. There were several settlers there at the time this trial took place and they knew that the jury was rigged. He was found guilty and condemned to death. When he realized that the Indians intended to kill Leatherlips, John Sells offered to give them his prize black horse if they would spare him. The Indians considered the offer and it appeared that they were tempted to agree, but they refused the offer and went ahead with the blood-letting. Leatherlips readied himself by bathing at a nearby spring. He dressed in his best apparel and painted his face. He sang a death chant as he was led to a grave that the warriors had prepared for him. He knelt and prayed; Chief Roundhead knelt with him and also prayed. Then one of the warriors executed Leatherlips by smashing his skull with a tomahawk. Leatherlips died as a martyr on June 2, 1810, and the Sells family and the other settlers lost a good friend. The execution was witnessed by John Sells and his brothers, Benjamin, Peter, and William. George Ebey was with the Sells brothers at the execution. Other settlers who were witnesses were Peter Millington who had settled in what is now Perry Township and Elias Lewis a lay minister from Worthington. Perhaps other settlers witnessed it also.

William Sells was 20 years old at the time. Sixty years later, in 1870 when he was 80 years old, he gave the following account of what took place, which is quoted here, exactly as he wrote it, and a copy of his original writing is inserted after the typed copy:

"There was thirty or forty of Indians on Indian Run & all around Dublin or where Dublin now stands. There was a squaw here called the Deer faced squaw. She was deformed & could not talk. The Indians made sugar on Indian Run in large quantities. Before the Battle of Tippecanoe there was an old Indian Chief by the name of Letherlips who was opposed to the Indians fighting & there was six young warriors who came out on the hunt of This Old Chief and found him three miles above Dublin on the east side of the Scioto River & we understood they were going to kill him and me & four Brother & several other of our neighbours. We all went up to the camp where the Indians went to kill the old chief And made an offer of a stable horse of my Brother worth about one hundred & fifty Dollars & the consell man told the old chief what the whites had offered for his life And The Old Chief came round & took all the white men by the hand and ponted up to Heaven as much as to say you will be rewarded by your maker. He then started up to where they had dug his grave where there was a tree blowen up by the roots & there he nelt down & prayed and as soon as he gave the signal he was ready the Indian behind him struck him with the Tomahock & nocked his skull in & he fell back dead. I helped to lay him in his grave. He is buried on the line between Delaware & Franklin Counties three miles above Dublin on the east side of the Scioto River. The concelman after we had offered the horse said no no to much Squaw. maby bad white man Indian say nothing. I am the only one living that was there at the time of the Tomahock of Letherlips."

116

OHI

12th There was ~~two hundred~~ Thirty or forty of Indians on Indian Run & all around Dublin or where Dublin now stands. There was a Squaw here called the Deer faced Squaw She was deformed, & she could not talk. The Indians made sugar on Indian Run in large quanties. Before the Battle of Tippecanoe There was an Old Indian Chief by the name of Letherlips who was opposed to the ~~Indians~~ ~~fighting~~ & there was six young warriers two came out on the hunt of this Old chief and found him three miles above Dublin on the east side of the Scioto River. & we understood they were going to kill him and me & four Brother & several father of our neighbours. We all went up to the camp where the Indians went to kill the Old chief. And made an offer of a stable horse of my Brother worth (for his life) about one hundred & fifty Dollars & the consell man told the Old chief what the whites had offred. And the Old Chief came round & took all the white men by the hand and pointed up to Heaven as much as to say you will be rewarded ~~~~. Then started to where they had dug his grave where there was a tree blowen up by the roots & there he nelt down & prayed and as soon as he gave the signal he was ready the Indian behind him struck him with the Tomahock & nocked his skull in & he fell back dead. I helped to lay him in his grave. He is Buried on the line between Delaware & Franklin Counties three miles above Dublin on the east side of the Scioto River. The concelman after we had offred the horse said no no to much Squaw, maby bad white man Indian say nothing. I am the only one living that was there at the time of the Tomahock of Letherlips.

13th I have no Old Newspapers or file of Newspapers or Map Hand-Bill or phamphlet Almnace or book published ~~~~,

14th There is one 1½ mile South of Dublin one 2½ miles South west of Dublin on Anson Davis farm. & one on the east side (River Scioto) a very large one about 2 miles north east of Dublin. No Stone in my possesion no arrow head or other artical in stone of the mound Builders

On November 7, 1811, not long after Leatherlips was executed, United States forces led by William Henry Harrison, then Governor of the Indiana Territory, and later to become the President of the United States, attacked and defeated the Indians at Tippecanoe, whereupon the Indians who had gone there to be a part of Tecumseh's alliance went back to their homes and the alliance fell apart. Tecumseh was not at the village at the time of the battle. He was away recruiting. Tecumseh did have his fight against the United States. He fought with the British against the U. S. in the War of 1812. Tecumseh died "by the sword," on October 5, 1813 near Windsor, Ontario in the Battle of the Thames. The Indians buried him there, but have kept the exact place of his burial secret to this day. Some Indians believed, and perhaps there are still Indians who do believe, that Tecumseh will someday return and lead the Indians to a victory over the Americans.

I think destiny dealt both Tecumseh and Leatherlips losing hands. Leatherlips believed that it was good to be friendly and that, if the Indians made friends with the settlers, the Indian way of life might be preserved. In contrast, Tecumseh, the charismatic warrior chief, believed that the white men would not keep promises made in treaties and that if not driven out, they would eventually occupy the entire Indian homeland and the Indian way of life would be destroyed forever. I think Tecumseh was proven right about that, but he also believed that by uniting the Indians and rallying them to his alliance, he could bring about the total and permanent removal of all white settlers from the Indians' homeland. He believed that if the Indians united, they could defeat the whites and have ultimate and total victory. He wasn't able to complete his alliance and wage the war he was planning, so we can't know for sure what the outcome would have been, but it's hard to believe he could have succeeded. In any case, I think of both Leatherlips and Tecumseh as heroes who died for what they believed.

There is a monument marking Leatherlips' grave just south of the zoo at the Delaware County and Franklin County line on the east side of Riverside Drive. Joseph Thompson, an early settler in Perry Township, became a good friend of the Wyandot Indians remaining in the Dublin area. For some time he lived in a cabin just east of Leatherlips' burial site. He took it upon himself to maintain the grave and protect it from desecration. His children and grandchildren continued to do so after Joseph's death. In 1887, his son, Colonel Samuel Thompson, gave a speech to the Wyandot Club of Columbus concerning Leatherlips and his execution. Thereafter, the club acquired an acre of ground surrounding the burial site, and in 1889 erected the monument that is now there and built the wall around it.

LEATHERLIPS MONUMENT & GRAVE MARKER – RIVERSIDE DRIVE – AT DELAWARE & FRANKLIN COUNTY LINE

According to all of the accounts of the execution of Leatherlips, he went to a spring and bathed before he was executed. Joe and Margaret Ryan and their daughter, Laura, my friend Mike Ryan's family, live along the Scioto just south of the Leatherlips' grave and monument. A spring fed creek runs through a culvert under Riverside Drive from the east side of the road, and then runs across their property and empties into the river. The spring that feeds that creek is probably the spring at which Leatherlips bathed.

On the west side of Riverside Drive, about two miles south of the Leatherlips grave and monument, there is another Leatherlips monument made of limestone in Scioto Park, at what used to be the location of Bill Butler's swimming pool. I have seen it, and it's very impressive. Many Dubliners are unaware that there is a special feature in the newer Leatherlips monument. The Wyandot Indians in Ohio were relocated to Upper Sandusky soon after the conclusion of the war of 1812, and in 1824 a Mission Church was built there which was used to educate the Wyandots until they were forced to leave Ohio for Kansas in 1843. The sculptor who built the monument in Scioto Park was given a special piece of limestone from the mission school in Upper Sandusky which he incorporated into the monument just above the nose on the face of Leatherlips.

It must have been discomforting to the Dublin settlers when the local "friendly Indian Chief" was executed by a group of Indians who wanted to drive the settlers out. The defeat of Tecumseh's forces at Tippecanoe must have been good news for the settlers, but the beginning of hostilities with England and their Indian allies in the War of 1812 must have been very bad news.

The Indians never attacked Dublin, but the folks had a scare at about the time of the beginning of the War of 1812. It seems that 18 year old Susan Sells, Samuel's daughter by his first marriage, decided that in view of the situation she should learn how to shoot a gun, and 19 year old, Jacob Ebey, George and Magdalena Ebey's son, decided to teach her. She fired off a round and you might say it was "The Shot Heard Round the Town." Elizabeth Sells, Samuel's wife, heard it and thought the Indians were attacking. She sent 12 year old Daniel, Samuel's son by his first marriage, to spread the alarm. The news spread and the settlers headed for Franklinton, where they thought they would be safer. When Jacob Ebey realized what was going on, he went around and explained what had happened and the settlers returned to their cabins.

Even after the War of 1812, Indians were frequently seen in the Dublin area. There was a large settlement of Wyandots at Upper Sandusky and they carried on trade with the settlers and traders at Franklinton. They traded furs and maple sugar for guns, ammunition and blankets. So they were often seen on the Scioto Trail or in canoes on the river heading for Franklinton loaded with furs or heading home with their guns and blankets. Think about that the next time you are looking down at the river while you are crossing it on the Dublin Bridge! The Indians also traded in Dublin. John Ashbaugh, Sophia Sells' husband, ran a pottery in Dublin and the Indians were good customers of his.

I'm told that some people in Dublin believe in the "Curse of Leatherlips." They believe that Leatherlips makes it rain when Mr. Jack Nicklaus has his Memorial Golf Tournament. I suspect some people will believe anything you tell them. From what I have read about Leatherlips, he wouldn't want to spoil a good time. He was a friend of the white man. Enough about curses.

Back in 1810, Zanesville was the capital of Ohio. Some legislators complained that they had to travel too far to do their legislative work for the state. You know how some legislators can be; if they aren't complaining about something, they don't feel that they are earning their salaries. Anyway, in February 1810, the Ohio General Assembly passed an act to locate the state capital within 40 miles of the geographic center of the state, and appointed a special commission to recommend a site.

Everybody understood the economic advantages that they would enjoy if the state capital was moved to their town. Delaware, Worthington, Lancaster, Dublin, Newark, and Franklinton, among others, lobbied for the prize. Dublin and Franklinton were the top contenders. John Sells argued that Dublin was the better place because Franklinton was prone to flooding and Dublin was not, and that because of good drainage, the Dublin area had no swampy or marshy areas and therefore had a healthier environment. The commission eventually reported to the General Assembly that they thought Dublin was the best place to locate the capital. However, some men with investments in the Franklinton area, and across the river on "Wolf Ridge," including Lucas Sullivant, Lyne Starling, John Kerr, Alexander McLaughlin and James Johnston were not willing to give up. These men had considerable financial resources behind them and had political connections in the General Assembly. Starling, Kerr, McLaughlin and Johnson offered that, if the General Assembly agreed to locate the capital on "Wolf Ridge," they would agree to give the state 10 acres of land for a capitol building and 10 acres for a penitentiary, and that they would build the penitentiary and all of the state offices, at their expense, up to $50,000, and that they would establish a town at that location by the name of Columbus. "Wolf Ridge was well above the river level, and so at least the statehouse wouldn't go under water with heavy rains. Wolf Ridge was where High Street is now, in Columbus. The only thing John Sells had to offer was the Black Horse Tavern, the spring, the distillery, and some vacant lots. So now the legislature had to choose between Dublin, the recommendation of the commission, and this "sweetheart offer" from the "men of money."

There are various stories about how the issue was finally resolved. Here is the story I like best. It was decided that the issue would be resolved by a two man poker game, with my Grandpa John Sells representing the Dublin interests, and a "Dr. Smith" representing the Franklinton/Wolf Ridge interests. They would play one hand of poker—winner take all. John Sells turned over three kings, and I imagine emeralds were sparkling in his eyes—for a split second. Then Dr. Smith turned over three aces, and that's how Columbus got to be the capital of Ohio, or so the legend goes. Do you suppose the deck might have been stacked? The "sweetheart offer" was agreed to by the legislators and the deal struck on February 14, 1812, Valentine's Day!

For years and years we had a sign on the east end of the Dublin Bridge which read: "Dublin, Leading Contender as Site of State Capital, 1810-1812." Well, Dublin lost that one; but really, isn't Dublin a whole lot better off the way she is now? Didn't we really end up with all the "green?" Maybe the Leprechauns had a "hand" in that card game. You never know. There's a lot of mystery in the world.

When Columbus was established in 1812, John Shields and other enterprising people turned their attention away from Dublin and toward Columbus. In 1813, Shields built a saw mill in Columbus on the east bank of the Scioto, near where the Federal Courthouse on Marconi Blvd is located today. In 1814, he laid out an addition, which later became German Village, and in 1815 he built a flour mill on the river. Columbus officially became the state capital in 1816.

SIGN ON THE EAST END OF THE DUBLIN BRIDGE

John Sells' argument that Columbus/Franklinton could flood and could have health problems due to poor drainage has been validated by historical events subsequent to the establishment of Columbus as the capital. In the 1830s, the 1840s, and in the 1850s several hundred Columbus residents died of cholera, due, in part, to the swamps and marshes east of 4th St which existed because of poor drainage. In 1913 the Scioto River flooded and some neighborhoods in Columbus were under 9 to 17 feet of water. The flood killed over 90 people and destroyed about 4,000 homes, the Bottoms (Franklinton) being hardest hit. I don't know of any deaths from cholera in Dublin, and I don't think there was any damage at all in the Dublin area during the 1913 flood.

Losing out on having the state capital in Dublin must have been a big disappointment to the Sells family and the others who had invested in property in Dublin. People's interest in Dublin must have diminished and land values must have dropped.

Most of the early Franklin County recorded deeds were destroyed by fire at the courthouse, but the Indexes to Deeds survived. I find no indication in the Franklin County Deed Indexes that Grandpa John sold any lots in Dublin during the decade from 1810 to 1819.

In March, 1818, he placed a notice in the *Columbus Gazette* that he would offer the new town of Dublin for sale in April. Was he just trying to sell lots or was he so discouraged he was trying to sell out the whole development? Read the notice and see what you think.

A NEW TOWN FOR SALE - The subscriber will offer for sale on the 10th and 11th of April next about 200 town lots, laid out and recorded as a town known by the name of DUBLIN, lying on the bank of Scioto River 12 miles above Columbus, and on the very place that the commissioners of the state made choice for the seat of Government: and at the expiration of the time specified by contract, it is probable that the legislature will turn their whole attention to said town, for as much as the conveniences for building is equal to any part in the Union. The best quality of building stone, lime, sand and excellent clay for brick or pottery ware. There is several remarkable large springs breaking of a lime stone rock in sundry places, and two excellent saw mills and a grist mill adjoining, and conveniences for a great number of other water works. This town stands on a high bank and known to be remarkably healthy. There will be also a number of out lots sold. A credit of one year will be given for the first payment and a balance in two yearly payments. The conditions will more fully explain the terms. A general warrantee deed will be given on the day of sale, where security for the payments are made. JOHN SELLS. March 12, 1818.

JOHN SELLS
OFFERS TO
SELL DUBLIN

There apparently weren't any lots sold—unless the buyers didn't record their deeds. I say that because I found no transfers of lots in Dublin listed in the grantors index until the 1820s. There apparently wasn't any acceptable offer for the whole town either, because John was the grantor of the lots when they did start selling in the 1820s and 1830s. The first conveyance of a "lot" in Dublin was in 1822 and was from John Sells to Samuel Sells (Lot 110).

Why would John Sells hold off on selling the lots (if he did)? Did he have hopes that the "sweetheart deal" would go "sour" and that the Ohio General Assembly would pick Dublin to be the capital after all? That would certainly have increased the value of his lots. Did he not give up hope until after the capital was actually moved to Columbus in 1816? What did he mean when he said in the newspaper notice: "at the expiration of the time specified by contract, it is probable that the legislature will turn their whole attention to said town?" I don't know the answers to these questions. Remember, I'm just a story teller.

But, what about Ludwick & Catherine Sells, and their children? What can I tell you of them?

[**Warning:** Most of the information I have on my family, I got from the internet at Ancestry.com. Most of the information that is on that site was supplied by my relatives, Sells descendants, from around the world. Because of the nature of the data collection process, there could be some errors in what I am telling you. With that warning, I will continue as though I know what I am talking about, and tell you all I can about the Sells family that settled Dublin.]

Ludwick Sells served in the Revolutionary War with a company from Pennsylvania under the command of Captain Martin Bowman. Ludwick and Catherine moved themselves, and those of their children who were not yet out on their own, to the Dublin area sometime shortly after the beginning of the 19th century. I don't know exactly when the move was made, but most accounts of early Dublin say that by 1803 the Sells Settlement was established. So, let's consider the family from that point in time.

In 1803, Ludwick was 60 years old, Catherine was 54; their son, Samuel, was 32, widowed, with two children; John was 29, married, with three children; Benjamin was 26, married, with two children; and Peter was 23 and unmarried. The other six children were unmarried and probably still living with Ludwick and Catherine at the time of the move to the Sells Settlement: Mary was 21; Susanna, 20; Sophia, 18; Margaret, 16; William, 13; and George was 11. Ludwick and Catherine built a house in Dublin and planted an orchard.

In 1808, Ludwick and Catherine, along with George Ebey and his wife, Magdalena, organized the first church in Dublin, the Methodist Episcopal Church. The congregation met at the Ebey home until the death of Mrs. Ebey, in 1815, and after that they met at Ludwick and Catherine's home. In

1837 a church building was constructed at 155 South High Street on land donated by Mr. and Mrs. Daniel Wright. At the request of the Wrights, the church was renamed "The Christie Methodist Church" in memory of Mrs. Wright's father, the Reverend John Christie.[13]

Like the Sellses, the Ebeys were from Huntingdon County, Pennsylvania. The Ebey family, including 6 children, moved to the Dublin area in 1805. Four additional Ebey children were born in Dublin. I don't suppose that it was just a wild coincidence that the two families from Huntingdon County, PA ended up in Dublin. Their part of Pennsylvania is mountainous and not heavily populated; the City of Huntingdon, the county seat, today only has a population of about 7,000. The families probably knew each other in Pennsylvania and were friends and may have gone to the same church. In Pennsylvania, they probably discussed the pros and cons of "upping stakes" and going "west" to the "Ohio Territory" and eventually both families decided to do so.[14]

Samuel Sells (1771-?), the oldest son of Ludwick and Catherine, married in Huntingdon, Pennsylvania, in 1794, before moving to Ohio. I don't know his Pennsylvania wife's name. They had two children: Susan (1794-?), who, while getting instruction from Jacob Ebey on using a rifle, triggered—literally—the "Indian Panic of 1812"; and Daniel (1800-?), Dublin's version of Paul Revere, who spread the word—"The Indians are comin', the Indians are comin'! In 1807, after coming to Dublin, Samuel married Elizabeth Woolcutt, (born in 1791), his first wife having died. He and Elizabeth had three children: Abraham (1808-1885); Elizabeth; and Jane.

I tracked down George and Magdalena Ebey's son, Jacob, who, in 1812, at age 19, taught Susan Sells, age 18, how to shoot a gun. Shortly thereafter, Jacob went off to fight in the war of 1812. He served under General William Henry Harrison. After the war he returned to Franklin County—probably

---

13   In 1912 a tornado severely damaged the Methodist Church, as well as the Presbyterian Church, which was located on North High St. where Tucci's now sits. The congregations of those churches and the congregation of the third church in Dublin, The Christian Church, organized a new church which they named the Dublin Community Church. The new church took over the church building of the Christian Church, located at 81 West Bridge Street. The Dublin Community Church is still active.

14   In 1818, after 13 years in Dublin, George Ebey and some of his eleven children moved "west" again, this time to Illinois. Three of his daughters who married Dublin men, were among those who remained in Dublin.

to Dublin. I decided to track Jacob down because I thought he and Susan Sells might have gotten married. It seemed logical that Jacob would have come home from the war and married Susan, his childhood friend. Remember, there were very few girls in Dublin back then. But, it didn't happen.

However, what I found out about Jacob and his family is worth noting. In 1815, he married Sarah Blue. (Maybe he met and fell in love with her while he was off fighting in the war.) They had 6 children while living in Franklin County. Their second child, Isaac, who became an important west coast historic figure, was born in 1818 and lived in Franklin County (probably in Dublin) until he was 11 years old.

In 1829 or 1830 Jacob and his family moved to Illinois where their seventh child, Winfield Scott Ebey, who also contributed to west coast history, was born in 1831. In 1832, while living in Illinois, Jacob served in the Black Hawk War, alongside of Abraham Lincoln.

In the mid-1830s the Jacob Ebey family moved west again, this time to Missouri, where Isaac, became a lawyer. In 1848 Isaac continued the family tradition of moving farther and farther west. Isaac went all the way to Puget Sound and settled on Whidbey Island, now a part of the State of Washington, where he took up 640 acres for homesteading. The land he homesteaded and farmed is now known as Ebey's Prairie. On part of his land Isaac established Ebey's Landing, a docking facility for boats. Isaac was a major political force in the area and a vital player in territorial affairs. He is credited with having named the city of Olympia, Washington, and was an important voice in separating the Oregon and Washington Territories. He was a Colonel in the Washington Territorial Volunteer Militia.

Isaac was shot to death and then beheaded in 1857 by Indians who were seeking revenge for the killing of one of their chiefs and 26 other Indians in a naval attack by the USS Massachusetts. Isaac had nothing to do with the attack; the Indians just wanted to kill someone important in retaliation, and chose Isaac to kill because they considered him to be the "white man's big chief." The Indians kept Isaac's head and danced around it at ceremonial feasts. After 3 years, a friend of Isaac was able to purchase the head from the Indians and lay it to rest with Isaac's body.

In 1942, during WWII, Fort Ebey was established on Whidbey Island and named in honor of Colonel Isaac Ebey. In 1978 the federal government established Ebey's Landing National Historical Reserve. The reserve includes 17,572 acres on Whidbey Island and was the first historical reserve established in the United States. The 1999 Academy Award nominated movie, *Snow Falling on Cedars,* was filmed, in part, on Whidbey Island and contains shots of Ebey's Prairie.

Jacob, his wife Sarah, their other son Winfield Scott Ebey, two daughters, and two grandchildren followed Isaac to Ebey's landing in 1854. Winfield wrote a book entitled, *The 1854 Oregon Trail Diary of Winfield Scott Ebey* about the family's trip from Missouri to Whidbey Island. Jacob and Sarah built a house and homesteaded on a 320 acre claim adjacent to Isaac's land. For protection from the Indians, they also built a block house. Both the house and the blockhouse have been preserved and are now part of Ebey's Landing National Historical Reserve along with Jacob and Sarah's 320 acres. Jacob died in 1862 on Whidbey Island.

It's all on the internet, complete with pictures of Isaac, and also pictures of Jacob's house and blockhouse. Check it out. Winfield's book is available through Amazon.com. I wonder if there are people in the Dublin area today with Ebey blood in their veins?[15]

Now let's get back to the Sells family. Ludwick and Catherine's son, Benjamin (1777-1837) was married in Pennsylvania to Rebecca Skidmore (1777-1842) before coming to Ohio. They had five children: Catherine (1797-?); Ephraim (1802-1834); Rachel (1803-?); Ludwick (1806-?); **and Peter (1809-1884). It was Peter's sons who founded, owned and operated the Sells Brother's Circus which you read about earlier in the book.**

Benjamin served as the first Franklin County Commissioner, being elected to that office in 1804. He was also a justice of the peace for Washington Township. I found that information in *History of Franklin County, Ohio,* by Opha Moore.

Peter Sells (1780-1832) was married in 1807 to Sarah Casey (?-1834) in Franklin County. Sarah was born in Marietta, Ohio, and was known by her nickname, Sally. They had five children: Miles; Sarah; Cyrus; Benjamin (1813-1880); and Luke (1829-?). Benjamin married Elizabeth Ann Davis. They lived in the beautiful brick house at 4586 Hayden Run Road, which was built for them by Elizabeth's father. The house is still there and is still beautiful.

15   When George Ebey left to go to Illinois, three of his daughters stayed in Dublin: Elizabeth Ebey (1791-1867) married William Sells (1790-1872). Mary Ebey (1796-1886) married Amaziah Hutchinson (1792-1847). Susannah Ebey (1803-?) married Daniel Hutchinson (1795-?).

The *History of Franklin County, Ohio* says that Peter Sells was a contractor in charge of building one of the Ohio Canals in the late 1820s. You may not know that between 1825 and 1852 a series of canals was built in Ohio which connected many Ohio towns and cities, including Columbus, by water, with Lake Erie and the Ohio River. After they were built, it was possible to travel by water on the canals from Columbus to Lake Erie and then cross Lake Erie to Buffalo and on to Albany by way of the Erie

BENJAMIN SELLS HOUSE – 4586 HAYDEN RUN ROAD

Canal and then down the Hudson River to New York City, and from there to about any place in the world, all without ever having to step on dry land. However, you would have had to change boats, from a canal boat to a schooner, back to a canal boat and then to another schooner, and perhaps to a square rigger for your ocean voyage. Or if you wanted to go the other direction, you could have left Columbus and gone to Portsmouth on canals and the Scioto River, and from there on the Ohio and Mississippi Rivers to New Orleans, then on to the Gulf of Mexico. In those days most freight coming into Ohio, or being shipped from Ohio, was transported on the canals. The trains ran the Ohio Canals out of business during the last half of the 1800s. The canals just couldn't compete. The last Ohio Canal was abandoned in 1913.

In 1809, at the age of 19, William Sells (1790-1872) married George and Magdalena Ebey's 18 year old daughter, Elizabeth (1791-1867). They had twelve children: Katherine (1810-?); Mary (1812-1845)[16]; Elijah (1814-1897); Elizabeth (1816-1899); Louis (1817-?); Francis (1819-?); William (1822-?); Sarah (1824-?); Sophia (1824-?); Joseph (June 5, 1826 - August 5, 1826); George (1827-?); and Ludwick (1830-1831).

---

16   Mary Sells married Brice Hays. She is buried in the northwest corner of the Indian Run Cemetery. Her tombstone is one of only a couple in that cemetery that are legible.

WILLIAM SELLS HOUSE
6028 DUBLIN ROAD
BUILT IN 1830S – 1915 PHOTO

WILLIAM SELLS HOUSE
RECENT PHOTO

The only information I found on Ludwick and Catherine's son, George, was that he was born in 1792 and that he is buried in the Indian Run Cemetery. There is no death date listed on his record of interment.

Ludwick and Catherine had four daughters. Their daughter, Mary Polly, born in 1782, married Jacob King and had three children: Sophia, Margaret and John. She died in 1814, and was the first person in Dublin to die. She was buried in a cemetery her husband established on a portion of their land on the south bank of Indian Run. It's now known as the Indian Run Cemetery.

Ludwick and Catherine's daughter, Margaret, born in 1786, married Henry Coffman (1782-1846) in 1808 in Franklin County. They had two children: Matilda (1809-1885) and Fletcher (1817-1902). Margaret died in 1869.

FLETCHER COFFMAN AND HIS WIFE, MARINDA
THEY BUILT THE "COFFMAN HOUSE"
NOW THE HOME OF THE DUBLIN HISTORICAL SOCIETY

I don't have any information on Ludwick and Catherine's daughter, Susanna, except that she was born in 1783.

Their other daughter, Sophia, born in 1785, married John Ashbaugh in 1806, and died in 1847.

I found no record of Ludwick owning real estate in the Dublin area or any other place except for one parcel in Franklinton that he conveyed to John Boyd, sometime between 1804 and 1813. (He may have built his home on property belonging to one of his children.) However, the surviving courthouse records indicate that five of Ludwick Sells sons speculated in real estate: Benjamin, Peter, Samuel, William, and John. Benjamin bought and sold many properties in Franklinton and in Columbus after it was established in 1812. The Deed Grantor Index lists Benjamin as grantor (seller) on about 40 separate deeds of real estate between 1804 and 1843. (After his death in 1837, properties were transferred by his executor.) Most all of these deeds were for conveyances of real estate in Franklinton or Columbus. Only a few were for Washington Township/Dublin properties. The Deed Index for the period from 1804 to 1833 lists Peter as grantor in about 23 real estate conveyances. About half of those properties were in the Dublin area, and the other half were in Franklinton or Columbus. Not only did Benjamin and Peter buy and sell real estate in Franklinton, so did Samuel and William. The courthouse records indicate that between 1804 and 1813, Samuel conveyed a property to John O'Harra and another property to Lucus Sullivant. In 1839, William conveyed property in the "City" (which I think would mean Columbus) to Amon Jenkins. William also conveyed property in Truro Township in 1826 to George Shoemaker and another property in Truro Township in 1830 to Peter Sells. This Peter Sells may have been Benjamin's son who would have been 21 at the time. William and Benjamin acquired considerable real estate between the southern boundary of Survey 2542 and the present location of Hayden Run Road. Samuel also bought and sold real estate in the Dublin area.

I told you earlier that Ludwick's other son, **John Sells (1774-1841) and his wife Elizabeth Stroup Sells (1777-1852) were my great-great-great-grandparents.** I listed their children and I told you about their coming to Dublin and building the Black Horse Tavern and a distillery, and founding Dublin on the property John acquired from his brother, Peter.

On November 3, 1809, before buying land on the west side of the river, John purchased 350 acres from Peter Mills on the east side of the river, about 1 mile north of where the Dublin Bridge is, in what is now Perry Township. There is a log cabin still standing on this property. The cabin is now part of a newer house and I was recently in it. It's between the end of Bright Road and the river. Did John Sells and his family live there until he bought the property on the west side of the river and built the Black Horse Tavern? I don't know.

Shortly after John Sells sold the property, the cabin became the home of Joseph Thompson, the man who maintained Leatherlips' grave, and it was later occupied by Joseph Thompson's descendants[17]. One of Joseph's living descendants, Jim Thompson, the author of *Last of the Wyandots*, believes the cabin may have already been on the property when John Sells purchased the land because, according to the Ohio Historical Society, the type of construction used in building it, had become obsolete prior to 1809.

John Sells paid $700 for the 350 acres and then sold it to Joseph Smith in 1816, for $1,875. The increase in value of that property may indicate that a house was built on it while he owned it. But if the log cabin I have already mentioned was on the property when John bought it, that cabin couldn't explain the increase in value of the property during the 9 years John Sells owned it. However, there was another log house on this property. Dublin Scioto Park is located on a portion of the 350 acres Grandpa John bought from Peter Mills, and there used to be a log house on the Scioto Park property. The house sat about 50 feet southwest of where the amphitheater stage now sits. This would have been a desirable place for a settler to have his home because there is a good spring just down the hill, about 50 feet from where the house sat. I was there recently and the spring is still flowing abundantly. The Butler family owned the property and lived in the log house when I was growing up. Bill Butler put in a public swimming pool on the property in about 1950 near where the playground equipment is now. That is where I used to go swimming with my girlfriend, Kay. The log house was still there when the pool was built, but was torn down a few years later. Was that house built while John Sells owned the property? Is that why he was able to sell the property after owning it only 9 years for almost three times as much as he paid for it? If so, who lived in it? Who knows?

---

17   Jennie Hall, a descendant of Joseph Thompson, told about being born and
      raised in that cabin in an article that appeared in the Summer 1989 Shanachie

John Sells and George Ebey owned the first grist mill in Dublin[18]. It was on the west bank of the Scioto River at the south end of town. It operated until 1898.   The last owner was Joseph Corbin and today it is commonly referred to as Corbin's Mill.   In the spring of 1821, John loaded a flat boat with 500 barrels of flour and some bacon and headed down the Scioto bound for New Orleans. The boat was 15 feet wide and 60 feet long. He and a hired pilot, and one other man, were the crew.

GRIST MILL OWNED BY JOHN SELLS AND GEORGE EBEY – LATER KNOWN AS CORBIN'S MILL

He also hired his 13 year old nephew, Abraham, Samuel's son, to be their cook. Fletcher, John's 12 year old son, went along too. News that John was going to attempt this journey caused quite a stir in Franklinton. The people there questioned whether he could make it over their mill dams, including the two mill dams of his friend, John Shields. When word spread that the boat was "a comin'," a crowd gathered at the river bank to watch. They succeeded in making it over the dam. In fact they made it to Maysville, Kentucky. However, they aborted their trip at that point, sold their load, and returned home. What an adventure for all of them!

John also owned a sawmill located near Indian Run. He also bought and sold real estate in Columbus and Franklinton. He is listed as being the grantor on about 15 conveyances of Columbus and Franklinton properties. But of course, being the founder of Dublin, most of his transactions involved Dublin area real estate. And, like his brothers, William and Benjamin, he also acquired considerable real estate between the southern boundary of Survey 2542 and the present location of Hayden Run Road.

---

18   It appears, based on information contained in the real estate abstracts for "Old Dublin" properties, that the grist mill was built while John Graham or Peter Sells owned the property. When Peter deeded the property to John, John received a half interest in the mill. George Ebey, a miller by trade, was John's partner in the mill and, perhaps, had acquired his half interest before John bought the land.

As I said in CHAPTER 2 – THE DAVIS FARM, John and Elizabeth's daughter, Matilda, married John and Ann Simpson Davis's son, Samuel, and they lived on the east side of the river near his parents.

John and Elizabeth's daughter, Lucy, married Dublin's first physician, Dr. Albert Chapman, who began his practice in Dublin in 1830.

**109 SOUTH RIVERVIEW STREET
BUILT IN 1822**

John and Elizabeth's son, Charles, married Amanda Hutchinson. Charles and Amanda's daughter, Marilla, married the second Dublin physician, Dr. Eli Pinney, who practiced in Dublin for about 60 years beginning in 1842. The house at 109 South Riverview Street was originally the home of Charles and Amanda Sells. After they died, it became the home of Marilla and Dr. Eli Pinney. Dr. and Mrs. Pinney aided runaway slaves at their house as part of the Underground Railroad. Dr. Pinney built a speaking tube that extended from his living room through the exterior wall of the house and into his nearby barn where the runaways hid so he could communicate with them.

John and Elizabeth's son, Eliud Sells, was in the hat making business with his brother Charles. In the early 1820s Eliud built the first stone house in Dublin at 83 South Riverview Street. After his father's original Black

**THE 2ND BLACK HORSE TAVERN
83 SOUTH RIVERVIEW STREET**

Horse Tavern went out of business, Eliud opened a tavern at his house and named it the Black Horse Tavern. He operated the tavern at that location from 1832 until 1842. After the bridge was built across the Scioto River in 1840, Eliud had very little traffic going past his place and therefore very little business. He then moved the Black Horse Tavern to a new location on South High Street.

In 1835, John and Elizabeth's daughter, Caroline, married Zenas Hutchinson. Grandpa John built the large limestone building on the south-east corner of Bridge and High Streets as a wedding present for Caroline and Zenas. It was operated by Zenas as The Hutchinson Hotel, and served the folks who traveled on the stagecoach road connecting Greenville, Granville and Pittsburg. That was a good way for Grandpa John to show off Dublin's excellent limestone. Furthermore, he needed to do something nice for Caroline and

THE 3RD AND FINAL LOCATION OF THE BLACK HORSE TAVERN NOW OCCUPIED BY THE STATE BANK AT 109 S. HIGH ST.

Zenas because when Lucy married Dr. Chapman, in 1833, he built them a nice house located north and west of Bridge and High Streets. The Chapman House no longer exists, but the Hutchinson Hotel building has been a Dublin landmark ever since it was built, and is still a fine looking structure. During the late 1800s, it was one of Dublin's many notorious drinking establishments and was known as the Old Stone Tavern. Now it houses Donato's Pizza. Zenas Hutchinson was elected as Dublin's first mayor and served during the period of Dublin's first incorporation as a municipality (1855-1856).

DONATO'S PIZZA – 6 SOUTH HIGH STREET ORIGINALLY THE HUTCHINSON HOTEL - BUILT IN 1835

John and Elizabeth's son, **John, Jr. (1803-1879) married Marinda Hutchinson (1804-1881). They were my great-great-grandparents.** They also had 10 children: Priscilla (1825-1880); Amaziah Hutchinson Sells (1826-1860), (this is not "The Old Man" who I have told you about. This Amaziah became a doctor and then died at 34 years of age); Nancy (1829-1858); Mack (1832-1887); Ann (1835-?); Warren (1837-?); Matilda (1838-1927); **Richard Hannibal Sells (1840-1916)**; Amanda (1843-1914); and John, III (1847-1920).

Since the "Hutchinson" name has come up several times in connection with the marriages of some of the children of John and Elizabeth Sells and some of the children of George and Magdalena Ebey, I want to take a few lines to tell you about the Hutchinson family. Amaziah Hutchinson, Sr. (1762-1823) was born in Connecticut. He moved to New York where, in 1791, he married Elizabeth Mack (1775-1853). They had 10 children, all born while they were living in New York. Sometime between 1813 and 1822 the family moved to the Dublin area and settled on the east side of the river, in what is now Perry Township. Like Ludwick Sells, John Davis, Ann Simpson Davis, and George Ebey, Amaziah Hutchinson, Sr. also served in the Revolutionary War. The Hutchinson family was closely tied to the John Sells and George Ebey families through marriage. Five of the children of Amaziah, Sr. and his wife, Elizabeth, married into the Sells and Ebey families: Amaziah Hutchinson, Jr. (1792-1847) married Mary Ebey; Daniel Hutchinson (1795-?) married Susannah Ebey; Amanda Hutchinson (1802-1881) married Charles Sells; Marinda Hutchinson (1804-1881) married John Sells, Jr.; and Zenas Hutchinson (1813-1890) married Caroline Sells.

Richard Hannibal Sells (1840-1915), married Amanda Rachel Bower (1840-1927). They were my great-grandparents. They had eight children, Peter, born in 1863; Lottie, born in 1865; **Amaziah Hutchinson Sells, born April 22, 1867;** Mary, born in 1869; Jacob, born in 1871; Florence, born in 1875; Ella, born in 1877; and Richard, Jr., born in 1879.

The son of Richard Hannibal Sells and Amanda Rachel Bower Sells, named Amaziah Hutchinson Sells, is the old man,—the husband of my Grandma Polly. He was named after his great-grandfather, Amaziah Hutchinson, Sr., my great-great-great grandfather.

Now I want to tell you a little about the family of my Great-Grandmother Amanda Rachel Bower. Peter Bower (1799-1876) was born in York County,

Pennsylvania. He came to the Dublin area and settled on the east side of the river near where Don Scott Airfield is now located. He was a farmer. In 1829, he married Mary Davis, the granddaughter of John and Ann Simpson Davis. Mary was the daughter of William Davis and Mary Sullivan. (See CHAPTER 2 – THE DAVIS FARM.) Peter and Mary had 11 children, one of whom was Amanda Rachel Bower, my grandfather Amaziah's mother. Therefore, Grandpa Amaziah was the great-great-grandson of John and Ann Simpson Davis. My Grandma Polly was their great-granddaughter, making Amaziah and Polly 2nd cousins, once removed.

William Henry Bower (1837-1918) was another of the children of Peter and Mary Bower. One of his children was Anna May Bower (1882-1938). She was the "Annie" of the "Ballad of Pat and Annie" which I told you about in CHAPTER 5 – MY AUNTS AND UNCLES. So, Uncle Pat and Annie, besides being husband and wife, were also 2nd cousins, once removed.

William Henry Bower was also the great-grandfather of Leona Jones, making her my 3rd cousin.

Another of Peter and Mary's children was Joseph Bower (1832-1881) who married Laura Case. One of their children, Gladys Bower (1872-1954), married Jacob Leppert and was the mother of Lester Leppert and Bertha Leppert Headlee. That means the Lester and Audrey Leppert family and the Earl and Bertha Headlee family are descended from John and Ann Simpson Davis. It also means that Bertha Headlee and my Dad were 2nd cousins and my old friend Gary Headlee is my 3rd cousin, once removed.

John Simpson Bower (1838-1912), another of Peter and Mary Bower's children, was the grandfather of Count Bower, making him a 2nd cousin of my dad and Bertha Headlee.

So now you've learned a little about the early history of Dublin, the early Sells family, and some other families the Sellses were closely connected to. I think you would agree with me that Dublin's early history is unique, interesting, colorful, and on some points, downright confusing.

Walking through the cemeteries in the Dublin area is one of the best ways to be reminded of Dublin as it used to be. When I take a stroll through the Dublin Cemetery, and see names of some of the Dublin clans who made Dublin great—the Headlees, the McCoys, the Tullers, the McKitricks, the Geeses, the Lepperts, the Thompsons—I regret ever leaving Dublin. There's even a monument for the famous Dublin Cornet Band in the cemetery; and when I read some of the names of the people who were in that band, whose families I am familiar with—the Davises, the Thomases, the Coffmans, the Eberlys, and the Pinneys (to name a few)—well, it makes me want to come back home. Thomas Wolfe, the author, said that you can't go back home, and Bob Dylan, the singer and songwriter and poet, said that you can go home, but you can't go back all the way. I don't know; I just know Dublin is in my heart and on my mind.

During the 1800s the Sellses and the other pioneer families I have mentioned, along with others, such as the Corbins, the Mitchells, the Hirths, and the Karrers, were buildin' Dublin up, and during that time, it seemed like the Sellses were busy marrying into the Davis family, or vice versa, and that all the clans were marrying into other clans. When I was growing up it seemed like Dublin had its own unique breed of people, sort of like it had spawned its own "Dublin DNA," and that the DNA was a mixture of all the clans. When you met Dublin people back then, you could just tell they were special by the way they walked and talked, and always had time for you. I can still remember shaking the rough-hewn hands of the farmers when my dad introduced me to one of them. To tell you the truth, I usually thought they might be one of my uncles who I hadn't met yet, or at the very least, I figured that they must somehow be related to me. It seemed like everyone else was. My cousin Danny Lee Sells told me to never get in a fight with someone from Dublin because you would probably find out later that you were related to him.

Anyway, there was a strong foundation being laid back in the 1800s for when Dublin would later become a sleepy little Irish village. Who would have ever guessed back then that someday Dublin Would be Doublin'.

What can my readers make of Ludwick Sells and his sons? What inspired them to set out and found a village? Was it curiosity? Wanderlust? Boundless energy? Grandiosity? Impulsivity? Or, was it that original Dublin blood pumping through their veins?

CHAPTER 11

MY HEROES

We had a lot of interesting characters in Dublin when I grew up there, When It Wasn't Doublin'. I guess if I tried to tell you about them all, I would never get this little book of stories finished. What I would like to do now is to tell you about just two more, my heroes...my dad and my mom.

The way my dad met and married my mother, and then got shipped over to England, fought his way through France and Germany, and eventually made it back to Dublin reads a little like a script from a Hollywood romance, and it could only have happened during World War II. My dad joined the Ohio Army National Guard in Delaware and the attack on Pearl Harbor quickly ensued. Then he really was in the Army. Since most military posts are in the South, my dad gradually moved in that direction, in and out of various camps, until he ended up in Austin, Texas. And this is where my mother enters the picture...

My mama grew up as the baby of the family, just like my dad was the baby in his family. Her father, Charles Williams, was forty-seven when she was born, and her mother, Alice, was forty-two. She had seven brothers and sisters who just doted on her: Earl, Elmer, Vivian, Violet, Irene, Flourine, and Noddy. As people would say now days, my mama was a "love" child and, she was always treated accordingly. The Williams family was basically a sharecropping family who lived on a farm near a very small town in Burnett County in Texas, called Bertram, about forty miles or so northwest of

Austin. The population in Bertram now is around 1,300, so in 1922 when mama was born it couldn't have been very big. The Williams family made their living sharecropping; that is, picking cotton.

My mama grew up with her cats and her puppies and her horses. She loved to ride horses, and probably could ride better than her husband to be. She would dress up her cats and dogs in ribbons and lace and put little bows in their hair just like, I suppose, her big sisters would dress her up in ribbons and curls. My mother was very straightforward and inno-cent in her thinking as she grew up in Ber-tram, maybe because of the sheltered life she led on a sharecropper's farm. I am sure that she was naïve as to the ways of the larger world. Bertram was isolated, and I am not sure if Grandpa Williams even had an auto-mobile. The story her family liked to tell and laugh about was that mama once got kicked in the head by a horse when she was a little girl and that's what made her a little different. They loved to tease her about that. But, my mama was quite smart in her own way. She

MAMA IN BERTRAM TEXAS

always did very well in school, even though in Texas during her time there were only eleven years of schooling required to graduate. She always prided herself on her penmanship and loved Texas history. I don't think she ever had to work very hard picking cotton. She never once complained to me about the heat or the sweat involved in picking cotton in Texas when she was young. My guess is that her mama and papa and brothers and sisters just let her do what she wanted when they took her out to the fields. Oh, they may have given her a little sack to fill, but I doubt they cared very much whether she filled it or not. They probably were content to just watch her sit under a shade tree and see her play with one of her dolls or kittens that she had brought along with her. She loved bluebonnets, like most Texans do; they were her favorite flowers.

I don't know how many boyfriends my mama had while she lived in Bertram, but I suspect not many. She was guarded by a very close-knit fam-ily, and there were not that many boys her age in Bertram, or even Burnett

County for that matter. Also, her big brother Earl was a county judge in Burnett, and that tended to dissuade prospective suitors. I do remember her talking about a certain young man by the name of "Hot Shot" who pursued her, but I think he was nothing more to her than an amusement, like another cat or dog.

During her age of innocence in Bertram, my mama developed into a beautiful young Texas woman. She had thick dark, long, auburn hair, long legs, a beautiful figure, and that innocent, enchanting, Texas smile. After graduating from Bertram, she left and went to live with my Uncle Elmer and Aunt Minnie in Austin. She once worked as a carhop on roller skates in a drive-in restaurant in Austin. I would have given anything to see her roller skating around the restaurant and taking orders. After a while, she found a job working in the Selective Service Office. The pictures that my dad had of her in a bathing

MY PRECIOUS MAMA

suit standing on the piers of Galveston and the beaches of Corpus Christi probably took his breath away. No wonder he fought so hard to get back home to her.

My mama loved to dance. You name it and she could dance it, especially the jitterbug. After work at the Selective Service, she and her best friend Thelma would go dancing. My mama used to love to go to the United Service Organizations (USOs) to dance with the movie stars who came in there. She would dance with any serviceman who wanted to dance. "Who was the greatest dancer that you ever saw, mama?" I once asked her. "Bojangles, that man could dance," my mama used to always say. She loved the movie stars of her era and went to all their movies. Her favorite movie stars were Ronald Colman and Clark Gable. "Now Clark was a right handsome man (as if she knew him personally), he surely was," she used to say, "but nobody was as good looking as Ronald Coleman."

Anyway, one night my mama and Thelma were in the Longhorn Saloon in Austin, dancing, and just having a good time after work when in walked this blond haired, blue-eyed Yankee technical sergeant and his friend, another sergeant. They were standing at the head of the stairs, looking down over the saloon. Their entrance was dramatic. My mom took one look at the blond haired soldier, and then looked at Thelma, lowered her eyes quickly, and said, "Thelma, I'm going to marry that man." Thelma looked over at my mom, shook her head like my mom was crazy and said, "Darline, you can't marry him. He's probably one of those Yankee boys from way up north, and you don't even know him!" "I don't care," said my mama, "he looks just like Van Johnson, the actor, and I'm going to marry him!" Somehow they got together quickly, this young sergeant from Dublin, Ohio, and this beautiful Texas belle. They courted for a very, very short while, and my dad asked her to marry him. Now he and the old man sort of "patched" up their difficulties after my dad went in the Army, so my dad called the old man up and asked him if he could get married to this Texas girl—right fit and proper of my dad, don't you think? The old man paused for a while, and then asked my dad one question: "What's her politics, Son?" My dad muffled the phone against his arm and asked my mama whether she was a Democrat or a Republican. "I don't rightly know, honey. All I know is papa voted for FDR. "She said her papa voted for FDR," my dad shouted through the phone line. "That's good enough," the old man said, "bring her on home, soon as you can." They were married a week later at Camp Swift, Texas, on the Fourth of July, 1942. They stayed married until my precious mama died in 1987. Such is young love, and such was romance in World War II.

Right after their marriage, my dad was sent to Camp Shelby, Mississippi. In those days, Mississippi was a "dry" state; that is, it was illegal to sell alcohol in the state. That didn't stop my dad. He was in charge of a motor transport unit at the time, and he would commandeer Army trucks and have them driven to New Orleans, where the drivers would pick up whiskey and distribute it throughout Mississippi. I don't know why he did it. Maybe for the thrill, maybe because he didn't think he would ever make it out of the War alive, or maybe for my mom. Anyway, I guess he made a lot of money, and he didn't get caught. He used the money to buy War bonds. At least he was patriotic.

After that, my dad got sent to England. Shortly after arriving in England, in December, 1942, my dad sent a V-MAIL to my Aunt Nancy and Uncle Ken Hovey describing the trip and the conditions in England. I believe the "Muz" referred to in the V-MAIL is Aunt Nancy's dog, and it is very probable that "Muz" was named for Muzak, Uncle Ken's canned music. (Uncle Ken graduated from Brown University as an electronics engineer. He invented and patented canned music and named it Muzak.) Anyway, here's the V-MAIL:

"Dear Sister; how are you & Ken & Muz? Miss all of you and sure would like to have Ken here playing gin rummy. The game would be interrupted every once in a while but he would get used to that.

"We arrived here in England all OK. No trouble at sea outside of a few stormy days of weather that rolled us around a little bit. I turned out to be a pretty good sailor, didn't get sick but was awful light-headed the first two days. Some of the fellows were sick the whole trip and couldn't seem to keep down anything they ate. I felt sorry for them and asked if they cared for a piece of fat meat on a string so that they could swallow it and pull it back up. The suggestion was very much appreciated and brought up everything. I was to be shot no less than ten times per sick man. They are all OK now and laughing over it.

"I met a lot of English soldiers on the way over and heard all about the War. Some of them were guards who had taken prisoners to the States. They were always wanting me to have tea. They have it twice a day over here. The English are the poorest coffee makers I have ever run into. They make it weaker than tea.

"The towns and all the farm houses are blacked out at night here and all over England. It seems funny walking around and not knowing what you are going to step into or where you are going. The blackout starts about an hour before dark and lasts until daylight. I saw some bombings the Jerries did and they sure tore the hell out of things. I am as safe here as I am in the county jail; so far this place hasn't been touched. I was assigned to a machine gun crew last night but it seems like the only thing we will be shooting at are rabbits.

"Nan, did you and Ken go South. The weather is about the same here as it would be down there. I wouldn't mind it here so much if it didn't rain all the time.

"The way they do things here reminds me of the way we used to do things back in 1925. The women are doing a wonderful job here of helping us win the War, and most of them are in uniform.

"Give my love to Muz and tell her I will always love her. Love to all.

"(P. S. Answer Via V-MAIL it's faster.)"

My dad said that he really liked England. He was there for a year and a half before the invasion of Europe. He liked to go to the Piccadilly Circus, of course, and liked driving on "the wrong side of the road." He said that about the only thing he didn't like about England was mutton. "I just couldn't eat that stuff," he said, "and I can eat about anything."

He first served as a supply sergeant where he was in charge of all the cigarettes going to the Allied Forces in Europe. "If I had been a thief I would have been a millionaire," he once told me. He then became a technical sergeant in a motor transport unit. But what my dad always wanted to be was a belly-gunner on a B-17 Bomber. However, he just couldn't slim down enough—I guess by now you know how Sellses like to eat. Anyway, he really wanted to get a piece of Hitler, if not by the ground, then by the air. I think that my dad saw Hitler not only as an evil being, but also as someone who was keeping him from getting home to his Texas beauty in Austin. My dad did bring home those heavy leather and wool mittens and caps that the crews of the B-17s wore. When he was working at a supply center outside of London, he said that the roar of the bombers getting in formation would wake him up at 4:00 AM. He said the vibration of their engines was such that it shook the water out of the fire buckets in the barracks.

After the invasion, my dad fought his way through France and Germany, and was there until the Germans surrendered. He had accumulated enough time and combat points in Europe that he didn't have to go to the Pacific Theater and fight the Japanese. After V-E Day he sailed on the Queen Mary with a bunch of other soldiers, headed for Fort Dix, New Jersey.

Shortly after my dad's arrival back in the U. S., he and my mother were reunited, and it was another of those World War II moments. My dad sent my mama a telegraph from Fort Dix, telling her to meet him at the train station in Philadelphia on such and such a day and time. So my mama left from Austin to meet him. The reader must bear in mind that the two had known one another only for a short time, and that intense combat can certainly take its toll on a man. Anyway, they arrived at the train station in

Philadelphia at roughly the same time. The trains emptied their passengers, but Bob couldn't find Darline and Darline couldn't find Bob. They waited and looked, and looked and waited, but there was just no Bob nor Darline. They kept on looking. Finally, after just about everyone had cleared out of the train station, my dad walked up to this beautiful, brown haired girl and asked: "Are you Darline?" "Why yes I am," she responded, "and you must be Bob, my husband."

When the war was over and dad got out of the army, he returned to Dublin and became a well driller. He and a guy named Mutt Plummer drilled about all the wells in Dublin and around central Ohio. As soon as my dad would drill a well and set the pump, he would walk right into the kitchen and drink the biggest glass of water he could. He did that every time he drilled a well. He wasn't a chemist, but he could tell you what was in that water. He loved to drink well water. I think that my dad would like to have been an oil well driller—a 'wildcatter'. I remember we visited the oil fields in Texas and Oklahoma during a vacation there.

After drilling wells, my dad went into the water systems business, "Sells Wells and Water." After that, he had a small plumbing company, and for quite a while, working with Housing and Urban Development (HUD), he made a lot of money. My dad never worked for anyone else, and he hated the Internal Revenue Service. I guess he figured that the government owed him for what he went through in the War, and it seemed like he was always being audited by the IRS.

I cannot recall him ever missing a day of work. He gave me my work ethic. He was an astute businessman and was no "shrinking violet." He aggressively looked after his business. He had a real good attorney, and he wouldn't hesitate to sue people when they didn't pay his company for the work that they had done. He knew people in City Hall and perhaps, on some occasions, that worked to the advantage of his business. There were times when he used his fists when someone would try to beat him out of the money that he needed to feed his family and pay his workers. One time when one of his laborers was complaining about not getting paid on pay day, my dad wrote him a check on a three foot, two-by-four, and told him to take it down to the Huntington Bank at Arcadia and High Streets and have it cashed. Then he fired the guy. Huntington cashed the two-by-four. The president of the Huntington Bank at the time was friends with my father.

My dad really liked President Kennedy; maybe it was because of the fact that he had been in the War. Anyway, when President Kennedy was assassinated, my dad wrote Mrs. Kennedy a letter of condolence, and she (I'm sure it was actually her secretary) sent him a thank you letter back. He kept that letter under his glass-topped desk forever. He went and listened to one of my heroes, Robert Kennedy, speak when he was here in Columbus, and shook hands with the Senator from New York. He was the first person to tell me that Robert Kennedy, too, had been assassinated. My dad was Dublin When It Wasn't Doublin'.

When we lived in River Forest, we had a very narrow driveway, and there were overlooking hills in the road both to the north and south. It was Dublin Road, and it was very dangerous to pull in and out of the driveway. My dad called up the Department of Highway Safety and asked them to come out to the house so he could show them the problem. Well, after a while a representative did come out to inspect the situation. I guess he said that, although it was dangerous, there wasn't anything he could do. My dad asked him to come inside. They talked for a while, and later my dad asked the inspector if he would like a drink. Apparently the inspector was officially off duty. Well, the long and short of it is, that after about ¾ of a bottle of whiskey, our house at 5175 River Forest Drive ended up with the widest driveway entrance to a major road in the State of Ohio. It made for a great basketball court, too.

He worked hard and he played hard and he drank hard. He loved to go deep-sea fishing in Florida and Mexico. I remember that one morning he woke up and announced: "I think I'll go catch some sailfish today." He hadn't made any plans; he just called the airlines and booked a flight to Mexico for that day, and off he went. I think my dad was the most interesting person I have ever known.

My dad always did things to the extreme, or was "obsessed" as they now call it, even when it came to flying kites. My dad would take a box kite with a tail and attach it to about two hundred yards of monofilament line on his big Zebco 88 fishing reel and pole. He would then wait for a real windy day, and let that kite go. The stronger the wind, the quicker the line would whir off that fishing reel. Up, up, up those kites would go until you could just barely see them. After the kite had been high up, waving in the air for what seemed like forever, my dad would give it its freedom by cutting the fishing line. Anyway, the kites would fly away, free as a bird, and my dad would get a big smile on his face. For my dad, it was just like fishing, I guess. He would catch a big carp and then let it go, or put it in the bathtub to scare my mama.

Also, my dad loved to set fires. He would set huge fires to burn trash down at the Blankenships' and later at the Snouffer's because we had big trash dumps. He also liked to burn the spring grass. He would go out in the big fields behind the Blankenship house with his plumber's blow torch and set long, long lines of fire and watch the grass burn. One time a wind caught hold of the fire and the Dublin fire truck had to come down and contain it before the fire burned up all of Dublin. He loved to clean; he loved to keep things "neat as a pin," because, I guess in his mind, cleanliness was next to Godliness. And if that is true, he certainly has a place in heaven. He used to take his blowtorch and burn all the cobwebs in our basements. How he did this without ever setting our houses on fire, I don't know. Maybe he wanted to set them on fire, who knows?

And chemicals? He loved about every chemical compound that could be used for cleaning purposes. Among his favorites were: ammonia, Clorox, muriatic acid, sulfuric acid, and Armor All. I don't know how many "old" toilets he pulled out of Bexley and Upper Arlington, Ohio, for people who wanted to replace their old toilets with new "water efficient" toilets, but it was a bunch. He would then clean the old toilets with muriatic acid, and sell them back to other people who found out that their "new, water efficient" toilets really weren't that efficient and weren't very good at flushing. I don't know how much money he saved his customers when he told them to just pour bleach down their drains about once a month and they wouldn't have any drain problems. But, he really fell in love with Armor All. He used Armor All on everything, but most dangerously on his kitchen and bathroom floors. You really had to be careful when you walked on his kitchen and bathroom floors in your stocking feet. But, nothing for him, could hold a shine like Armor All, and he loved that shine.

My dad always liked to be the first person to have a new invention, and I am sure, that if he were still living, he would be texting and facebooking and cell phoning all over the place. After all, we had one of the first television sets in Dublin, and one of the first color television sets in Dublin, and one of the first microwave ovens. He brought the first ditch witch to Columbus to dig and lay drainage pipe. He "invented" the wide circumference, white plastic pipe mounted on the sides of plumbing trucks so that lengths of copper pipe could be carried safely and securely inside. He built, by hand, the first steel "pontoon" boat, that I know of, the African Queen. Funny though, he also got one of the first "labeling" machines that ever came on the market. I suppose one normally uses a labeling machine for things like remembering specific combinations or codes, or for identifying switches or valves, but my dad didn't use his that way. When you walked into his apartment, you immediately saw labels all over the place: for examples, on a lamp there was a label "lamp"; on a picture there was a label "picture"; and on a box of index cards there was a label "index cards." I don't know why he liked his labeling machine so much because his mind, at that time, was still very sharp. Maybe it turned into an obsession, or maybe he just liked to play with his labeling machine.

And, to be sure, my dad was an excellent plumber and mechanical engineer in his own right. I was amazed at how he could read schematics and blueprints and bid jobs. He never let architects dazzle him, and he always made sure that he received his draw on jobs (got paid) when he was supposed to. As a plumber, his work was immaculate. With the proper tools, there was nothing he couldn't do. I was always fascinated at how he could walk through the rough of a new apartment complex, take his time, and then bid a job to the dime. He could sweat a copper fitting "neat as a pin." And, like most plumbers, he was a strong man physically, who could contort his body into all types of tight, awkward positions. Many times at night he would have me come into his room and rub his back down with alcohol because his muscles ached so badly. To be sure he yelled like he was still in the army, and he cussed like he was still in the army, and when he wanted something, he wanted it now, but in the end he was a professional; and this brings me to a story that truly illustrates his character...

My dad bought a mobile home down in Malta, Ohio, close to McConnelsville, close to where my Uncle Don, or Uncle Dolly, or Uncle George lived – he went by three different names. Try to figure that out; I never knew what to call him. Anyway, the mobile home had no gas or electric. I think my dad bought it because, besides being nice, it was close enough for him and my mama to go to whenever they wanted get away, and he loved to fish in the Muskingum River, renowned for its giant catfish. My dad also had a boat, which he kept docked there. Anyway, it was in a beautiful location:

quiet and bounded by the great Muskingum River. The fact that the mobile home had no gas or electric when he bought it was of minor significance to my dad: didn't his crew of men consist of some of the best electricians, plumbers, and pipe fitters in central Ohio? So, one Friday evening after a day of work, his fleet of black AAA Plumbing's trucks headed south toward McConnelsville to complete a daunting mission set for the very next day: completely plumb, wire, and run the gas for the mobile home. My dad was paying his men double time for this job. The crew consisted of my cousin Dick Sells, Hammy Myers, and my brother Mike. They packed a cooler of sandwiches, pop, and beer for the next day, but they were under strict orders that they were not to eat until the job was done, and it was to be done by 6:00 PM. The crew was to arise at 6:00 AM and were to forgo breakfast and lunch and work straight through to 6:00 P.M. The men slept in the trailer, and the next morning my dad stood on the steps of the mobile home and addressed his "troops":

"I know it ain't goin' to be easy, men, but I'm goin' to be workin' right beside you. I wouldn't ask you to do anything that I wouldn't do. Dick, you're in charge of all the electric; Hammy, you're in charge of all the plumbing; and, Mike, you've got all the gas lines. You know how to do this; you've done it a thousand times before. At 6:00 PM I am going to go to the stove and turn on a gas burner so that I can have a hot cup of coffee. Do you have any questions?" There were no questions; they were all seasoned veterans; they all knew what to do.

Now, what my dad was asking for was no small feat. Just to plumb the trailer in one day, free from the interference of other workers, was no small task. But, to coordinate the efforts of all three workers at the same time was a Herculean task. On the other hand, my dad must have felt that not only they, but he, the boss, was up to it. As I have detailed, my dad was a lot of things, good and bad, but he never shied away from hard work, or the "Army" way. I don't know if my father ever served under General George Patton in the Third Army in Europe, but on that day, on that one day at the mobile home in Muskingum County, Ohio, my dad was George Patton. The only things that my dad lacked were a swagger stick and a pith helmet. He was literally everywhere driving his men: cutting and threading black iron pipe, sweating copper fittings, stripping electric wire, installing traps, checking fittings and couplings. "Go, men, go," he would yell out, "you only have three more hours left." Then, "onward, men, come on, you only have two hours left." And, then "one hour left; check your work, men, check it again." Finally, 6:00 PM (or 1800 hours) came. "Lay down your tools, men, you've got 'er done."

My dad walked into the mobile home, and an exhausted Hammy, Mike, and Dick followed close behind; everyone was drenched with sweat. My dad calmly went to the stove, filled the teakettle with water, placed it on the back burner, and then turned the knob for the gas stove. However, instead of a blue flame, out of the gas burner jumped a jet of water that almost reached the ceiling. No one said a word; they just hung their heads. I thought I saw a smirk on my Cousin Dick's face, but I sure didn't say anything. Finally, dumbfounded and in shock, my dad looked at the senior man of the crew, Hammy Myers, and asked, "Hammy, how in the heck could that have happened?" "I don't know, Bob, we must have crossed the water and the gas lines somehow, somewhere," Hammy said. "Well, men, we aren't done 'til the job's done. Let's go out and find the problem and fix it," my dad said, in an amazingly calm voice. They all went out, and they all went under the mobile home with flashlights until they found the problem and fixed it. Then they all went back inside and attacked their sandwiches, chips, cheese, pop, and beer while my dad drank his hot coffee, prepared on his gas stove. He looked across at his crew and addressed them.

"Men, when you do a job, do it right the first time; do it "meticulous." I don't know where my dad learned that word "meticulous," but sometimes a word or phrase would get into his mind, and he would never let it go: like the phrases, "Cleanliness is next to Godliness," and "Do something even if it's wrong." "You want to be meticulous, men, because if you're not, like tonight, I get call backs on jobs. And all call backs do is cost me money. So take your time, and do the job right the first time, and always be 'neat as a pin'. Don't think that I'm not proud of you, I am, and you will be paid well for your work. Thank you, men." At that point I expected my dad to say "Men….Dismissed" like in the army; but he didn't.

My dad always kept a lot of cash on him, just like Al Delewese and a lot of other people did when Dublin Wasn't Doublin'. He had a roll of a couple thousand dollars that he kept in the rafters down in the basement of our house in River Forest. When my dad sold that house, he forgot all about the loose cash that he had in the basement rafters. When he finally remembered, we were living at the Snouffer's on the river. He paid the new owner of our old home a visit, under some pretext. Diverting the new owner's attention to the outside of the house, he quickly crept down into the basement and snatched his money back.

He would forget things even when he was younger. I think it's a Sells' trait. He once bought a Lincoln Continental, the one with the suicide doors, from a friend at a bar (of course), and forgot that he had bought the car. He was called about three days later by the bar owner to come and get his new car.

He was sharp, though, even when he was somewhat under the influence. One night, or early morning, he was driving home in his RV, and he must have been weaving a little as he was going north on Dublin Road toward our house. He was only about a mile away from home when he was stopped by a Franklin County Sheriff's Deputy. The Deputy told my dad to get out of the RV, which my dad did. The Sheriff then proceeded to give him a sobriety test by laying two quarters, two dimes, and a nickel on the side of the road. "Sir," the Deputy said," please tell me how much money I have placed on the berm." My dad looked down at the coins, reached into his pocket, pulled out a quarter, and flipped it on the ground. "There, there's a dollar," my dad said, "now, go buy yourself a hamburger." My dad got in his RV, drove home, and that was that.

Like I said, my dad quit wearing regular clothes when he got older, just like the old man, his dad, did. My dad ordered a whole bunch of jump suits from Nieman Marcus down in Texas. These jumpsuits were really something—red, blue, yellow, orange, and even purple— and you could just about see the real loud boxer undershorts that he wore under them: polka-dot, stripes, and paisley. The jump suits bordered on the transparent, but it didn't seem to bother my dad in the least. One time

DAD AT MY COLLEGE GRADUA-TION PARTY IN ONE OF HIS JUMP SUITS

he had his "getty-up" on, and he asked me if I wanted to go with him to the airport to pick up my mama. "You're going to have to change your clothes, dad, before I go out in public with you." He went by himself.

Like I said, my father made a lot of money real fast when he was working with the Department of Housing and Urban Development. He bought this huge recreational vehicle, which he used to work from. Doubtless he wrote it off as a business expense. He would pull up in front of an old HUD house, literally jump out of his RV with his tape recorder in hand, go inside, and list all of the repairs needed to bring the home up to code in order to make it nice and livable. I remember one day when I was with him. He was in his "getty-up": yellow see through jump suit with a big gold buckle and blue boxer shorts beneath. He pulled up in front of a HUD house, and jumped out of the bus with his tape recorder in hand. There in front of him sat this little African-American boy on a bench, waiting for the bus; he was probably eight or nine, maybe ten. He sat there and looked at my dad from head to toe, and then he looked at him again. Then, in the softest, most respectful voice that I have ever heard, he stared at my dad with his big brown eyes and asked him one question: "Pardon me, Sir, is the circus in town?" It was one of the few times that my father was ever at a loss for words, but he didn't quit wearing his jump suits, or his loud underwear beneath them. Seemed like we couldn't shake off our circus ancestry.

My dad lived when Dublin Wasn't Doublin', and he and all of the other people there were giving and fun loving. I can remember him with Al Delewese in the Nite Club and how they would sit and talk and just laugh and laugh and drink beer all night long. And, I can remember, that my dad, and some farmers, when they came into town, would just stand behind a car parked on the curb, tell stories and relieve themselves whenever they needed to. I remember one night that my mama made two lemon meringue pies, and Jughead Sharp came over to play gin rummy with my dad. During the course of the gin rummy games, Jughead ended up eating both pies. He used to tease my mama about that. I don't think she held it against him. Jughead was a huge man, a tractor-trailer driver, and he had a big appetite.

My dad was a real giving person. Like I said, we had about the first TV set in Dublin, and everyone in Dublin came over to see it, even the old man. We had one of the first color TV sets in Dublin when we lived on Marion Street, and everyone was invited to see that peacock from NBC spread her tail feathers. My dad told me that one night when he was out on the road (he always wanted to become a truck driver, so after he "retired" from the plumbing business, he bought an 18-wheeler), he pulled into a buffet where there were a couple of busloads of high school marching band members standing in line, waiting to eat. "Put it all on my bill," he told the cashier. Sounds like something he would do. He probably didn't even know the name of the high school. I remember that when we lived down on the river at Blankenships' we had an old Chris Craft boat. She was a real beauty. He would drive it down the river under Fishinger Bridge, and would offer boat rides, especially to little children standing on the bank with their parents. He loved Christmas and always went to great lengths to decorate the house with big Santas and candy canes. For Thanksgiving, he always made sure his workers had a turkey or a ham. But it wasn't just him; that's the way it was with everyone in Dublin: giving, kind and forgiving.

After he retired from plumbing work, my dad did some really neat things. Like I said, he drove a tractor-trailer, mainly back and forth from Columbus to Chicago, and back and forth from Baltimore to Columbus. He hauled boxed freight. Later, he became the treasurer for the Jaymar Corporation, and went out West, to Winnemucca, Nevada, and drilled core samples to explore for gold. My dad told me that if you ever get involved in a corporation, don't worry about being the president or the vice-president; be the treasurer, because he is the one who signs the checks and knows where the money is going and that is the most important thing. They didn't find any gold, but my dad had a lot of fun driving around in the desert in his pick-up truck, which the company paid for. My dad sent me a postcard with a picture of a "jackalope" on it and at first I believed that they really existed. I am still pretty gullible.

One time when I was first in the Chillicothe VA Hospital, in the fall of 1973, my mama and my dad came down in their motor home to visit me. Though he wasn't supposed to, my dad took me for a ride, and we ended all the way up in Jerome, Ohio. "Darline?" he asked, as he was reading a sign on the side of the road "do we have a turkey yet for Thanksgiving?" "No, Bob, we don't." she replied. "Well," he said, "I'll just go get one." The sign was advertising a turkey shoot that was being held that day, and at that time, in Jerome. So, we went to it and what followed really amazed me. He borrowed someone's shotgun to shoot clay pigeons. I was afraid he would embarrass himself. He wasn't a spring chicken at the time, and it was a borrowed shotgun. Well, the first time he shot, he hit nine out of ten clay pigeons; the second time he shot, he hit ten out of ten; and the third time he shot, he hit ten out of ten. He won three turkeys; kept one, and gave the other two away.

Another time we were up at a guy named Ted Spooner's house north of the zoo off Riverside Drive. Ted had a real nice pond, and we were fishing. I was fishing across the pond from my Cousin Dick. Nobody was catching anything. Ted, who owned a car dealership, and my dad were out on the back porch of Ted's house. Ted had an M-1 rifle and asked my dad if he had ever shot one. My dad said that he had, a few times. My dad took aim at my Cousin Dick's bobber, which was about one hundred and ten yards away from my father across the pond. "Be careful, Bob," Ted said, "that gun's loaded." "Ted, that's the only way to keep 'em. It's just the 'empty' ones that kill people." And with that, he looked down those open sights, and gently squeezed off a round, and there was a big bang, and my cousin's bobber jumped about three feet out of the water. That was all the action we got out of that pond that day, but it was enough.

When my dad was in his seventies and couldn't move around like when he was young, he lived in a little apartment on Ferris Avenue in the northern part of Columbus. This was after my mama had died. He liked to sit in his big chair in the living room and put birdseed out on the balcony for the birds to eat. My dad became a bird watcher. My Uncle Ted did about the same thing when he got older, but he fed peanuts to the squirrels when he lived down on Maynard Avenue. Anyway, my dad would lie back in his recliner and look through the sliding glass doors and watch the cardinals and blue jays and finches and even the sparrows eat his birdseed. There was one problem: a rogue chipmunk that would raid the concrete balcony floor and eat all the birdseed and scare the birds away. My dad didn't like that. What he devised to solve the problem truly would have made Rube Goldberg, the famous inventor, proud. I apologize to the members of PETA in advance, because I am going to offend them. My dad took an electric skillet with an extension cord and plugged it into an electrical outlet inside his apartment. He turned the skillet up to the highest heat setting, and propped it up at an angle, with a piece of wood on the balcony floor. He tied a long cord around the piece of wood, and ran it all the way back to his recliner. Then, he put lots of birdseed under the electric skillet. Then he reclined himself in his chair, held the cord in his hand, and waited, just like he was fishing. He didn't have to wait too long. The chipmunk scurried under the skillet to grab the bait and my dad just yanked on that cord. Fried chipmunk! But the birds lived happily ever after.

There was another thing he once did, and this was when mama was alive and they were living in an apartment on Cleveland Avenue that I thought was pretty neat. One afternoon he was alone in the apartment working on the window air conditioner, and he heard someone rattle the front door knob. I don't think it bothered him at first, because he said he just kept on working on the air conditioner. But, then, when he heard the doorknob rattle again, he slipped into the bedroom and pulled out his German luger. Ever since I could remember, we had that luger, and we used to shoot it a lot when we lived at the Snouffer's on Dublin Road, or Donnegal Cliffs, as it is now called. My dad walked quietly to the side of the kitchen door, held up the luger, and put his left hand on the doorknob, holding the luger in his right hand. As soon as the door handle started to rattle again, my dad jerked the door open and onto the kitchen floor, head first, flew the would-be burglar. Needless to say, he had come to the wrong place. My dad "politely" told him to get down on his knees, made him put his hands behind his head, and then my dad placed the barrel of the luger right up against the would be burglar's temple. "Please don't kill me!" the man cried out "Please don't kill me!" "I ought to kill you for being so stupid, you dumb son-of-a-gun!" my dad calmly said, "That door wasn't even locked; you could have walked right in if you had just turned the handle." My dad called the Sheriff's Department, and they arrived right away. It turned out that the burglar was on parole, and they just hauled him away.

There's one more little story about my dad that I'd like to share. My wife and I were living in Clintonville on Longview Avenue, and we were having electrical problems. We had that old knob and tongue groove wire running through the house, and we were having electrical shorts or something. Anyway, I called up my dad. "Don't worry," he said, "I'll be right over." He came into the house and stomped down the stairs like King Kong looking for a big banana. "Where's your electrical box?" he asked. "Over there," I said. "Tim," he bellowed, "go get me the biggest Phillips screwdriver you've got. "Dad," I cautioned, "are you sure you know what you're doing? "Tim," he bellowed, a little insulted, "I've fixed more electrical boxes than Carter has little liver pills." So, he began poking around in that electrical box with that big screwdriver—poke, jab, poke. And then, all of a sudden, there was an explosion the likes of which I had never heard before. There were sparks like fire crackers everywhere; skyrockets in flight; the screw driver was frozen in my dad's hand; and he went back pedaling, doing the Texas two-step, at a tremendous rate of speed toward the back wall of the basement. He hit the wall with great force, and slid down to the basement floor on his rear end. What made the whole scene even funnier, afterwards of course, is that he was wearing one of his jump suits. It was circus time all over again! Anyway, he was OK. He looked up at me with a "shocked" look on his face and just said, "Tim, that wasn't supposed to happen." I looked at the head of that Phillip's screwdriver, and half of it had melted. I still have it, and think of my dad every time I see it. It's not good for anything, though, just a souvenir.

He had probably the greatest sense of humor I have ever seen, one that rivaled Jim McCoy's. "Don't ever take this life too seriously," he would tell me, "You'll never get out of it alive." Another one of his favorite sayings, probably derived from his military experience was the following: "I'm just living on borrowed time." I guess he knew that from all the fighting he had seen and done during the War. Whenever I was indecisive or in a quandary about something, he would say, "Do something, even if it's wrong!"

He had all of his teeth pulled (on the same day and without Novocain) and then got a set of false teeth. Soon afterwards, he went down to the VA to have his prostate checked. When the VA physician told him to roll over and inserted his hand up my dad's rectum, my dad's new teeth shot out of his mouth like a missile and went clear across the examining room. The physician went over and calmly picked them up. "How's my prostate?" my dad inquired. "I don't know about your prostate," the doctor replied, "but somebody made you a pretty good set of teeth!" He liked to tell that story. My wife had once made a beautiful Thanksgiving dinner, and my dad came over to eat with us. We said grace and began to eat. "Heck, Debbie (my wife), I forgot my teeth," and he just leaned back in his chair and laughed and laughed.

I remember one particular lunch Dad, Danny Lee and I had at Reeb's Restaurant on East Livingston Avenue in Columbus. I had been working with Danny Lee that morning, and it was a really hot June day, almost 90 degrees. Danny Lee and I, please let me rephrase that, Danny Lee was digging a trench to lay some PVC drainage pipe. As usual, I just stood there transfixed by his skill with a shovel and a spade. Only Him Frank Kelly could out do Danny Lee when it came to digging. By the time 11:30 AM rolled around, Danny Lee was just drenched in sweat. He always just wore a white T-Shirt. While he was wringing wet, I had managed to remain pretty cool.

Now, back in those days, people weren't obsessed with "hydrating" themselves with water like they are now days. Heck, Danny Lee had managed to dig about a three and a half foot trench with nary a slug of water. My dad came cruising over to our job site about this time in one of the big black plumbing trucks, and hollered out to my cousin, "Danny Lee, do you want to go down to Reeb's and eat some liver and onions with your Uncle Bob?" "I sure do, Uncle Bob," he answered. I was half ashamed. I loved liver and onions, but I hadn't even worked up a sweat. I was hoping that my dad didn't notice, but by the beauty of the hole that was dug, I guess he figured out, as usual, that Danny had been doing all the work.

As soon as we got into Reeb's and sat down, Danny picked up a glass of water (those were the days when restaurants sat out glasses of water before you asked for them), threw back his elbow, and made all of that water disappear down his esophagus in one big gulp. Another waiter happened to stroll by. "I'll have another glass of water, please," Danny politely asked. The waiter brought him another glass of water, and he downed the second one even faster than the first. Finally, the waiter arrived to take our order and Danny quickly looked up at him, "I'd like another glass of water, please."

I could tell that my dad was hungry. You eat with a man all of your life and you know when he's hungry. But, my dad loved his nephew; Danny Lee could do no wrong in his eyes. Danny always kept his big black plumbing truck spotless, and cleanliness was next to Godliness in my dad's eyes. My dad folded his menu (he knew what he wanted anyway) and looked up at the waiter:

"Do you know somethin'?" my dad asked the "water" waiter.

"No, Sir" replied the waiter.

"You'd save yourself a heckuva lot of time if you'd just run a garden hose from the kitchen to this table for this kid, because if you don't, he'll wear the soles off your shoes askin' for more water; and none of us is goin' to get anything to eat. Well, Danny Lee didn't get a garden hose, but we did get three big pitchers of water set on our table. The bacon on the liver and onions was extra crispy—just the way I like it.

Danny Lee himself tells a pretty good story about my dad, but first let me preface his tale. In all the years that my mama and dad were married, through all the fights that I heard them have, the subject of infidelity never arose—not once. To the very best of my knowledge, my mama and my dad stayed true to one another. But, back to Danny's story. My dad's plumbing company, AAA Plumbing Supply and Service, was located at 1000 Dublin Road, just north of the Franklin County Engineers Building. There was at that time, a real nice steak house called Jack Bowman's. Jack's was right across the road from the Grandview Inn. Anyway, on his way home, my dad passed Jack Bowman's, and since they had a nice bar, and my dad was certainly no stranger to alcohol, he stopped there frequently, and thus became a close friend of the owner, Jack Bowman. Jack was a real nice fellow, had a pretty daughter who I always wanted to take out, but she was out of my league, and Jack served succulent steaks and seafood. My mama and dad took me there after my high school graduation for a lobster dinner. They took me to Seafood Bay on North High Street for a lobster dinner when I graduated from the 8th grade. My dad always took me out for lobster dinners when we went up to Cleveland to watch the Yankees play. But, enough of lobsters, my favorite food, and back to Danny's tale…

Behind the bar at Jack's was a nice old lady. She was a pretty good bartender, or barmaid, as they say now. Mary was up there in years, but nobody ever gave her any lip. She had been around and she knew how to handle herself. Mary liked my dad, and the relationship was mutual. They both respected one another; they both had led hard lives. Mary had heard just about everything behind that bar, so what my dad had to dish out was totally harmless to her. I think my dad must have thought of Mary as an older sister, of which he had many.

"Mary, would you please shake me up a martini?" Now, the Suburban was one of the few places where my dad would order a martini.

"Right with you, Bob"

Could you please put three olives in it for me, Mary? I think my blood pressure's low, and I need some salt in my system. You know, Mary, I'm just livin' on borrowed time."

"I know that Bob. We all are."

"Mary, when I come in here and see you, I don't feel like I need to see a doctor."

"Thank you, Bob. That's kind of you."

"Mary, can I tell you something?"

"Bob, you know that you can tell me anything."

"Mary, you look marvelous tonight."

"Thank you, Bob."

"And Mary, your beautiful black hair—did you have your hair done today, Mary?"

"I did, Bob, and thank you for noticing."

"Mary, could I please tell you one more thing?"

"Anything, Bob."

"That is the most beautiful red dress that I have ever seen in my life, and I have been all over England and France. You wear that dress so well, Mary."

"Thank you, Bob."

For a long while, my dad just sat at the bar, twirling his olives around with his stirring fork. A quiet fell over the bar at Jack Bowman's Suburban Steak House."

"Mary."

"Yes, Bob."

"There's only one thing that red dress needs."

"What's that, Bob?"

"My arms around it so I could give you a big kiss."

Mary laughed, "Bob, go on home to that beautiful Texas wife of yours and that horse you call a dog before I call the sheriff on you. No more three olive martinis for you."

"Good night, Mary."

"Good night, Bob; sweet dreams."

Well, in regard to my dad, I've saved the best story for last. I have heard the story recounted many times by him. You see, When Dublin Wasn't Doublin', the game was baseball. Dublin had some real good football and basketball teams too. We had some good old, corn-fed ball players, but as long as I can remember, Dublin has always been known for baseball. Bobby Joe Bailey and Benny Deleweses' team was the runner-up for the state championship in 1955 and David Bakenhaster and Mike Ryans' team was the runner-up for the state championship in 1964. My dad sponsored an independent baseball team once, and I remember them playing down at Jet (Clipper) Stadium. I remember Chuck Roll pitching and Dick Termeer playing first base. I remember that Benny Delewese almost hit one over the fence. I remember when David Bakenhaster struck out twenty-two men in a seven inning game—a passed ball. Of course, I grew up with probably the greatest all-around athlete and baseball player of them all, Mike Ryan. As I said before, there is no doubt in my mind that he would have become a major league second baseman if he had not gotten injured. So we played baseball, and we loved baseball. In many respects, it was our religion. Long before Bobby Joe Bailey and Benny Delewese, of course, we had Dublin's Dirty Dozen, and remember, my Uncle Ted and Louie Geese played for them. You could say that baseball ran through Dublin's veins.

In regard to the professional teams, most of the baseball fans in Dublin either leaned toward the Cincinnati Reds, the Cleveland Indians, or the Saint Louis Cardinals—the old Columbus Red Birds having been the farm club of the Cardinals. But my dad, well, he was different; he loved the Yankees. I don't know why he loved the Yankees; maybe because during the War he was a "Yank." I don't know. All I know is this: when the Yankees came into Cleveland to play the Indians, he would take my big brother Mike and me to watch them play. He would also sometimes go up with Al and Nardine Delewese, but they were Indians fans. We would stay in the Cleveland Sheraton Hotel (my mama went too), and we always got real good seats. My earliest memory of being a Yankee fan was when Don Larsen threw his perfect game in the World Series against the Dodgers in 1956, and Mantle made that great catch in centerfield. I remember listening to the Yankee games every night on the radio and keeping score. I loved Red Barber. I remember staying up into the wee hours of the morning when the Yankees played on the Coast.

He loved, and we loved it, when he would take us to Cleveland to watch the Yankees play. He even managed to befriend some of the Yankee ballplayers. My dad said that he got to know Ralph Terry, a pitcher for the Yankees, on one of his trips to Cleveland, and he said that Ralph, being from Oklahoma, used to like Westerns, so they went and saw *Last Train from Boot Hill* together. My dad also said that up in Cleveland he got the opportunity to meet Ryne Duren, a relief pitcher for the Yankees, who was notorious then for a blazing fastball, poor vision, and a strong taste for alcohol. I guess that Duren was pretty wild when he pitched, and hitters would not "dig in" against him. I heard that he once hit a batter in the on-deck circle, and that he once threw a warm-up pitch over the screen behind the plate. Anyway, my dad really liked Ryne Duren, and I am happy to say that Mr. Duren finally forsook alcohol, and lived the rest of his life in sobriety. But, I am getting way ahead of myself…

When I was ten or eleven, my dad took our family to Cleveland to watch a doubleheader with the Yankees. We got there real early, so we decided to have breakfast in the dining room of the Cleveland Sheraton Hotel. We had just sat down and ordered, when in walked Mickey Mantle, Roger Maris, Whitey Ford, and Tony Kubek. Mickey Mantle sat down at the table right beside me. I was scared to death and afraid to speak—or eat. Asking him for an autograph was out of the question. I remember the following things about that baseball icon of the 1950's and 1960's. He didn't seem to be six feet tall as he was always listed; rather, he was more like five feet ten inches or five feet eleven inches. I remembered that he ordered a pink grapefruit. And last of all, he had the most massive neck and shoulders that I had ever seen on a human being. I don't remember what the rest of the players did—I just remember that Mickey Mantle ate a grapefruit.

So, my dad would take us up to Cleveland when the Yankees came in. I once nervously asked a waitress if she thought the Yankees would win that day. "Honey," she said, "the Yankees win as soon as their train pulls into the station." That was good news.

As was his custom after a ballgame, especially a night game, when my mama and brother and I were tucked safely away in the Cleveland Sheraton, my dad liked to go out carousing, or drinking, for lack of a more appropriate term. He would frequent bars in and around the hotel district, and one night he hit it big, one night his gift of gab was surpassed by the ultimate gift of gabber, who once testified in front of a Senate Select Committee regarding baseball. As I said before, it was an epiphany for my father, and may have been the closest thing to a religious experience that he ever had. He met his idol, and this is how the story goes. I will do my best to give you the dialogue as my dad told it to me, and others, many, many times.

My dad walked into the Old New Englander, a downtown Cleveland Bar, around midnight. This time he was appropriately dressed in a suit and tie, not in one of his jumpers. I think the year was 1960; the same year I had "breakfast" with Mickey Mantle. My dad could always light up a room just by saying, "Hello!" I don't know how he did it, maybe it was just a manic charisma, maybe it was years of country charm refined by World War II; but he could certainly light up a room. However, this room was already lit up when he entered it. There, sitting at the bar, talking to a reporter, was the master of circumlocution, the man who had once managed the Great DiMaggio, the master of "Stengelese," none other than the manager of the famed New York Yankees himself, Casey Stengel. My dad immediately recognized him, and did not hesitate to make his acquaintance. Dad was never bashful. Once he asked the King of England if he would sign a blank check for him. I'll tell you about that shortly.

"Excuse me, Mr. Stengel, my name is Bob Sells, and I have a small plumbing company in Dublin, Ohio. I just want to thank you for all of the happiness that you and the Yankees have brought to my family and me over the years."

"Did you go to the ballgame today?" Casey asked my dad.

"I did," my dad replied.

"Did you pay to get in?" Casey asked?

"I did," my dad replied.

"Well, sit down then," Casey said, "and we'll talk a little baseball."

And so they talked and talked and talked into the wee hours of the morning. My dad said that Casey very seldom referred to any ballplayer by name, and if he did, he would use their last names properly. My dad said that you really had to pay close attention to what he was talking about because he rambled a lot, and that it was easy to get confused listening to him speak:

"Well, we ain't got no bad team this year. We got that big moose over there on the first base, and he fields the ball real good (Bill 'Moose' Skowron). Big feller and can hit the ball to right field when we need it, when you got a runner on first. He can hit it over the left field fence too when you make a mistake to him. At shortstop and second, we got what I call the 'milkshake boys' (Tony Kubek and Bobby Richardson) because you never see them in a place like this especially at this hour. They make the plays, that we need, and they turn the double play about as good as it can be done. At third, we are set real good, as we have what is called a human vacuum cleaner down there who can make just about everything look easy and who can hit the ball over the fence when the occasion arises (Cletus Boyer). In the outfield, in the left field, we have two pretty good fellers in Mr. Cerv and Mr. Lopez, who can make the plays in the field and hit pretty good too, which is always an added attraction. Now, Mr. Howard and Mr. Berra can share the catching position, and the both of these two can also be called upon to play the left field, and I appreciate them for their flexibility and team spirit in that matter. Now, everyone thinks that Mr. Berra is not too smart because he talks a little different and sometimes says things, which can be taken in two or three different ways. I find that a funny thing myself because I have never seen him forget to cash his World Series checks, or make bad investments with the money he has earned. In centerfield, well, we got that feller from Oklahoma who can hit the ball out of any park, including Yellowstone, from either side of the plate (Mickey Mantle). I keep asking him why he swings so hard all of the time; you just need to hit the ball over the fence for a home run, not out of the ball park. I tell him that. I'm an old man, but he looks at me like I was born yesterday, like I was always old, like I was born old. He can make the plays in centerfield, too; you just need to ask Mr. Larsen who pitched that perfect game for us in the World Series about that. In right field, well, as soon as I seen that short, sweet swing of his, I told Mr. Weiss, my boss, that we had to have this feller playing for us, that with that little porch we have in our stadium, he would hit a lot of home runs (Roger Maris). Pitching—we got some pitching; of course, we got that little left-hander they call the "Chairman of the Board" (Whitey Ford). He's pretty slick, which is another name for him. I don't pitch him much against teams like Kansas City and the Senators; I spot him up 'cause he just don't rattle in those big games. Lots of time they accuse him of putting things on the ball, or cutting it; maybe he does and maybe he doesn't. It's a mystery to me. You will probably want to ask me who was the greatest which I ever managed. Well, let me save you the question. It was the Great DiMaggio. I never had to tell him nuthin, nuthin. He managed himself. So, now we have talked a little baseball...."

Well, my dad was never quite the same after his conversation with Casey. He returned to Dublin and regaled all of his friends and enemies about what had happened. I was so happy for him. It was like he had become an astronaut or something. He still drank a lot and he could still get mean, but there was a softer side to him. We still kept going up to Cleveland. My dad always wore a suit when he went to the ballgames up there; you can figure out why.

My dad never talked about the War until much, much later in his life I don't know exactly how much combat my father saw in World War II, but I do know that he saw a lot. His Department of Defense Form 214 states the following under Battles and Campaigns: "Northern France and Rhineland." Under Decorations and Citations, it reads: "Good Conduct Medal, American Defense Service Medal, and European African and Middle Eastern Service Medal with 2 Bronze Stars." In his last Will and Testament, my dad stated that he fought at Cherbourg, France, and at the Battle for the Bridge at Remagen, Germany. World War II was the defining epoch in my father's life, and it is inscribed on his footstone in the Dublin Cemetery.

I asked him once if he had been afraid to cross the English Channel to go into France. "Heck no I wasn't afraid," he practically shouted, "before we went over there, they kept us in the hold of an Arabian ship for seven days and seven nights. I would have fought anybody just to get off that darned ship!"

He told me that one time, after he had crossed the Channel and was in France, he and his company marched all day and most of the night to rendezvous with another company. No one in my dad's platoon could get to sleep that night because there was a big German shepherd dog barking nearby. My dad went into the orderly room and told the company clerk

that if he didn't get somebody to shut that dog up, he would shoot it. "You can't shoot that dog," the clerk said, "that's the company commander's dog." "I don't give a rat's a** if it's the General's dog. We're tired, and we need to sleep." The dog didn't shut up, so my dad just went up and shot that dog right through the head. He lost a stripe for it, but since the combat was so fierce where he was, he quickly earned it back.

DAD AND ONE OF HIS BUDDIES WITH DAD'S JEEP "MISS DARLINE"

My dad said that the German soldiers were good soldiers, especially their Non-Commissioned Officers, but said that they lacked the initiative of the American soldier. "The Germans were very punctual. They would fire their artillery right on the second, and so we knew when they would start and could be sure to be done with our lunch before they began. Also, the German soldier seemed to lack the quick, fighting intuition of the American GI. It seemed as though the Germans were always waiting for a command from their Non Commissioned Officers (NCOs) to move, whereas a GI would just react to the situation automatically. It seemed to me that the Germans were always afraid to make a tactical error, a mistake. So, to make a long story short, their NCO's made good targets. I never thought that I could shoot another human being, but you lie there and see your best friends get shot up and blown to bits and then it's not hard. For me it was like shooting deer on the Farm."

My dad got lost behind German lines once after an assault, and for eight days he survived on just spring wheat. He finally made it back to his unit. I'm glad he did.

During the Korean War my dad's old first sergeant called him up and asked him if he would re-enlist. My dad told him that he had a wife and a family and a business—and that he had already killed enough people for one lifetime.

In my dad's later years I liked to go over to his apartment and listen to him tell stories. He became a rather well-known local raconteur in the service organizations he frequented, the American Legion and the Veterans of Foreign Wars. His stories were also enjoyed at our home when he came to visit. In his apartment, he kept a little display of ivory like elephants beneath his television stand. The elephants were in procession, just like in the circus, holding one another's tails. He never lost his love for elephants. As he talked, he would lean back in his chair, close his eyes, let out a sigh of air, put his fingers together with a cigarette in one hand and begin (every story) the same way. I wish that I could describe for you the manner and tone in which he spoke; it was kind of between a soft bellow and a sweet sigh. He would begin: "Tim, when I was in the Army, I had a friend, he was the best friend that I ever had, he was like a brother to me, we did everything together, I will never, ever forget him…what in the h— was his name?"

My dad had some good Army stories—the lighter ones. He was in the Army with Billy Conn, the heavyweight fighter who fought Joe Lewis twice for the Heavyweight Championship of the World. Conn had Lewis out boxed twice and was up on Lewis on points until the later rounds. My dad said that he gently asked Conn how he let Lewis get away from him. Conn looked at my dad and said, "You have to knock the Champ out, and I couldn't do it." He also told dad that Joe was so strong that when he hit you on the arms it hurt.

While my dad was in the army in England, he actually met the King and Queen. It seems as though my dad was in charge of a motor pool and some of his men had gotten into trouble at a hotel. I think it was the Savoy Hotel, and my dad was called to come and retrieve them back to their unit. They had been locked up in a little room down in the basement of the hotel after becoming quite rowdy the night before. Anyway, my dad and another soldier drove to the hotel in the morning, and when they arrived, there was quite a commotion. It seems as though the King and Queen were on their way to the hotel to pay a visit. Everyone was standing in line, so my dad and his friend took their position at the end of the line. Down the line went the King and Queen saying hello and good morning to everyone. All the ladies curtsied, and the men shook hands. When the King came to my dad, the King asked him, "And how are you enjoying your stay in England, Yank?" To which my dad replied, "Well, Your Highness, I'd be enjoying it a lot more if you would sign this blank check I have in my back pocket." He said that the King chuckled, and said that it really wouldn't be "quite proper."

At this point, I would take a moment (and a few lines) to acknowledge and thank a friend of mine and a friend of my father, Roger "Buddy" Essig. Buddy was a true and faithful companion to my father during my father's later years, and I will always be indebted to him for his kindness. "Buddy" is the son of Roger Essig, Sr. who owned Carr Manufacturing down on Naughten Street in Columbus. Buddy's father was just a wonderful gentleman, and he and my dad were close friends and did a lot of business together. After Mr. Essig passed away, well, I think my dad sort of "adopted" Buddy (or would have liked to). My dad and Buddy had two great things in common: they loved to drink beer, and they loved to eat. They loved eating and drinking together, and I think that Buddy liked to listen to my dad's stories. I don't know which of them could drink more beer; Buddy was a lot younger, but my dad had much more experience. Buddy was a great basketball player at Dublin High School. He had this beautiful, left-handed jump shot with a perfect rotation on the ball. He always reminded me of Gail Goodrich from the Los Angeles Lakers when he shot. Buddy would have scored a lot more points if Mike Ryan had passed him the ball more. He also had the prettiest girl in high school for a girlfriend, Trudy VanArsdale. She was a cheerleader, and I still like to tease Buddy about her when I see him.

I once thought of going to a function to hear General Colin Powell speak, and told my dad that I bet he hadn't ever seen a four-star general before. "Tim," he said, "you have to remember this. When I was in England, before the Invasion, all of us knew we were going over the Channel, we just didn't know when. England, then, was like one gigantic aircraft carrier. The Allies had commandeered everything in the Western Hemisphere that could float and taken it to England. So, I saw Eisenhower, Mark Clark, and Patton." That was the last "bet you" question that I asked my dad.

One day I was watching a war movie, and the name of the movie was "The Bridge at Remagen," the battle he had fought in. "Look at this, dad, look at this. This is cool." He never lifted his head; he just kept pecking away on his electric typewriter, typing up bills to be sent out to his customers.

I used to love to work with my dad on the plumbing trucks even though I didn't know what I was doing, and he would yell at me a lot. I used to enjoy going down to Carr Manufacturing and seeing Mr. Essig, Buddy, and Big Jim, the warehouse man. I used to enjoy sitting on the stools at the front counter while other plumbers came in and got their supplies. Most of all, though, I used to enjoy going to lunch with Mr. Essig, Buddy, and my dad. There was always a lot of food to eat and it was really good, and it was "real" food. In fact, my dad knew just about all the best places in Columbus to eat since he worked on the water systems of a lot of the restaurants. On some occasions we would walk into the kitchens and eat right there with the cooks. But, even if we had our work clothes on and my dad felt like eating in the more formal dining rooms, that's where we would eat. The best restaurants I remember eating at with my dad when we were out working were the Jai Lai, Reeb's, Plank's, and at the Biltmore, when we were on the west side of Columbus.

When I worked for my dad, we usually ate lunch together, and invariably he would ask the waiter or waitress, "Do you know what the Germans used to make Sauerkraut (one of his favorite dishes) out of during World War II?" They would hesitate, and then timidly say, "No." "Cabbage," my dad would say, and then he would laugh out loud. I guess he had earned the right to make that joke.

Like I said, my dad had a water systems business, and he had accounts with everybody from surgeons to Saint Brendan's Catholic Church. My personal favorite was Gable's Dairy Farm on Godown Road because they always gave me as much ice cream as I could eat when I went there with my dad. My dad had all kinds of different clients, but one in particular stuck out in his mind, and when he got a little "oiled" up, he loved to tell the story of the convent. He assumed the position. He leaned back in his recliner, cigarette in hand, the tips of his fingers touching one another, making a little tent as he riffled the tips of his fingers back and forth in sequence. He took a deep drag on his cigarette, exhaled slowly, and closed his eyes:

"Tim, I remember an afternoon, it could have been in the late morning of the Spring—or, maybe early Summer—when I got called over to the Catholic Convent there on Olentangy River Road at Henderson. I took care of all their water systems, and Sister Mary was there—and what in the heck was their problem? It could have been in the drains—it could have been the hot water tank—or, it could have been that they were not getting enough water pressure in the convent. It was a big place. Anyway, Mary was showing me around the place and explaining the problem to me like she always did. I liked Sister Mary; she was a tough old gal, but was always nice to me. Anyway, she's explaining to me what's wrong when, all of a sudden, I hear in the background a voice I know I have heard before, a long time ago. I'm listening real close to this voice in the background all the while and trying to pay attention to what Sister Mary is saying at the same time. I know that I've heard this voice before, and it's driving me crazy. Finally, I can't take it anymore, and I excuse myself from Sister Mary and watch this other nun as she is talking. It took a while to register, but it finally hit me, as the voice was unmistakable. I took one more long look at that nun who was talking, and just said: 'Axis Sally (the official propaganda voice of the German Third Reich), what in the heck are you doing in here; and how in the heck did you ever get out of Germany?' Quickly, Sister Mary stepped between us and told me, 'She's no longer Axis Sally, Bob; her new name is Sister Magdalene (or something like that), and she's with us now.' Well, my dad looked at Sally, and then he looked at Sister Mary—for a long time. Finally he spoke, 'Sister Mary, whoever you take in here is none of my doggone business, but for three years while I was in England and France and Germany I listened to her mouth go on and on about how Hitler was going to defeat us and how us GIs ought to surrender because the German soldiers were so much better than we were. Personally, I ain't got nuthin against her; she just rooted for the wrong side. But I will say this: keep her away from any microphones in here or she's liable to start a riot.'"

I once asked my dad if he would like for me to take him down to Columbus for the Red, White, and Boom fireworks display. He leaned back in the recliner in his apartment, took a deep drag off his cigarette, and put his hands together, the tip of each finger touching the corresponding tip on the other hand. He riffled the tips of his fingers back and forth, and got a faraway look in those cold blue eyes. Then he spoke: "Tim, I laid on my back one night in France, my rifle right beside me, my head against my helmet, and I saw one of the biggest naval bombardments of a country in the history of warfare. I think there were more ships in the ocean than there were stars in the sky. All night long I saw those big muzzle flashes and heard that deep rolling thunder, {whoom-boom-boom, whoom-boom-boom, whoom-boom-boom). It was a great lightning storm, and the night was day…Why in the heck do you think I would want to go to downtown Columbus and watch somebody shoot off some firecrackers and skyrockets?" And that ended that.

When my dad came home after the war to become a well driller, run a water systems business, and to be a plumber, he brought my mama and she became a housewife and mother in Dublin, When It Wasn't Doublin'. I guess that she was just about the prettiest thing anyone had ever seen in that little town, and she had that Texas drawl that she kept with her until the day she died. One time a new friend called me up and my mama answered the phone. "It's for you, Timmy," she said. My friend's first words were: "I didn't know you had a maid in your house!" "That's no maid," I said, "that's my mama!" She spoke a lot like Laura Bush, the former President's wife. She used words like "tarry" for wait, or linger, and "tradin" for shopping at a store and "child" for son. And she had that pervasive tenderness, and overriding compassion and kindness in her voice that people from the South have, and which is just not as apparent in people from the North. Everyone seemed to love my mama.

When she and my dad got to Dublin, they started having babies right away. She had four sons: Mike, Pat, me, and Kelly. I was supposed to be the girl of the family, and I guess when Doctor Karrer said that I was a boy, my mama cried and cried. But bein' good old me, she quickly got over it.

Back then, she couldn't believe that there were no "Fritos" in Columbus, and that people up North didn't drink Dr. Pepper, and that we didn't know what a "hamburger deluxe" was. She was just as proud of her Texas lineage as my dad was of his Dublin Sells' blood. She just loved Texas. She didn't know a football from a fastball, but she always rooted for the Aggies or the Longhorns when they were on TV. She taught me Texas history, and always stressed to me the fact that Texas was the only state that could still divide its counties into five different states if it so desired, and that everything is bigger in Texas—and better. She loved to go back to Texas, especially when the bluebonnets were in bloom. She loved LBJ and she loved Lady Bird, which was about the extent of her politics.

During the day, the TV was my mama's entire life, and besides watching *Ruth Lyon's Fifty-Fifty Club*, my mama was a soap opera queen. Many times I would come home from school, and she would be sitting in a chair with a TV stand in front of her, eating some Fritos and drinking a Dr. Pepper, and she would be glued to a soap opera. Sometimes I would see a little tear dribble down her cheek, she was so involved. That was my mama. At night, though, my mom and my dad watched *The Price Is Right* and *Wheel of Fortune*, and later in the evening, *The Johnny Carson Show*.

The prettiest picture I have of my precious mother is when she got baptized in the Hilliard Baptist Church. It reminded me of the movie with Robert Duvall, *Tender Mercies*.

My mama never lost her *naivete*. One day I was over at the Snouffer house and happened to have a tire pressure gauge in my pocket. I pulled it out and started running my fingers up the shiny silver sides.

"What's that you have in your fingers, child?" she asked.

"Oh, mama, what I have here is a "life expectancy gauge." You just blow into this little hole at the end, and it will tell you about how many more years you have to live." I blew into the hole, and deftly slipped the inner white stick way out.

"Mama, says here that I'm going to live at least another fifty years."

"Child, would you please hand that device over to me." She blew and blew into the tire gauge hole, but of course the inner white stick never budged.

"Child, call the emergency squad and don't tarry. I don't think I have a second more on God's beautiful earth." After I explained my joke on her, we both had quite a laugh together.

Another one of my favorite memories of my mama involves my wife, Debbie. Debbie hails from around Cincinnati and is a big Reds fan. One afternoon the three of us—Debbie, my mom, and I—were watching the Reds on television. Of course, my mama had her eyes on her matinee idol, Johnny Bench. Johnny wasn't from Texas, but he was from Oklahoma, and to my mama that was the next best thing. Then, right out of the blue, Debbie said, "You know, Darline, I'm from Cincinnati, and I used to date Pete Rose."

"My Lord!" my mama exclaimed, "if that's not the cat's pajamas. What was he like?"

"Well, he was OK," Debbie said, "but not nearly the gentleman Tim is."

Debbie and I have had a lot of laughs about that, because when we told mama we were pulling her leg, she refused to believe it wasn't true, and to her dying day she would tell her friends and kin, "Did you know that my daughter-in-law picked my son over the great Pete Rose?" Of course, if the player in question had been Johnny Bench, I'm sure things would have been different with my mama. "Child, I know Timmy is a fine young man, but the great Johnny Bench…?

Many times, when I was working down at the Federal Building in Columbus, my mama would call me up and chat with me in that Texas drawl of hers. "Mama, how did you sleep last night?" I would ask her. "Well, child, I don't rightly know. I went to sleep on the couch watching Johnny Carson, and I never did make it to bed." "Did you sleep well?" I would ask her. "Well, I don't rightly know if I slept or not. Maybe I did. It's hard to tell sometimes," she would say. For years after she died, whenever the phone rang, I would think it was my mother calling.

When we lived in a beautiful home in River Forest, I don't think she ever walked out of the front door of the house. She just used the kitchen and side doors. She could drive a car, and some of my earliest memories of her, when we were living right in the middle of Dublin, were when she drove our Pontiac convertible with us in it. I remember the truck drivers, like I said earlier, would look down into our car and whistle at her when she drove by. I couldn't figure out why—then. Her longest road trips were to see my Aunt Vivian and Uncle Darrel who lived in West Virginia. I believe that she always stayed off the freeways.

She loved to go back to Texas to visit her family. Her people were poor, but since she was the baby of eight children, they always doted on her. When we would visit her family in Austin, my mama took on a whole different air. Her Texas accent became more pronounced, and there was just something extra delicate about her. Many times mama and Aunt Minnie, my Uncle Elmer's wife, would get in the kitchen and cook up a storm: fried chicken, fried okra and green tomatoes, biscuits with chicken gravy, with a pecan pie thrown in for good measure. Her sisters Violet, Noddie, and Vivian would take her for rides in the Hill Country by Lake Traverse, where she would look in awe at the blue bonnets, her favorite flowers.

But, despite what I have told you up to this point, our home was not always peaceful and harmonious. My dad drank a lot when I was growing up. He was also sometimes abusive. I think he drank to medicate himself from the manic depression and post-traumatic stress that he suffered from. Very seldom would he come straight home from work. He normally stopped at the Gloria, the Nite Club, the White Cottage, or the Wyandotte Inn before coming home. He seemed to have to unwind first. Maybe he needed alcohol to numb himself from what he had seen and done during the War. Maybe he had a constant surge of energy that caused him to feel a need to talk and engage others in conversation. Also, many times he had trouble falling asleep. Perhaps there was a constant flight of ideas that caused this sleeplessness. I don't know.

My dad was a business owner. He never worked for anyone else. He always had a payroll to meet, and he had a wife and four sons to feed. Later, the beautiful girl that he wed from Bertram, Texas, his "Yellow Rose of Texas," who really never left Texas, developed problems of her own that my dad had to deal with. So, my dad lived under a lot of stress. I can now understand some of the underlying causes for my dad's drinking to excess, and his abusiveness at times in the home. I don't condone abuse of any kind in the home, or anywhere else for that matter, but I can understand that there are underlying causes. I hated my father when he was drunk; I hated him, and could not stand the sight of him when he would slap my mother, or my brothers, or me.

Also, dad used to embarrass me a lot; and at times made me feel ashamed of him because he was just so outspoken and so indifferent to the likes or dislikes and the feelings of others. Some people loved my dad to death, but a lot of people avoided him entirely. I don't believe my dad ever cared what other people thought of him. I, on the other hand, became quite the "people-pleaser," perhaps to compensate for my dad's ways.

I don't know what caused my mama to drink and become an alcoholic. I don't think she could ever really adjust to life in the North, even in a quaint, friendly village like Dublin. I am sure that she missed her close-knit family in Bertram, Texas. My mama should have never really left Texas, because Texas never left her.

When we were living in the little house between Cole's and Herron's right in the center of town, and my big brother Mike was three years old, my other big brother Pat was eighteen months old and I was just about a month old, my mother left Pat in his crib in his room for just a short while. When she came back to get him, he had pulled down the window curtains above his crib and had suffocated. To this day I have never gotten the exact details. Neither my mom nor my dad ever recovered from Pat's death.

Around that same time, my mama got a hook lodged in her eye during a fishing trip. Her beautiful deep brown eyes had now become a source of disfigurement for her, and she remained self-conscious about her blurred eye the rest of her life. Doubtless, for someone who prided herself on her beauty, this was a crushing blow to her self-esteem. My mother later had an artificial eye inserted to replace the injured eye, but it wasn't the same for her. Whenever my mama would see a movie star like Elizabeth Taylor or Paul Newman, she would immediately say, "Look at those eyes!"

So, while my dad was drinking at the various bars which he frequented, my mama turned to drinking beer at home. Given the circumstances, even though it hurt me, I don't blame her for it, and she is still my Yellow Rose of Texas.

But I hated it when my mother drank and got drunk, and I hated it when I would find empty beer bottles hidden around the house. I can remember sitting in school and being afraid that my mom would be drunk when I came home, and that my dad would come home and slap her around. I also became ultra-sensitive to what others might think about me and my home. I tried hard to make things appear "normal" by being an excellent student and athlete. I was so afraid that someone might find out what was really going on at our house. On the other hand, I always hoped that someone would intervene; a social worker perhaps, and save us. A boy should not have to grow up, afraid to bring his friends over to his house for a sleepover for fear that his mom or dad might be drunk.

I became very co-dependent on my father and mother. When they were sober and happy, I was happy, but when the opposite prevailed, I was sad and very anxious. I wasn't able to be free of their circumstances of the moment, or to live independently from their actions. I had no internal foundation. I craved the love and attention of my parents when they were sober.

I believe that I was blessed to have role models, and the normalcy, steadfastness, and yes, even love, of such men and women in Dublin as Louie and Virginia Geese, Sherm Sheldon, Chi Weber, Jim McCoy, Bob McCoy, and Bill and Sally Wolfe. "It takes a village...."

I remember like it was yesterday the first time I got really sick with my first case of full-blown mania. It was right after I was discharged from the Army. I had flown from Oakland Army Air Base in California down to Austin, Texas, to see my mama. My mama was always fine and happy in Texas. Anyway, when I arrived back in Columbus, there was no one to meet me at the airport. Lack of communication, I suppose. I took a cab home. I remembered that my old friend and roommate, Phil Hill, was having a party at his house on Summitview Road in Dublin, so, and I don't know why, I took over my stereo speakers, turntable, and receiver that I had bought in Korea. Even then, I knew it was kind of weird.

I remember walking home from that party by just crossing the shallow part of the Scioto River and walking up to our house at the Snouffer's at 7700 Dublin Road. The next day, after a sleepless night (I was feeling more and more energy and felt like I didn't need sleep), I remember going to my brother Mike's house. He had a Mossberg .22 caliber pistol lying around. With an air of self-importance, I told him and his wife, Mary Beth, that I had spent all of my time in Korea working for the CIA and I fired the pistol up in the air. I suppose I really did look wild and dangerous to them. I had gone a long time without sleep and couldn't stop talking. I was hallucinating and was afraid that someone or something would come along and just take away this "great, euphoric" feeling that I had. They ended up calling the Franklin County Sheriff's Department, and they came and took me to jail. I remember screaming and hollering the whole night that I was in jail.

The next morning I appeared before Judge Georgina Howell, and she ordered that I be taken to the Columbus State Hospital on the Hilltop in Columbus for evaluation. I was handcuffed, hands behind my back, and placed in a paddy wagon. I remember screaming and hollering; I just had so much energy and I did not want to be confined. On the way to the State Hospital, the two police officers pulled the paddy wagon into an alley, got in the back of the paddy wagon, and with their night sticks, proceeded to just beat the living you-know-what out of me. To this day, I can't understand why. I was no threat to flee or harm them. I believe they were just sadistic. Then they took me to Grant Hospital where I was given seventeen stitches to close a wound in my head. I was then taken to the State Hospital.

When this happened, my mom and dad were vacationing up in Port Clinton, Ohio. My dad had an old Army buddy up there, John Burkhart, who owned a bar. What could be a better combination for him? Anyway, as soon as my brother told them what had happened to me, they came right home. Shortly thereafter, I was transferred to the VA Hospital in Chillicothe, Ohio.

The Sells family had a reputation for fighting with one another, but when someone picked on a Sells, or treated one of them unfairly, the family was quick to come to the defense of the mistreated one. When Mt. Carmel Hospital sent a bill for stitching me up in the emergency room, my hero, my dad, sent the following response:

> "In regard to this bill, dated September 10th, 1973, under the circumstances, it is my belief that the medical services performed on the above patient, my son, should be paid either by the Franklin County Sheriff, 380 South High Street, Columbus, Ohio 43215, or by the County Commissioners, Franklin County Court House, Columbus, 43215. The wounds received by the patient were inflicted by Deputy Sheriffs M. E. Williams and R. V. Vandergriff of the Franklin County Sherriff's Office. The patient was being transported from the City of Columbus Municipal Building to the Columbus State Hospital after being committed by his brother. The patient wasn't violent nor under the influence of alcohol or

drugs. He was alone in the back of a patrol wagon with both hands cuffed behind his back lying on the floor. They stopped the patrol wagon and beat him with clubs in route to the Columbus State Hospital. There were no charges of any kind filed against the patient. The patient has had a mental depression since his return from Korea. The records at the Columbus State Hospital and Veterans Hospital in Chillicothe, Ohio, will show same. I have always paid my taxes, and debts, including bills from your hospital (your records will show same), but I refuse to pay this bill because of the BRUTAL way of its occurrence by county employees. As in the past, your medical services were of the very best quality, although the scar will always be there for the rest of my son's life. My entire family and my friends thank you for the services performed."

The letter was signed by my father, Robert L. Sells, and he sent copies to The Franklin County Sherriff's Department, The Franklin County Commissioners, the News Media, the VFW, and others.

After I was released from the VA Hospital at Chillicothe in November of 1973, I returned to our home at the Snouffer's in Dublin. I was in a state of deep depression, and I remember taking my dad's German luger and holding it in my hands and considering ending it all. However, I was afraid that there just might be a God, and I didn't want to go to Hell. During the next couple of months, a county health nurse came to our home and gave me injections of either Prolixin or Haldol. These medications built up in my system to the extent that I was almost paralyzed by New Year's Day, 1974, and had to be rushed to the old VA Clinic at 700 Bryden Road. That's where I first met my psychiatric nurse Patricia Seeger. She was to be my God-send for more than the next thirty years. She took me off Prolixin and Haldol, and I started feeling better.

The depression lifted by the late winter of 1974 and I felt well enough to travel back to Colombia to see my friends there. I stayed with them until the Spring of 1974. Although I didn't feel well enough to return to the rigors of graduate school, I did think I could hold a job. I started off as a supervisor at the Franklin County Juvenile Detention Center and later became a supervising probation officer. However, the stress of the job led to another manic episode in the Spring of 1976. I was hospitalized at the Mt. Carmel Psychiatric Center for mania and was released a few months later. I convalesced from a state of depression, again, until February of 1977 when I again started feeling better. I then took a job with the Franklin County Welfare Department as an Income Maintenance Worker. The job was extremely stressful, and I landed back in Mt. Carmel for mania.

I was so ashamed and utterly crushed and depressed after I got sick again and couldn't do my job at the Franklin County Welfare Department that I decided I would become a barber. I wanted to learn to do something with my hands and not have to think so much, be more like my dad and brothers, I guess, and I had never forgotten Mose Myers, and those good days when I shined shoes in his barber shop. I was living in Reynoldsburg at the time and the Ohio State Barber College was nearby, so I enrolled. I was in barber school from July, 1978 until March, 1979. My dad used to come to the barber college a lot and have me cut his hair. I was still feeling pretty depressed, because I didn't feel I was doing anything worthwhile, since I wasn't doing anything "academic," but my dad seemed to be really proud of me. That seemed strange to me at first because, when I was in high school and college and I was in my room at night studying and studying, trying to get good grades, he would come in from a night of drinking and lecture me, telling me that you can't learn everything from a book. He would ramble on and on, not making any sense, for which I rejected and despised him. But in the end, he was right.

MY BARBER SCHOOL CREDENTIALS
I WANTED TO BE LIKE MOSE

A change took place in our relationship during my time at the barber college. The more I cut his hair, the more relaxed I became toward him. I think it had to do with touching his head. It seemed as though I was getting to know him better. Even feeling the dent in his head from when he had fallen down the quarry gave more meaning to that story, which I had heard since I was a small child. And the more I cut his hair, the more at ease he became with me. Many times he became so relaxed he would fall asleep, like the farmers at Mose's. It was a strange thing and I can't explain it, but it was almost as though a door had opened and we had gone into a much more comfortable and relaxing room together. I quit feeling embarrassed by him, and started looking forward to seeing him come into the barber college. I actually became proud of him for the first time in my life. And, I think he really started loving me more as he realized that I was learning to love and serve him. It definitely had a positive impact on our relationship. So I learned something amazing from that experience and it wasn't something that could have been learned from a book.

When I was going through my bouts of mania and depression that were resulting in hospitalizations, my dad stood by me all the way. He made it a point to spend more time with me. I guess we hung out together more than we ever had before. We played cribbage, listened to Yankee games together, and watched the *Dean Martin Show* and the *Johnny Carson Show* together. He loved those shows and would laugh and laugh. I loved to hear my dad laugh.

During my barbering days and afterwards, I spent a lot of time thinking about my dad and our relationship and I began to view him differently. I came to appreciate that, although he was very busy with his work and in meeting all of his responsibilities, he still found time to take us to ball games and watch us play ball. He also occasionally took my brother and me to see movies at the RKO Palace Theater on Broad Street in downtown Columbus. I came to realize that the things that I love to do to this day, my dad had taught me, or modeled for me: baseball, fishing, being a New York Yankees fan, playing cards (especially cribbage), and just spending time with my friends. Like I said, my dad never told me he loved me; he just built me that raft, the African Queen. When I was a boy, I loved it when he would rub his hand over my little burr head (and maybe he had been drinking a little) and say, "I wouldn't trade you for a million dollars." That came pretty close to saying "I love you."

I also thought about the difficulties dad had had to deal with. He grew up with many challenges, which I decided helped to explain his faults. He was the youngest of fifteen children born to my Grandma Polly and Grandpa Amaziah Sells. Based on the stories I have heard about him, I believe Grandpa Amaziah was a very unusual fellow and that he wasn't the ideal father. Also, there is little doubt in my mind that my dad suffered from some form of manic-depression, the same malady that I live with. I have talked this over with my psychiatrist, and after describing my dad to him, he is more or less in agreement. And then there was the impact that his experiences during WWII had on him, and I believe that the impact was profound and that it affected him until he died.

I really came to forgive, love, and appreciate him (isn't it amazing how your parents "grow up" and how wounds heal?). I think he tried to be the best dad he knew how to be.

He helped me through my difficult times and counseled me as best he could. His particular form of mental therapy was a bit different though. Concerning my sickness, he would say: "It's all in your mind." That wasn't too comforting since I knew my sickness wasn't emanating from my feet. But then he would say, "Tim, your mind is the strongest part of your body." And when I would be seeing doctors and taking all kinds of pills, he would say, "What you need is the 'Big Medicine'." I never knew what he meant by the "Big Medicine"; he never told me, but maybe it was something that he had taken or experienced before that had helped him get through life or death experiences: Maybe, just maybe, he had had a personal experience with Jesus that he didn't want to, or could not share with anyone. I really hope that was it. I have faith that someday I'll know. Or, sometimes he would tell me what to do when I was real anxious and scared, "Tim, when you feel that way, just say 'Get the hell away from me'!" He never told me who it was I should tell to leave me alone. He never explained his "religious" beliefs to me, only that "Cleanliness is next to Godliness." and "God helps those who help themselves." To this day, I never have been able to find those lessons in the Bible.

I have forgiven my father and have come to accept the weaknesses that he had. We all have shortcomings. We are all in need of the saving grace of our Lord.

Dad began as a farmer, and what he learned on the farm stayed with him his whole life. He worked hard, played hard, and fought hard. He was never afraid to do something even if it might be wrong. He became a shrewd businessman, but he was generous at the same time. He made a lot of money, and he spent a lot of money. It might be said that dad was the good, the bad, and sometimes the ugly, of Dublin when it wasn't Doublin'.

But dad never took himself too seriously. He knew he lived on borrowed time. He knew that he would never get out of this world alive, and he didn't. He died in 1998. I still really miss him, and would give anything to hear just one more story, and I pray that someday I will.

He did accomplish a lot of things that people doubted he could: He survived as the youngest of fifteen kids, he fought his way through France and Germany, he succeeded as an independent businessman and met a payroll, he maintained a difficult marriage with my mother "until death did them part," and he even dug a patio for his friend and mayor Joe Dixon while hanging on the edge of a limestone cliff using a back hoe. My dad said that your mind is the strongest part of your body, and that is the way he lived.

So, flawed as they were, my dad and my mom were, and still are, my heros. All heroes have their strengths and weaknesses; just ask Superman about kryptonite.

CHAPTER 12

CONCLUSION

Well, that about ends When Dublin Wasn't Doublin'. After I left the barber college in 1979, I took a job as a Disabled Veterans Outreach Specialist for the State of Ohio, where I worked for the next 30 years until my retirement in 2009. In 1982 I met my beautiful wife, the former Debbie Yockey of Sardinia, Ohio, in a Bible Study (better to meet 'em in a Bible Study than in a bar). Somehow she and I started talking about fishing. She showed me she had a fishing license, and that's why I took her out—I took her crappie fishing up on Mohawk Drive on the O'Shaughnessy Reservoir. We married in 1987 and will be celebrating our 25th wedding anniversary on August 22nd of this year.

Debbie earned a Masters Degree from The Ohio State University in Social Work while she was working full-time as a social worker for Franklin County Children's Services. Subsequently, she felt a calling to work at Tree of Life Christian Schools in Columbus. She has been there since 1997, and is presently employed as the elementary school secretary. Debbie makes sure that everyone is well-fed in our home with her Southern Ohio cooking and gardening skills. She plays the piano quite well and used to teach it.

Debbie and I have two children. Our son, Ryan, was born May 22, 1989. He is currently serving as a combat medic for the 684th Medical Supply Company in Bagram, Afghanistan and is due to return to the United States this August. Ryan attended Columbus State Community College for two years prior to his deployment, and would like to become an emergency room nurse upon his return from Afghanistan.

THE FAMILY AT ELIZABETH'S HIGH SCHOOL GRADUATION

Our daughter, Elizabeth, came along three years later. She was born April 17, 1992. I was working downtown at the Federal Building, when, early that morning, Debbie called and said that she felt like she was going to have the baby right away. I ran all the lights on my way home, picked her up, and dropped her off at the emergency room at Riverside Hospital. I parked the car as quickly as I could, but by the time I got up to the birthing room, Elizabeth had already made her entrance into the world. She's been a feisty little thing ever since. Elizabeth is a junior at Miami University in Oxford, Ohio, on a full academic scholarship and is a straight A student majoring in nutrition. She's a member of the *Alpha Phi Sorority*.

Elizabeth recently became a member of the National Society of the Daughters of the American Revolution, as a descendant of Ann Simpson Davis. It is my hope that, upon his return, Ryan will pursue becoming a member of the Sons of the American Revolution, as a descendant of John Davis or Ludwick Sells.

Debbie and I also have a nice little house and friends and two cats, Curly and Chloe, and a dog, Lily, a Springer Spaniel. If I ever get another dog, well, I'll just name that dog Enuf because God's been gracious to me and given me enough of everything I could possibly need.

I am happy to say that, thanks to the Lord, some good doctors, and my precious wife, my health has been pretty good these past thirty-some years, although I did get sick in the spring of 1982, which I will tell you about in the Epilogue. I started this storybook saying that everybody is waitin' for somethin', and I'm no different. I'd like to have some more little Sellses running around. I'd like for Ryan or Libby to give Debbie and me some grandkids. I'd love to teach my little grandchildren to fish and play ball and play cribbage. I know that I'd spoil them, but that's of no account. I'd leave the learning part to "Grandma Debbie" since she's the brains of the family. I wouldn't even mind crossing the two rivers (the Olentangy and the Scioto) like Indian Bill used to and find a little house back in Old Dublin where Debbie could plant a nice garden. I don't like to work in gardens, but I sure like to eat what comes out of them. Some things never change.

I told you that my grandpa, the old man, Amaziah Sells, just quit wearing clothes when he got to be up around sixty—just wore a different colored robe for each day of the week, as the story goes. And remember how my dad sent away to Nieman-Marcus to get his color-coordinated, see-through jump suits when he reached about the same age? Well, the strangest thing happened to me when I got to be about their age. I quit buying clothes. I didn't mean to, it just kind of happened naturally. One morning, I saw one of my co-workers wearing a real nice maroon Eddie Bauer coat into work and I said, "Charlie, that's about the nicest coat I ever did see. I most certainly would like to have a coat like that." A few weeks later, he gave me his coat. He probably had a lot of coats. The same thing happened to me with this Indian woman I worked with. She had this beautiful silk shirt on one day, and I complimented her on it. It turned out that it was her husband's shirt, and I'll be darned if she didn't give me that shirt. After that, and you may think this is brash, when I would see something nice on someone, I would just tell them right off that I would like to have it. You would be amazed at all of the clothes people have given me—maybe I look destitute and desolate. I just hate to go shopping, or "tradin," as my mama called it.

I've gotten ties, shirts, pants, and shorts. When my best friend from work, Command Sergeant Major Dave Turner died suddenly, his beautiful wife, Jan, just opened up his closets for me, and Dave had a lot of top of the line suits and other wearing apparel. After getting his things, I didn't need any more clothes. But, every now and then, somebody will give me a shirt for Father's Day or Christmas.

I'm ashamed to say that I didn't make it out to the Dublin Cemetery or the Davis Cemetery on Memorial Day which just passed. But I intend to visit them both before the end of the summer. It's hard for me to find my way around in Dublin anymore with all the new streets and changes in the routing of the old streets. And all of that traffic congestion is just hard to bear. It seems like there's not enough room to go anywhere. It's like everybody is rushing around in their cars trying to get to the Dairy Queen before it closes. But since I'm retired now, I can slip up to the cemeteries some evening. I want to take Ryan and Elizabeth with me to see the cemeteries and some of the other places mentioned in the book. It's high time they learn about their heritage. Maybe I can even get them to read the book! (Ryan read an early draft of the manuscript and said he liked it!!)

It's very sad to me that my precious and tender mama never got to know my children and they never got to know her since mama died before they were born. Mama probably should have been buried under a bluebonnet field out in the high country of Texas. She was very proud of being a Texan. It's like she and her family used to say: "Don't ever ask anybody where they're from. If they're from Texas, you'll know it, and if they're not, there's no sense in embarrassing them." I plan to get a little Texas flag from the Flag Lady here in Clintonville and put it beside her footstone and if I can find any bluebonnets at a flower shop, I'll take her some.

So, there you have it: When Dublin Wasn't Doublin'. Thank you for reading these stories; I hope they made you smile. Nice talkin' to all of you, and as my dad said in his Last Will and Testament: "Adios, Amigos," or "Go with God, friends."

EPILOGUE

In the spring of 1982 I got sick again and was hospitalized at the VA in Chillicothe. But, two important things happened as a result of this episode that changed my life for the better and so I call it "my good sickness."

First of all, my Dublin High School friend and fishing buddy, Mike Holmes, invited me to go with him to the Covenant Baptist Church on Dierker Road in Upper Arlington. When I was young I attended the Dublin Community Church. However, it was not a very meaningful experience for me, and I didn't attend often. My experience at the Covenant Baptist Church was different. Perhaps this was because I was older, or perhaps it was because of the illness that I was struggling with. But whatever the reason, every word that Pastor Fred Glasser said seemed intended for me. I also remember forming the impression that the people in that church weren't as concerned with my background, such as my family, or where I had been raised, or my academic accomplishments, as they were with my understanding of Christianity and my beliefs. It was a whole new religious experience for me and I began to think that I might benefit from church. So I continued to attend.

One night, as I continued to be plagued with depression and couldn't sleep (and there were many such nights), I got down on my knees and prayed to God and promised that if he would just let me sleep and take this anxiety away from me, I would follow Him for the rest of my life. I really had no place else to turn at the time. I got up, opened my Bible from the Dublin Community Church, And turned at random to the following passage, Matthew 5: 16: "Therefore, I tell you, do not be anxious about your life, what you shall eat or what you shall drink…" That, as they say, sealed the deal for me.

I joined a Bible study class at Covenant Baptist and that is where I met my wife, Debbie. That's the second important beneficial life changing thing that happened. Debbie and I attended Covenant Baptist Church for eight years. In 1990, we started going to the Vineyard Church of Columbus. During the past twenty-two years I have been blessed to be under the teachings of Pastor Rich Nathan at the Vineyard Church, and to be a member of a small men's group at the church.

It was at Dublin Community Church where I was first introduced to Jesus. It was at Covenant Baptist Church where I accepted Christ as my Savior. And it was at the Vineyard Church of Columbus where I really fell in love with Jesus. Rich has made Christianity more understandable to me than anyone I have ever known. Mostly he just focuses his messages on Jesus, and I guess that's about all any preacher really needs to do.

Like I said in the beginning, I'm not a "deep" man. I leave all the heavy reading to the other men in my men's group, especially to my spiritual mentor, Steve Lander. Sometimes we talk about Jesus, and sometimes we just talk; but the love and compassion of Christ are always there. Like the place called "Cheers" in the old television series, it's a place "where everybody knows your name." I have always been able to find peace, compassion, understanding, and acceptance there. Everybody knows that I've been sick, but they don't care. They accept me for who I am, warts and all, and praise be to God, I have learned to do the same with others. There is always love there, so it's a good place to hang out. I firmly believe that my church and my men's group have been a great source of my continued good health.

A while back I read a Christian book, which ripped through me like a ball and chain. The book is called *The Great Divorce* by C.S. Lewis, and I would like to quote a passage from it (p.72):

> "There are two kinds of people in the end: those who say to God 'Thy will be done'. And those to whom God says, in the end, 'Thy will be done'. Without that self-choice there could be no Hell. No soul that seriously and constantly desires joy will ever miss it. Those who seek, find. To those who knock, it is opened."

When I graduated from Ohio State University, I had a lot of knowledge, but no spiritual wisdom, and no internal foundation. I was standing on shifting sand. Knowledge without wisdom is useless, and can even be dangerous. Most of what I now know comes from these sources: my church, my men's group, and of course, God's Word. During the past thirty years, I have found truth, which, indeed has set me free. I don't have a hole in my soul anymore. Jesus has made me whole, and I intend to do my best for the rest of my life, to do the will of God.

Now, please don't get me wrong; I still have my share of problems. What's different now is that I know where to turn, and I don't feel alone anymore. It's a terrible thing to feel alone. I feel that it was actually a good thing that I got sick, real sick, back in the Spring of 1982—so sick that I wanted to die. I may have never found the One who could not only save my soul, but could also help to heal me mentally and emotionally. Also, that girl I met in the Bible study at Covenant Baptist, Debbie, has played a big part in keeping me healthy. So you can see that I paid a very small price for what that sick spell in the spring of 1982 brought to me.

I feel that my life can be summed up by a hymn written by Bob Dylan. The hymn is called "Saving Grace":

> If You find it in Your heart
> Can I be forgiven?
> I guess I owe You some sort of apology.
> I've escaped death so many times
> I know I'm only livin'
> By the Saving' Grace that's over me.

> By this time I thought that I would be a livin',
> In a pine box for all eternity.
> My faith is keepin' me alive
> But still I keep on 'a weeping'
> For the Saving' Grace
> That's over me.

> Oh the death of life that comes with Resurrection.
> Wherever I am welcome is where I will be.
> I put all my faith in Him,
> My soul protection,
> And the Savin' Grace that's over me.

> Oh the Devil's shining light
> That can be most blinding.

But to search for love
Is no more than vanity
As I look all around the world all that I am findin'
Is the Savin' Grace that's over me.

Oh the wicked know no peace
And you just can't fake it.
There's only one road
And it leads to Calvary.
It gets discouraging at times,
But I know that I will make it
For the Savin' Grace that's over me.

27200605R00146

Made in the USA
Lexington, KY
30 October 2013